Also available at all good book stores

9781785313875

9781785315992

9781785317187

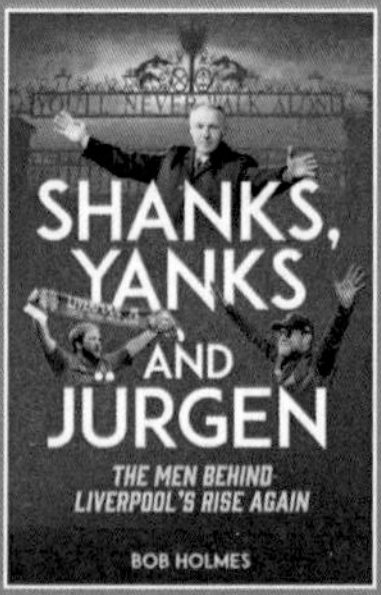

9781785316661

9781785313967

9781785319853

9781785313066

9781785311932

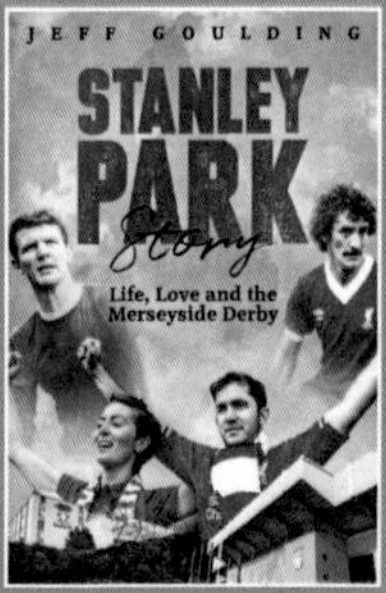

9781785314490

The Untouchables

The Untouchables

Anfield's Band of Brothers

Jeff Gouding & Kieran Smith

pitch

First published by Pitch Publishing, 2021

Pitch Publishing
A2 Yeoman Gate
Yeoman Way
Worthing
Sussex
BN13 3QZ
www.pitchpublishing.co.uk
info@pitchpublishing.co.uk

A CIP catalogue record is available for this book from the British Library.

ISBN 978 1 78531 863 4

Typesetting and origination by Pitch Publishing

Printed and bound in Great Britain by TJ Books, Padstow

Contents

Preface and Acknowledgements 9
Foreword 13

Part 1: **Origin Story: Three Boys, Their Club and Their City**
1. Football and the City 21
2. Walter Wadsworth, the Champions and 'Owd Tom' 36
3. Catastrophe and Revolt on the Mersey as Walter and Elisha Arrive at Anfield. 45

Part 2: **The Untouchables at War**
4. Private Tom Bromilow: from Flanders Fields to Anfield . . 67
5. Wounded on the Western Front: Private Danny Shone's Battle for Survival 80
6. The Home Front 90
7. Tales of Gallantry and Redemption 102

Part 3: **The Untouchables Assemble**
8. War Is Over but a New Foe Stalks the Land as Football Finally Returns .115
9. David Ashworth, His Captain, and the 1920s Boot Room 133
10. The Gentlemen of the Board 153
11. Creating the Band of Brothers 160

Part 4: **Liverpool FC 1921/22: All Hail the Champions**
12. Champions Again, at Last! 175
13. Celebrations and Speeches 196
14. Defence of the Crown 208
15. Matt McQueen to the Rescue as Ashworth Departs . . . 221
16. Glory and Adulation as Hero Tom Marries His Sweetheart . 234

Part 5: **All Good Things**
17. Whatever Happened to the Untouchables? 241
18. Farewell to 'Waddy,' Tom and Danny 262
19. A Legacy Worthy of Kings 273

Bibliography. 286

This book is dedicated to one of the greatest Liverpool teams ever to grace Anfield, 'The Untouchables', and to their families.

May they never be forgotten. They will never walk alone.

Those Were the Days

How well I remember.

The Kop without its lid
And Wadsworth giving it to 'Our Kid'.
The way Billy Lacey used to pass.
And Tommy Bromilow's class

How well I remember!

When Harry Chambers used to score
In Championships galore
Dicky Downs' overhead jinx
Everton nil Crystal Palace six!

How well I remember.

McKinlay's lethal free kicks
And Scott's excellence between the sticks
Dean's 60 – all in one season
Is yet another reason,

Why, those were the days I well remember.

Mr E. Lloyd Jones,

Liverpool matchday programme, 2 April 1982

Preface and Acknowledgements

FOR SUPPORTERS of the modern Liverpool Football Club, its history is dominated by the legacy of one man: Bill Shankly. The Anfield that Shankly stepped into was beset with decaying infrastructure and a boardroom seemingly content to wallow in the second tier of English football and overseeing a team unable to punch at its own weight, let alone above it. Given the transformation that followed, it is little wonder that the great Scot has since been endowed with almost messianic status.

We count ourselves among Shankly's most fervent admirers. However, this is a football club that not only survived, but thrived throughout the 67 years that preceded his arrival. It had already secured five league titles and appeared in two FA Cup Finals, it had survived two world wars, while its owners had not only overseen its birth, launching it into the Lancashire League with barely dozens of fans in attendance to see its first game, but they had also guided it to the top of English football, securing a first championship within a decade of the club's creation.

In the decades that followed, Liverpool FC signed a succession of incredible players and developed countless others. The stadium itself became architecturally one of the grandest in the country, and at one end of the pitch a vast terrace grew up on Walton Breck Road, becoming both fearsome and iconic long before its stone steps reverberated to the sound of Gerry Marsden's 'You'll Never Walk Alone'.

Our generation frequently chastises the modern football fan, lecturing them that the sport was not invented along with the Premier League in 1992. It was not, of course, but neither did Liverpool FC's journey begin in 1959. Alongside many others, we feel passionately that this football club has a rich and fascinating history that stretches all the way back to its foundation in 1892. Indeed, the seeds of its inception stretch back beyond that, to the creation of Everton Football Club in 1878 and the eventual boardroom split that set it off on its glorious journey.

Prior to the arrival of Shankly there are many tales to tell, managers to understand and revere, players to celebrate and championships that were as hard-fought as any since the war. The people and events brought as much joy to supporters then as they do now. That these moments in the history of our club could one day fade from view is an idea we find unbearable.

In the summer of 2020, locked in the grip of a pandemic, we were reminded that the world had endured a similar catastrophe a little over a century earlier. In 1919 the influenza pandemic would go on to kill more people worldwide than the world war it followed. The city of Liverpool had been among some of the hardest hit in Europe, yet its people had seemed to soldier on.

We found it remarkable that men who had fought amid the slaughter on European battlefields from 1914–18 could return to a country ravaged by disease and economic ruin and decide to play football. Had they merely found it within themselves to engage with sport for the simple joy of it, to find relief from the grim reality of life, that would have been enough. However, these men rose to become the best in the country, not once but twice in consecutive seasons.

Yet to all but a relative few among the vast ranks of Liverpool supporters, their story is largely unknown. To their families and descendants they are heroes and legends, their keepsakes, photos and medals are treasured possessions, but with each passing year their legacy is fading from view. There is barely any film footage of these men and those that exist contain no sound. We will never know their voices and hear their accents. They are mere images, records, match reports from a bygone era and occasionally they speak to us from the columns they wrote and interviews they gave.

They are so much more than that, and they lived in a glorious age, as complex, dramatic, comic and tragic as our own. After many conversations spent bouncing around ideas about how we could celebrate these men, the idea for this book emerged. It has become something of a mission ever since.

We were inundated with offers of support and practical help from a host of people dedicated to the history of our club, and others with a passion for football's lost stories. These dedicated historians gave up hours of their own time to furnish us with clippings, anecdotes and photographs, many of which have been used in this book and all of them have informed our thinking and research. Their sense of common cause has sustained us throughout what has been a monumental undertaking.

In the face of such generosity, a mere thank you seems insufficient, but to Mark Platt of LFCTV for his moral support as much as his willingness to share so much invaluable information; Jonny Stokkeland, Liverpool Football Club's official archivist, for his meticulous attention to detail; Stephen Done, Liverpool Football Club's museum curator, for his insights; Everton FC Heritage Society; Arny Baldursson editor of LFCHistory.net, for his time and support; Kjell Hanssen of Play Up Liverpool for his insights and time; the historian, author and journalist Stephen F. Kelly for his insights and for the photographs of Charlie Wilson; George Sephton for giving up his precious time; Adrian Killen for sharing his wonderful scrapbook – truly a treasure trove; George Scott; Tom Neal; Plunkett Carter; Brian Hayes Curtin of the *Cork Independent*; Dan Kay of the *Liverpool Echo*; Chris Lloyd of the *Northern Echo*; and Kerenza Moore of the *Cornish Times.*

We also appreciate the efforts of Fraser Kinnie, genealogist at Heir Hunter UK, who tracked down relatives of Fred Hopkin; the author Karl Coppack of *The Anfield Wrap* for his thoughts and insights; Omar Saleem, Steven Scragg and Will Sharp of *These Football Times* for their support; Joanna Durkan of This Is Anfield for her thoughts and insights; the historian Mal Holmes; John Pearman from *Red All Over the Land* for his insights; the author Andy Marsden for introducing us to programme collectors and for providing so many invaluable leads; match programme collectors Rob Gowers and Andrew Weir for their time and for sharing so much of their precious collections; Vicky Griffiths and Tina Ball of the Prescot Museum and Kirkby Gallery; the author and historian Chris Jones; Tony Zeverona of Prescot Cables FC; and Prescot football historian and author, Neville Walker. Thanks also to the author and musician Peter Hooton for his insights; and Liverpool FC blogger David Moen; we offer all of you our sincere gratitude.

When we set out on this journey, we were committed to getting as close as possible to a three-dimensional representation of the period, the game, the club and the people as we could. It was our desire to reveal these players not through statistics and grainy images, but as people who lived, loved, had adventures, struggled, had families and served their club and football with distinction. The record books, internet archives and online libraries could only take us so far along the way.

For us to really get close to these men, whose flame burned brightest a century ago, we knew we had to reach out to surviving relatives, listen to family stories and gaze upon the treasure trove of photographs, medals and caps. We are thrilled that we were able to find so many of them, but grateful beyond words that they took the time to furnish us with so much personal information and detail.

It is our sincere belief that we could not have produced this book without the cooperation and contributions of First World War historian and author Jacqueline Wadsworth and her father Bill Wadsworth (granddaughter and son of Walter Wadsworth), who have contributed so many wonderful images, shared their own stories, memories and research; Lee Tracy (grandson of Tom Bromilow), who was extremely generous with his time, shared family memorabilia and so many stories; the incredible creative talent of Anthony Tracy-Winson (ANT-OGRAPHY via Facebook) who colourised and enhanced so many of the images in this book; Brian Spurgin (nephew of Tom Bromilow) for sharing family memorabilia and being so generous with his time; and John English, Mike Hunter and Douglas Barlow (great nephews of Danny Shone) for sharing their own research along with so many precious memories, photographs and documents.

Thanks also to William Sinnott Lacey and Jacqueline Sinnott-Lacey (grandson and granddaughter in-law of Bill Lacey) for giving us their time and sharing so much memorabilia, photographs and memories; Mary Beadles, great niece of Harry Beadles; Kent Brothwell, nephew of Fred Hopkin; Dennis (grandson of Harry Chambers) and Karen Chambers for their support; Ros Tatton and the rest of Cyril Gilhespy's family for sharing their precious photograph of Cyril featured in this book; and to Ken Davies for his comprehensive research on Harry Beadles.

Finally, we would like to say farewell to Bill Wadsworth, the son of Walter, who passed away in July 2021 at the age of 91. May he rest in peace.

Foreword

OUR DESIRE to write this book stems from a need principally to tell the story of a football team. No ordinary team for sure, but one that rose to prominence after the end of the First World War, securing consecutive First Division titles in 1922 and 1923. Packed with incredible characters and led by a mercurial manager, this was a team assembled from near and far, blessed with individual brilliance and men prepared to roll up their sleeves and do battle when the occasion called for it. They were fighters, as fierce as any in the game, but to those who witnessed their rise, they were regarded as the finest proponents of their art in the game. They were, to put it succinctly, untouchable.

Maybe to some, particularly those with an affection for Liverpool Football Club or who have an interest in the history of football generally, a book that dealt solely with those two incredible seasons would suffice. To do that though would be to do a disservice to the protagonists in this incredible story, and it would deprive you, the reader, of something far more enthralling: the chance to really know these men and the lives they lived. Lives that were far richer and more intriguing than any football match could hope to be.

However, this is a story that goes beyond those two seasons, stellar though they were. It is about more than football matches, statistics and records. To do justice to the lives of 'The Untouchables' we are committed to telling the whole story, with respect and honesty, but to do so with warts and all. Though they were certainly heroes, they were also human beings who lived and loved, triumphed, and enjoyed the rewards, made mistakes, and paid for them, and whose journeys were replete with the fascinating and occasionally the mundane, as are all of ours.

Instinctively we all know that in any tale of heroes or villains, we must first address the origin stories. All acts of valour, feats of endurance, great triumphs and even those lives played out in the ordinariness of birth, work and death owe their roots to family, society, community, and geography. The character of all people is shaped as much by the events of their lives, the places they lived and the people they met as it is by their physical constitution.

So to focus only on the high points and pay no attention to what came before or after is to tell only a fraction of the story and would leave these men where they are now: as two-dimensional figures on the page of a book or a computer screen, only properly known to their families and doomed to fade into obscurity with the passage of time. To us, that would be a crime we cannot and will not let happen.

The men you will discover in these pages will be as real and as fully fleshed out as we can possibly make them. They will inhabit a time and a space that we hope you will come to know and love. It is our intention to create an accurate image of Liverpool Football Club, the players, the management and the board, before during and immediately after its glorious achievements. But we will go beyond that. Anfield did not exist in a vacuum, and as such we will paint a picture of the city that gave rise to this now iconic stadium. We will explore its culture and history and in doing so, we will drop you the reader into the epicentre of its sprawl and walk those streets with you.

The team who would become known as 'The Untouchables' were assembled from England, Ireland – both sides of the border – Scotland and Wales. Likewise, the men who built the club and led it to glory came from all corners of the British Isles. However, then as now, the club had a local heartbeat. Its supporters, drawn from the city's docks, factories and streets that were filled to bursting, had a love and passion for their team that would be instantly recognisable to all of us today, but few of us could comprehend the lives they lived.

To those who stood on the Kop in the early decades of the 20th century, watching football was as much an escape from mundanity, toil and the uncertainties of life as it is to today's supporters. For at least 90 minutes a stevedore working in the cold, dark warehouses of Liverpool's dockland could forget the daily struggle for survival and become part of a cause much greater than his own. However, if he were to be elevated from the terrace and be afforded the chance to do battle on the pitch, he would be given the chance to escape his lot altogether.

Today, on the side of a house in Sybil Road, off Anfield Road in Liverpool, is a mural dedicated to Reds defender Trent Alexander-Arnold. Trent is a native of the city, born in its West Derby district. His rise to prominence is one born out of chance, hard work and an insatiable desire to realise his ambition. Though the circumstances of his upbringing may not have involved the hardship endured by his 19th- and early 20th-century counterparts, such as Kirkdale-born Tom Bromilow for example, the pair would no doubt have recognised each other's desire to represent their boyhood club and achieve more than their accidents of birth had mapped out for him.

Jimmy Case, a hero of the 1970s and '80s, worked in a factory as an apprentice electrician before rising to prominence as part of Bob Paisley's all-conquering teams of that era. His football journey would see him playing for amateur teams in the Garston area of the city, much like Danny Shone did after the First World War. Shone learned his footballing trade playing for a shipping company called Grayson's of Garston FC in the amateur leagues, before later joining the Reds.

Indeed, the same Bootle streets that gave rise to the tough-tackling and deceptively cultured defender Walter Wadsworth would also spawn Jamie Carragher, who we will see was cut from very similar cloth to his 1920s equivalent. However, though Walter would taste acclaim and glory in a career that spanned two decades at Anfield, he could not have hoped to have the earning potential and career opportunities of his modern-day equivalent. Yet both men will have seen football as not only a calling but also as an escape. These are just some of the threads that connect our local heroes across the centuries.

And so we have chosen to explore this period in the history of Liverpool Football Club through the eyes of these three players: Walter Wadsworth, Tom Bromilow and Danny Shone. All of them were local lads whose lives ran in parallel to events that led to the birth of the club they would go on to represent with distinction, and who will have lived through its rise to prominence, supporting it on its journey, perhaps standing on the terraces of Anfield as young boys and doubtless dreaming of pulling on the shirt someday.

Perhaps if we could talk to them today, and we were to ask them to appraise their success in the famous red shirt, they would answer in similar terms to Trent Alexander-Arnold, each man describing himself as 'just a normal lad from Liverpool whose dream has just come true'. As you get to know them in these pages, we feel sure that you will share our view that this is probably exactly how they would have described themselves.

We choose to make these men the focus of this story not because they were necessarily the best players in that side, nor were they all the most famous. Although, as we will learn, Tom Bromilow was something of a superstar and celebrity in his own right. Instead, we want to witness the rise of the club and this team – as 'cosmopolitan' as any English team could be in its day – as it would have been viewed by the people of the city. So we will follow these three local lads as they meet and forge friendships, some of which will last a lifetime, with some of Anfield's greatest players, and fight alongside them as they rise to the very top of the English game.

You will learn of their early lives and, in the case of Shone and Bromilow, their military service in the First World War. Through Walter's eyes we will capture life at Anfield between 1914 and 1918, as conflict raged in Europe and a debate raged in society as to whether something as trivial as football should continue amid so much death and destruction. We will explore the players who played in those wartime games and explore the machinations at board level and how the club would eventually emerge from a war footing to plotting the conquest of English football.

This is a tale of heroism of both the ordinary and extraordinary kind. It is packed with drama, humour and intrigue. It is of course one ultimately of great sporting success. However, in telling it we have drawn on the lives and deeds of so many people who have helped to fill the pages of this book. It is a story with a cast of thousands, from the men in the boardroom, the players on the pitch and their families, to the supporters in the stands. We will attempt to paint a vivid image of them all, through the lens of these three young boys who would become Kings of the Kop.

As the adage says, all good things must come to an end, and the demise of this great team after 1923 can appear to some as a fall from a cliff edge. In dealing with this, we will show that like all great empires, the seeds of their downfall are often sewn long before their collapse. Factors both internal and external can be seen to have played a part, but in no way should the absence of success in the years after 1923 detract from the greatness of this team. Indeed, the relative mediocrity that followed, and the catastrophe on a world stage that preceded those years, only serves to illuminate this team's achievements at Anfield as something of a footballing oasis for the club, the city and its people.

The final pages of the book will concern themselves with legacy, and in doing so we will need to explore the onward journeys of these men. In some cases, we will see that football continued to provide a source of income and meaning. However, for others life became more complicated and filled with strife. In at least one case the end of a playing career meant a fall from grace, a brush with the law and incarceration and for others complicated family lives intervened and threatened to consume them.

This should not surprise us, as these were just normal men living – for a relatively short period – extraordinary lives. Without the riches and media opportunities of today's generation, the heroes of this story would be forced to carve out new lives with varying degrees of success. In telling their stories honestly, including the good and the bad, we seek not to diminish their legacy but to enhance it. To bestow upon them some superhuman strength and to portray them as latter-day paragons of virtue (something none of us can claim to be) would in our view conceal the true depth of their lives. Furthermore, we feel that their achievements are made all the greater by the fact that they were simple human beings beset with the same frailties and whose back stories are as littered with the same struggles as the people who went before them, and many of those who came afterwards.

And, of course, we firmly believe that to hide from view parts of their journeys, shining our light only on the success and the glory, while ignoring the hardships and missteps along the way, is to deny you one of the greatest stories in the history of Liverpool Football Club.

So we commend to you the story of The Untouchables, Anfield's band of brothers who for two years conquered all of English football. We sincerely hope you enjoy getting to know about their origins and their fate, and when you finally say farewell you will recall their tale with the same fondness and pride that we do.

Part One

Origin Story: Three Boys, Their Club and Their City

1

Football and the City

THIS IS the story of three working-class lads – Walter Wadsworth, Tom Bromilow and Danny Shone – born in 19th-century Liverpool near the dawn of a new millennium and who would grow up to conquer English football. Remarkably their birth and coming of age stories ran in tandem with the club they came to serve with such distinction.

They lived in a city that had come to dominate world trade, making great strides in public health and the arts, but which was also a place of staggering contrasts. A time traveller visiting Liverpool during this period would marvel at the immense wealth and Victorian splendour of the city centre and port, while being staggered by the unrelenting poverty and disease of its court housing.

Liverpool, a hotbed of political struggle and rising trade union activity, was also at the centre of resistance to Britain's colonial rule in Ireland. With such a large population of Irish immigrants of both republican and unionist traditions living in close quarters, tensions would often boil over, and the city's leaders were frequently on alert for weapons and explosives, which were smuggled into its port from activists in the United States.

Against that backdrop, the emergence of a sport that would later become synonymous with the people who inhabit the banks of the Mersey seems a trivial affair. However, as we will see, the game would have the power to lift the citizens of the city from their day-to-day struggles and elevate them and their teams on to the national stage.

Walter was born in 1890, Tom arrived in 1894 and Danny in 1899. And, while football was certainly not the game we enjoy today, it was at least played under a unified code of rules. Its development into what is now the nation's favourite sport was a rocky one – at least initially – and those rules and codes took time to settle down. Indeed, even the idea that the working classes should be involved at all had initially been a controversial one in the early days of the Football Association.

Our trio were born within a couple of miles of each other: Walter in Bootle, Tom in Kirkdale and Danny in the Edge Hill area. They each grew up in Liverpool's densely populated urban sprawl. The city had already enjoyed a century of unparalleled growth that saw the creation of a stock exchange located in an area behind the Town Hall, and the population would rise almost eight-fold from around 85,000 in 1791 to around 662,000 by the advent of the 20th century. It would continue to expand in the early years of the new millennium also.

A search through the photographic archives reveals yet more evidence of the contrasting fortunes of the city's people. Gaze upon the postcards of scenes from Lime Street, Bold Street and the area around Water Street, and we see elegantly clad ladies with parasols in hand and voluminous hats atop their heads. They often have children in tow who are equally well dressed. Gentlemen in suits, with pocket watches attached to their waistcoats and all manner of headgear on their heads, can be seen frozen in motion, perhaps scurrying to meetings or heading for boats moored at the waterfront, while others appear still, pipes of tobacco in hand, watching the world go by.

Then there are the grim portraits of squalor and want, with shoeless children roaming the cobbled streets in front of court housing, which was no more than a collection of hovels crammed into alleyways in the poorer districts of Liverpool. You see their mothers' gaunt expressions staring into the lens. Those images don't convey the smells or feel the hunger their bellies must have felt, but they do reveal that not everybody shared in the prosperity the city's port and their toil generated.

Rare film footage can be found. Two Blackburn-based film makers, Mitchell and Kenyon, regularly set up their cameras in Liverpool, filming its people at work or at the match. Their subjects would attend screenings at the city's St George's Hall, hopeful of seeing themselves on the screen. Some of these movies survive, and they reveal images of dockers clocking off from work. We see men and boys on the Kop. All of them are in their best clothes, and it seems that Kopites at the turn of the century would never be seen without a hat to cover their heads. Strikingly there are no scarves or rosettes either; such things would be reserved for cup competition.

In one film, as the camera pans along the crowd at Anfield, we see that the children are the forefront, eager to get their faces captured. Their cheeky grins are instantly recognisable, and you can imagine their journeys to the ground. Perhaps they paid to get in; perhaps they used their ingenuity to good effect and were enjoying the occasion for free. Then we notice one kid, a mischievous glint in his eye as he holds out his right hand to the filmographer and produces a gesture that seems to imitate masturbation. Though the film is grainy and monochrome, and this child is of another age, his irreverence would be right at home at any football ground in the 21st century.

An examination of contemporaneous speeches and the memoirs of notable figures from the period create a picture of a city in the throes of 100 years of continuous expansion, from a tiny hamlet on the banks of the Mersey to a port of global significance dubbed 'second city of the Empire'.

In 1791, Thomas Erskine, the 1st Baron Erskine, wrote, 'That immense City which stands like another Venice upon the water ... where there are riches overflowing and everything which can delight a man who wishes to see the prosperity of a great community and a great empire ... This quondam village, now fit to be the proud capital of any empire in the world, has started up like an enchanted palace even in the memory of living men.'

Yet even this remarkable vision of 18th-century Liverpool would soon be surpassed. Soon, some 40 per cent of the world's trade would pass through the city's port, leading to a growth in its network of docks and flooding it with people from all over Europe and across the globe. Trade in cotton, sugar, tobacco and shamefully slaves from Africa fuelled the explosion in wealth and funded the expansion of the city and the growth of its great works of architecture.

In 1846, shortly after the onset of the great famine in Ireland, which saw some half a million Irish people pass through the city, many of them settling in the Scotland Road area, Prince Albert – who had been invited to the city to open its magnificent Albert Dock – would address Liverpool dignitaries assembled at a huge banquet in the Town Hall, telling them, 'I have heard of the greatness of Liverpool, but the reality far surpasses my expectation.'

And, by 1886, an article published in the *Illustrated London News*, dated 15 May 1886, proclaimed, 'Liverpool … has become a wonder of the world. It is the New York of Europe, a world city rather than merely British provincial.'

However, such expansion would impact on the fabric of the place and on the lives of both the rich and the poor, though for very different reasons. Consider this statement from a book entitled *Reminiscences of a Liverpool Ship Owner*, a collection of essays written by William B. Forwood between 1870 and 1917: 'Speed is the criterion aimed at, calling for constant and strenuous work.'

Forwood goes on to mourn the loss of his leisurely strolls down to the waterfront, where he would survey his ships and the sailors at work, before returning to his office to ruminate about the great issues of the day. The author had lived through the demise of the sailing ships that once filled the Mersey until 1860, when they began a steady decline only to be replaced by the great steamships. They must have been a magnificent sight on the Mersey, at least far more romantic than their iron and steel counterparts.

Modernisation of course meant an increase in trade as transatlantic journey time was cut and capacity to transport goods from across the globe increased. Soon the city's ship owners and council leaders would see their coffers swell but work on the docks would become grim and brutal, particularly for stevedores and porters, with some suggesting that few men could endure it for more than five years.

Another curse of work on the docks was its virtually unregulated nature, with shipping companies concerned primarily with profit. The safety of the men who stood in line, hoping to be picked for a day's labour, was of little interest. Work was often long and arduous and hazardous in the dark warehouses and on the dockside. Accidents and even fatalities were commonplace. However, increasing industrial action over working conditions and casualisation, coupled with the activities of prominent reformers such as William and Eleanor Rathbone, meant that by the time Walter Wadsworth had found a position on the docks, work would have been less precarious and better rewarded than in the latter years of the 19th century.

The lives of Walter, Tom Bromilow – who would briefly become a shipping clerk – and the parents of Danny Shone, who owned a corner grocery store in the Edge Hill area, were shaped by the ebb and flow of business at the port. Though not employed on the waterfront, the Shones, and their customers, would benefit from the increasing availability of goods shipped from across the world.

Life for many in the city had for many years been tough. Liverpool, granted city status in 1880, had been home to diseases such as typhus and cholera, with the latter having led to riots in the 1830s. The seemingly continual presence of disease in its centre would push many wealthy merchants out to suburbs, like Anfield. It would also mean that Liverpool became a focus for medicine and advances in public health, with the city employing the country's first medical officer of health, Dr William Henry Duncan.

Duncan's work promoting the link between poverty and the spread of disease throughout the 1830s, led to the Liverpool Sanitary Act in 1846. The Act was sponsored by Liverpool's local government and led to improvements in the health of the city's population.

Additionally, Liverpool's growing wealth led to works of great architecture which continue to inspire and surprise visitors today. The city's leaders and business community were ambitious, clearly seeing theirs as a world city on a par with London, Paris and New York.

To the Victorians, the second half of the 19th century was marked by the relentless march of progress. They were proud of what they saw as their benevolence towards the poorer sections of society, pointing to improvements in the living conditions of ordinary citizens during the period.

Such observations are inevitably subjective and must be judged in the context of the era. Here we return to the prolific writings of Forwood, this time drawing upon his *Recollections of a Busy Life*, written between

1860 and 1910. In it, he points to the paving of streets, great sewer works, the building of libraries and parks, washhouses and public baths and workmen's cottages, as well as the closure of 25 per cent of the city's pubs, an act designed to curb 'the curse of drink', as evidence that the lives of its citizens were getting better.

Consumption of alcohol was a subject of great concern in Victorian Britain. And as we will see, their attempts to control and reduce its consumption in the latter half of the 19th century, driven by the growing temperance movement, would play a key role in the formation of Liverpool Football Club.

Forwood, who also served as mayor of Liverpool twice, could call upon the words of Professor Ramsay Muir, who in his *A History of Liverpool*, published in 1907, asserts, 'Thus, on all sides, and in many further modes the city government has, during the last 30 years especially, undertaken a responsibility for the health and happiness of its citizens.'

It is undeniably true that the lives of working people in Liverpool at the turn of the century saw some improvements, especially when judged against what went before. However, it is also clear that many workers felt that the immense wealth that their labours produced was not being shared equally. The prevalence of campaigns, strikes and other protests is evidence of this. Demands for reductions in the working week, aid for the unemployed, an end to casual labour and improvements in pay, were common features of labour relations and influenced political thinking greatly.

Indeed, the National Union of Dock Labourers in Great Britain and Ireland, which was formed in 1889, was so popular that by 1890 it had 34 branches in the city and would move its headquarters to Liverpool.

In 1890 stevedores and dockers in London and Liverpool struck for pay and better working conditions, with historians describing their struggle as having 'all the hallmarks of a labour war'.

The simmering tensions among the Liverpool working class and their employers, particularly on the waterfront and in the transport industry, would continue to boil over throughout the early decades of the 20th century, leading to improvements in working conditions and pay which would create new opportunities for leisure for working people and for football.

All of this is of interest to us, not least because we know that Walter Wadsworth would find employment as a stevedore in the early part of the 20th century. Had it not been for these movements he may never have found the free time to become a footballer. However, they are also important factors in the evolution and development of the sport on Merseyside.

Up until the late 1880s, football was played by the wealthy and professional classes, mostly for their own amusement. It was centred around public schools like Rugby and Eton. The game was played under varying codes and rules, such as the Sheffield rules or the Cambridge rules. Eventually these codes would settle into the sports we now call rugby and football. But in the early years, teams negotiating matches with rivals would often haggle over which rules they would observe. What seems to have mattered most to these early proponents was getting a game; the rules mattered far less.

Eventually the Football Association would be formed in 1863 and the movement towards a unified set of codes that would lead to the creation of the version of football we love today would be agreed. It is therefore important to understand that the game our heroes fell in love with and played with such distinction was in its infancy at the time of their birth.

Furthermore, the sport had been far from a working-class endeavour during its formative years. The wealthy classes who had come to dominate it in the mid-19th century had resisted professionalisation, fearing that 'working men, uneducated in the art of the game' would get to take part.

However, those issues were largely settled by the time Walter and Tom began playing football at school and were probably unknown to Danny's generation. At the point where all three had seriously taken up the sport, it was becoming an increasingly professional affair, meaning that lads like Walter, Tom and Danny could realistically imagine making a living, albeit a modest one by today's standards.

The football movement in Liverpool, like in other areas, was driven by churches of many denominations, with the local clergy establishing clubs to provide a healthy outlet for people, and to promote exercise, particularly during the winter months. In 1878 a team would be founded by Methodist clergy at a chapel on Breckfield Road North. Initially known as St Domingo FC, it would be renamed Everton Football Club just a year later. They originally played on Stanley Park before later moving to a field off Anfield Road. Around the same time, a team known as Bootle St Johns AFC came into being. They played their fixtures at Hawthorne Road. These two clubs would play the first 'Merseyside derby' more than a decade before Walter, Tom and Danny were born.

In 1888, Everton would become founder members of the Football League and would go on to win the championship of England in 1891. Bootle AFC were less fortunate. Denied entry to the Football League (as only one team from each city was allowed), they would go on to help found the Football Alliance, which eventually became the Second Division of the Football League in 1892 before resigning a year later due to financial difficulties.

By this stage, Everton had fractured in two, ostensibly after a row over the rent paid on the land owned by John Houlding, the then-president of the board. This story is widely known among supporters of Liverpool and Everton on Merseyside today, with Reds occasionally singing 'you should have paid the rent' at derby matches. For their part, Blues will point to the fact that Liverpool's founding father was a Tory to mock their counterparts.

However, the origins of the split are more complicated than that, and had their roots in politics, religion and the growing temperance movement as much as business issues. Houlding, who owned a brewery and many public houses in the area, was also elected as Conservative representative for the Everton ward and later became mayor of Liverpool in 1897. He was a member of the Orange Order and a prominent Freemason, belonging to several lodges.

Houlding's rival, and the man who succeeded him as president, George Mahon, was a Liberal politician, and in terms of religious affiliation, a non-conformist Christian who attended a Methodist church in Great Homer Street. While Houlding and his supporters were unionists in relation to Anglo-Irish politics, Mahon was a supporter of the Liberal Party's Home Rule for Ireland campaign.

The issue of temperance was also a divisive one among members of the board, with several men being members of the movement. Some have even suggested that there were objections to the club's players drinking in Houlding's pub, the Sandon, prior to games. This, it was argued, was responsible for Everton's failed defence of their 1891 title.

It is therefore likely that, rather than simply being an argument over rent, it was a combination of all these factors that contributed to the eventual breakdown and the vote in 1892 to remove Houlding as president, and move the club to an area called Mere Green Field on Goodison Road. Indeed, the dispute over finance feels more like a pretext for the split, rather than the primary cause of it. In any case, this failure by the board to hold itself together would unwittingly set in motion one of the most enduring rivalries in English football.

Houlding had now been left with a football ground but no team. Not to be outdone, together with John McKenna and William Edward Barclay, who had remained by his side after the split, he would go on to establish the city's second great football club. In doing so, he would cement his reputation as a dominant figure in the early development of the game on Merseyside.

Houlding's close alliance with Barclay and McKenna had developed over several years. Barclay was born into a middle-class family in Dublin, in 1857. His father, David, was the governor of the Malone Reformatory, an institution that provided an alternative to prison to young offenders. It was a position that would have ensured the family were comfortably off.

William took full advantage of his good start in life, achieving two university degrees – a Bachelor of Arts and one in Science – and his addresses show that he travelled extensively during his young life, making homes in Belfast, Aberdeen, Lancashire (where he married in 1878) and eventually in Liverpool.

He would marry Emily King, a Yorkshire woman, around the same time that St Domingo FC were being formed and started playing their inaugural games on Stanley Park. By now Barclay was following in his father's footsteps and was employed as the governor of an industrial school in Everton, a position he held until 1898.

His work would see him providing education, board and lodgings to poor and neglected children of the borough. He was now established in the city and clearly a man of some means, a factor that would have placed him in the same circle as other influential men like Houlding and John McKenna.

They are most likely to have connected through their involvement in both the Orange Order and Freemasonry. Houlding and McKenna were members of several Orange lodges including Kirkdale, Anfield and Everton, while both held the rank of Grand Deacon at the West Lancashire Grand Lodge. Furthermore, all three men were active Freemasons, and members of the following lodges: Anfield, Sir Walter Raleigh, Everton, Lathom, Hamer, Lodge of Sincerity and Cecil Lodge.

The influence of Ireland and Irish culture and politics on the character of the city of Liverpool is well known, and it is not surprising that this would have stretched to the development of the city's football clubs too. Upwards of 200,000 Irish families lived in the crammed streets on the city's Scotland Road area. The thoroughfare had previously been a stagecoach route taking passengers from Lancashire to Scotland but was now home to descendants of the great famine in the mid-19th century.

This concentration of people, who came from both unionist and republican traditions, in such cramped conditions created a volatile atmosphere and contributed greatly to the area's culture, influencing the accent of Liverpool's people, and no doubt helped create the city's radical spirit. However, the tensions between those communities led to sporadic outbreaks of sectarian violence and played a role in republican campaigns on the British mainland.

This is evidenced by the Liverpool Town Hall bombing in 1903, and a further attempted bombing of the customs house, which was foiled. The perpetrators had used a pipe bomb and made an unsuccessful attempt to escape by leaping into a canal boat filled with manure. They were eventually tried and sentenced to 14 years in a penal colony.

Events like these led to serious discussions in Whitehall and consideration was given to dispatching troops to the city. Local politicians referred to these issues as 'The Fenian Troubles', which was a reference to the Irish Republican Brotherhood, whose Fenian leader Jeremiah O'Donovan Rossa had been found to have shipped explosive devices described by the authorities as 'infernal machines' to Liverpool from his base in New York. They had been disguised and hidden in cement barrels.

The sense of fear and paranoia created among the city's local government and law enforcement led to an amusing incident later described in the memoirs of the lord mayor of the time. He had been sitting drinking tea in the mayor's parlour at the Town Hall when he became aware of a commotion outside. What appeared to be an angry protest was taking place. Suddenly, the window smashed and 'a large, black, ugly looking object fell on the floor opposite'.

A cry went up from a nearby porter, 'A bomb!' and much panic ensued. However, the offending item would comically turn out to be a pensioner's cork leg. Apparently the protest had been of a more mundane nature. The old gentleman responsible had thrown his false leg at the mayor's window in protest at the number of potholes in the city's pavements.

Nonetheless, it was Liverpool's proximity to Ireland, and the cultural impact of immigration from the nation that placed the likes of Barclay and McKenna in the orbit of Houlding. Their association would lead to Barclay becoming the first secretary of Everton Football Club during the inaugural 1888/89 Football League season. And the men played significant roles in the fortunes of both clubs.

McKenna, born in County Monaghan in 1855, is believed to have travelled to Liverpool as a youth to work in a grocery shop run by his uncle, John McArdle, at 53 Stanley Road, Kirkdale. Like Barclay, and after meeting Houlding, he would soon be invited to Anfield to watch an Everton game.

McKenna found work as a vaccination officer at the West Derby Poor Law Union and was also an enthusiastic rugby player. He had helped form a regimental rugby club before joining the West Lancashire County Rugby Football Union as a professional. No doubt this experience had caught the eye of Houlding who may well have thought McKenna's administrative skills would serve Everton well, and he would soon become a fixture on the board where he assisted with the expansion of the club.

As a result, attendances had risen to 8,000 and the team that then played in salmon pink shirts with blue shorts and socks would clinch the First Division championship in 1891. Following the split in 1892 Houlding would ask McKenna and Barclay to become joint secretaries of his newly formed club. It is said that Barclay took on the role of secretary-manager, while McKenna focused on team affairs and on-pitch matters. However, it was John who telegraphed the Football League, asking them to admit the club to the Football League; the request was promptly turned down.

Claims that the board of the newly formed club blundered in not simultaneously applying to join the Second Division, an error often laid at the door of John McKenna, may be wide of the mark. A letter written by Barclay to *Field Sport* in June 1892, and describing himself as honorary secretary of the Liverpool Association Football Club, tells a different story, and seems to have also been Barclay's way of announcing the club to the football world: 'We have joined the Lancashire League, and have thus provided a very interesting series of fixtures for our first team. We regret that we could not see our way to make application to enter the Second Division of the league, as we felt, after very careful deliberation, that the gates would be no better than the gates drawn with Lancashire clubs, while the traveling expenses would have been very high.'

Whether this was merely a party line, masking an error on the part of McKenna, we will never know. However, it is clear from the following passage that the newly formed board of Liverpool AFC meant business, and had lofty aspirations for the future: 'We hope to meet some of the league clubs during the season, and already engagements have been made with some of the leading Scottish clubs for odd dates. Cup ties – English, Lancashire and Liverpool – will fill vacant spots, and altogether I think the "bill of fare" at Anfield will not disgrace the past.'

Working alongside McKenna, who is credited as having recruited the 'Team of Macs' – players drafted from Scottish football to make up Liverpool's first team – Barclay as honorary secretary would have certainly approved the signings of these men. In his letter to *Field Sport*, he boasts, 'As to players, the following have signed: Andrew Hannah, Renton, back; Sydney Ross, goal, Scottish League vs. Scottish Alliance; half-backs James Kelso, John Cameron and James McBride (Renton), and F. Rogers (Liverpool); forwards, Jock Smith (Sunderland), Thomas Wyllie (Everton), John Miller (Dumbarton), Andrew Kelvin (Kilmarnock), and one or two men of less repute. In addition, we shall have at least four of the best players in Scotland, with whom we are now negotiating. Our supporters may rely on it that we shall take the field with men who can and will play football and good exhibitions of the dribbling code will be seen at Anfield.'

Scotland was regarded as the epicentre of association football, and its players were highly sought after and the subject of many scouting missions from English clubs. As we will learn, the practices employed to entice them south of the border were sometimes of dubious legality and often comical. Liverpool's hierarchy would have doubtless been confident of attracting crowds to see their new stars, a fact backed up by this passage from Barclay's letter: 'Subscribers' tickets will be ready in a few days at 7s, 6d, 15s and 21s, according to accommodation, and the prospects are very bright, and I anticipate a very satisfactory season on the old ground. Although we are the Liverpool club, all the old playing members of the old Everton, to whom Evertonians are much indebted for promoting the game in our midst, have been elected honorary life members. The plans for the dressing rooms and gymnasium are now under consideration, and visiting teams will be spared the trouble of dressing away from the ground, while our own players will not only have a clubroom, but admirable dining rooms and training quarters at the ground.

'In your next issue but one I hope to be in a position to give our friends a full list of our players for next season. The charge for admission to first-team matches will be 4d, and to second-team matches 3d, and only in very exceptional cases, when large guarantees are required, will 6d be charged. The ground is in better order now than it has ever been before at this season of the year, and is improving daily. We do not propose to lay the track this year, as it is too late, but a start will be made early next year.'

Clearly, Barclay and co. were ambitious men, and had every intention of matching their neighbours across the park. Their overture of honorary membership to the 'old playing members of the old Everton' seems to suggest that regardless of the acrimony of the split, good relations will have existed between at least some members of both clubs.

Despite this, it seems there was sufficient bad blood between them to ensure that the first encounter between the sides on the football field would be a feisty affair. The game took place at the end of the 1892 season, with both teams reaching the final of the Liverpool Senior Cup at Bootle's Hawthorne Road. The game was so eagerly anticipated and so much interest was generated that it soon became clear that the turnstiles could not cope with the volume of supporters trying to get in. Conditions and queuing outside the stadium were described as 'interminable'.

The result of the game, which Liverpool won, was as fiercely contested as the fixture itself. It was claimed that a Liverpool player had handled the ball and the subsequent protest by the Everton board would delay the presentation of the trophy to the Anfield club.

Under the stewardship of McKenna and Barclay, Liverpool graduated as champions from the Lancashire League and gained promotion to the Second Division after a victorious 'test match' against a certain team called Newton Heath, who would later become Manchester United.

After Liverpool won the 1895/96 Second Division title, McKenna stepped back into the boardroom, but not before he switched the team from playing in blue and white to red shirts and black shorts. From that moment, Liverpool would be variously referred to as the 'Reds' or the 'Anfielders'.

Utilising his role behind the scenes, McKenna made one of the club's most astute and influential acquisitions – the signing of Tom Watson as first-team manager. Watson was a serial winner at Sunderland and would lead Liverpool to their first two top-tier titles in 1901 and 1906. Walter and Tom would certainly have been old enough to be aware of their city's team becoming champions of England for the first time. Danny Shone may well have rejoiced in Liverpool's second championship. However, the next time all three would experience such joy, they would be lifting the trophy themselves.

There has been much debate as to whether Barclay or McKenna was the first 'manager of Liverpool Football Club', but what seems clear is that the term 'manager' did not really apply in the latter part of the 19th century, at least not in the way we think of it.

Liverpool, like most clubs, were 'managed' by a secretary who took care of the administration side of the game, recruited players and selected the team on matchdays. It is often argued that Barclay shared the role of secretary with McKenna.

However, documents published in 1892 show that Barclay was the club's honorary secretary while McKenna is referenced as being on the committee of directors. Barclay is also recorded as the secretary of Liverpool Football Club in the 1893/94 Football League Rule Handbook and is reported to have resigned the role in 1895 by the sports paper *Cricket and Football Field*. It seems that he was then succeeded by McKenna, who took over as secretary in 1895, and continued in the role until the appointment of Tom Watson in 1896.

'Owd Tom', as he would become known, would serve the club until his death in 1915 and had a hand in the development of several of the men who would go on to become the 'Untouchables' of the 1920s, including Walter Wadsworth. Barclay had led Liverpool from the Lancashire League to the First Division, before failing to save them from relegation in 1894. It would be McKenna who would restore their place at the top table and provide the platform for his successor Watson. As such, both men played pivotal roles in the early development of the club and paved the way for the success that followed.

By now, football had become the dominant sporting pastime in the city, overtaking cricket and certainly enjoyed by more than the game played under rugby league rules. As we will see it would soon attract the interests of youngsters Walter Wadsworth, Tom Bromilow and Danny Shone. Though we have no way of knowing for certain, it is intriguing to think that each of these boys would have followed the well-trodden paths of so many working-class lads of the period by regularly attending matches at Anfield or Goodison, and maybe both.

However, as we are about to see, their passion for the game would go beyond being mere spectators. And, though their journeys to the first team would take very different paths, the game of football would come to dominate the rest of their lives, introducing them to a succession of incredible characters and taking them to places they could never have dreamed of before.

2

Walter Wadsworth, the Champions and 'Owd Tom'

WALK WITH us for a while as we take you to the city of Liverpool at the turn of the 20th century. It is sunset and we are on Ranelagh Street, and the date is Monday, 29 April 1901. A huge crowd – some estimates say 60,000 – has assembled in front of Central Station. There is a faint drizzle of rain in the air but no one cares about the weather though as they stand on tiptoes, their faces caught in the glow of the street lamps and their necks straining for a glimpse of the newly crowned league champions, Liverpool Football Club.

The Reds were travelling back from The Hawthorns, in Birmingham, where they had defeated the already relegated West Bromwich Albion. The victory would see them clinch the title for the first time in their nine-year history and exorcise the ghosts of their agonising near miss just a couple of seasons earlier.

To today's visitors to Liverpool, Central Station is something of a nondescript building, almost hidden by the shops that cover its grand Victorian frontage. But at the turn of the 20th century it was an impressive, imposing sight, a tall structure standing 65 feet in the air and covering the great arched shed that lay behind it. In front, tall pillars 20 feet high held aloft the iron signage that carried its name.

Underneath it the champions would soon emerge, and if they could find a path through the throng, it would carry them all the way to Anfield, and the Sandon pub for an evening of celebration.

Walter Wadsworth, from Cowper Street in Bootle, just five miles away, would have been ten years of age by now. Tom Bromilow, whose home was barely three miles away, would have been six, while Danny Shone's family would soon be celebrating his second birthday. No team from their city had won a league title since Everton secured their first a decade earlier in 1891. And, while it may be romantic to think so, we wonder whether at least Walter and Tom were among that crowd, perhaps Danny's family too.

What emotion must have been unleashed in the hours after it became clear the Reds had delivered their first league title. Civic pride, yes, but there were also local bragging rights at stake too, and not just for the Liverpool board and their players. A keen rivalry between supporters of the Reds and Blues had already been cemented, and cartoonists of the day revelled in Everton's discomfort at playing second fiddle to their neighbours across Stanley Park.

After Liverpool had routed Aston Villa 5-0 earlier in the season, one artist had depicted an Evertonian, depicted as a thin, stooped character in ill-fitting kit, attempting to congratulate a smiling Tom Watson who is chugging on a giant cigar and appears like a giant in comparison. The caption reads:

LIVERPOOL'S WHOLESALE
SLAUGHTER OF THE VILLANS.
Everton – Ok-er-may I congratulate you on-er-your-um-what shall I say –
Liverpool – Tut, dear chap! Don't mention it.
Assure you it was a-er-very simple smash up – no exertion – dear me, no.

The championship, secured by great players like Scotsman Alex Raisbeck the club's giant, golden-haired captain, or Johnny Walker, a man who looked like a Wild West gunslinger and whose goal had won the league, would undoubtedly have earned the Reds an army of new admirers. Kids like Walter and Tom, already keen players for their local schools, would have dreamed of emulating these men.

Suddenly, a giant roar fills the air. 'They're here, the champions are home,' people shout. Eager children, their clothes scruffy and their feet bare, dart between the legs of men and women dressed in their best clobber. Some will have come straight from work; others will have dodged the night shift to catch sight of the title winners.

Then, they emerge, the men who would be forever immortalised in the history of Liverpool Football Club ride out of the station on the back of a cart, or 'brake', pulled by horses. They are immediately swamped. Raisbeck is hoisted aloft and the crowd sing and shout for him to make a speech. He declines, and the players continue their onward journey and the revelry that will surely last way into the small hours. This is how our first championship-winning captain recalls events: 'What a night after the match! We got a great send-off at Snowhill Station by the Brummagen folks who were good enough sports to cheer us off as league champions, but we were unprepared for what was waiting us at Liverpool. I should imagine there was a crowd of between 50 and 60,000 packed in front of the Central Station, and right along nearly as far as Lime Street.

'The street was literally black with people and in the time-honoured way, the horses were dispensed with, and our brake practically carried along by willing hands to our headquarters at the Sandon Hotel. As we went along the crowd yelled for me to make a speech from the brake. I was not to be found, however, as I found it convenient to lie low behind some of the others. Speechmaking was never in my line.'

Walter Wadsworth, a boy who would grow up to be idolised by a generation of Kopites who would christen him 'Waddy', the son of William and May, and the family lived in modest accommodation at 11 Cowper Street, Bootle.

The Wadsworths, who had moved from Rhyl Street in Birkenhead some time after 1881, were a large family and Walter was one of nine children along with his two older brothers, Frederick and Arthur, four sisters Edith, Alice, Jessie and Isabel and two younger brothers, Charles and Harold. We know that the four boys became footballers; Walter and Harold would see first-team action for Liverpool, while Charles would play briefly for the reserves. It is also known that Arthur played football, but he would never play professionally.

Walter's childhood was undoubtedly tough. Just five years after these memorable scenes in Ranelagh Street, in 1906, Liverpool were once again champions, but the Wadsworths were wrestling with great trauma. His mother was committed to Rainhill Asylum that same year after a struggle with mental illness. Her symptoms would likely have been visible for years, causing her to suffer greatly and placing great strain on her and the family. Sadly she would spend the remaining 14 years of her life in the asylum before passing away in 1920. She would never see her son's success.

Their home in Bootle was a place of contrasts in the late 19th century and early parts of the 20th century. Alongside the vestiges of prosperity lay poor housing, squalor and misery. Originally a seaside resort for wealthy merchants in the early part of the 19th century, the growth of the docks and railway saw Bootle rise into a prominent centre of commerce.

Today, its town hall still stands as an example of its past Victorian splendour and its significance as a centre of economic power in the region. The area would even elect a future Conservative prime minister, Bonar Law, to parliament in 1911.

However, life for families who relied on the docks for their living would have been very different. Living conditions in the terraced houses close to the waterfront were cramped, especially for large families. Many were used to going hungry, particularly as work was casual and precarious. Walter's granddaughter, the historian and writer Jacqueline Wadsworth, believes that her family were luckier than most.

She said, 'They grew up on the terraced streets of Bootle (addresses included Cowper Street, Hemer Terrace and Brook Road) in houses that must have felt pretty cramped for a family of that size. At the turn of last century when Walter was growing up, times were difficult economically – especially in Bootle where dockers' families often went hungry.

'But I don't think the Wadsworth family was touched by poverty because, despite fairly humble beginnings, Walter's father was determined to make a success of himself. Beginning life as a railway labourer, then an iron planer, he went on to start up a coal merchant's business, and ended up running the Wadsworth Lighterage and Coaling Company, which had its own fleet of barges which were used to refuel ships in the Mersey. He was also a Bootle councillor.'

Young Walter was therefore the middle child in a very large family, living in a tough neighbourhood, without his mother and with a father undoubtedly working long hours. This meant the older children would have had no choice but to take care of the home. Walter became very close to his sister Alice, who assumed the role of family matriarch. Walter, therefore, would have learned early on the value of collective effort to ensure group survival. However, living among such a large family meant that he would also develop an ability to speak up and fight his own corner. These are qualities that would shape the man and the player he became.

By April 1912, the Wadsworths had moved to nearby 63 Brook Road and the older siblings, Alice, Frederick and Arthur, had left the family home. Walter was now 21 years of age and had found work on Liverpool's extensive dock system in his father's business. Despite his work commitments, he had found time for football, which would have provided him with a relief from his toils. He had been playing at amateur level for some time and had featured for Lingdale and Ormskirk. It was while playing for the latter that he began to attract interest from Liverpool and the great Tom Watson.

Watson had become Liverpool secretary 16 years earlier in 1896 and remains the Reds' longest-serving manager. His capture represented something of coup for the Anfield board. Tom was already the most successful football manager in England, leading teams representing both the east and west ends of Newcastle, helping to found Newcastle United at St James' Park, before going on to guide Sunderland to three league titles.

His exploits in Wearside included back-to-back titles in 1892 and 1893 and three FA Cup semi-finals. His final championship for the Wearside club was secured in 1895, but by then he would have been the most sought-after man in football, and the Sunderland side he commanded were referred to as a 'team of all the talents'.

With Liverpool recently promoted back to the First Division at that time, the board were keen to show their ambition. So certain were they that Watson was the man to lead the club to glory they would offer to double his salary, making him the highest-paid secretary in the league. He would earn £300 per year at Anfield, a huge sum for the period.

Tom was more than a club secretary though, and arguably he was an early pioneer of the duties we most associate with a manager today. Modernisation was clearly on the agenda at Anfield. With John McKenna now firmly back at the directors' table, Watson became more involved in recruitment, team selection and tactics.

The *Cricket and Football Field* journal noted at the time that Liverpool had never had a 'boss off the field and there have been too many on', hinting perhaps that the players were calling the shots. If this were the case, they would more than meet their match in Watson.

Liverpool's new 'manager' was a believer in football science, he understood the importance of diet and exercise – though some of his methods and ideas would raise eyebrows today – and he was a powerful figure in the sport. He would have very quickly earned the respect of the dressing room. Whatever they were used to in the past, things were about to change dramatically, and his impact would be huge, if not instant.

On arriving at Anfield, even as a reserve, Walter would have quickly learned that football was more than a pastime. The players' day started early with them reporting to Anfield at 7.30am. Once there, they would complete a 30-minute stroll. It is not clear where this took place, but it is possible that the residents of Anfield would have seen them walking around the neighbourhood or in Stanley Park.

Breakfast was served at 8.30am and would consist of 'weak tea, chops, eggs, dry toast or stale bread'. Tom did not want his players indulging in butter, sugar, potatoes or milk. As in the modern game, training was split into two sessions, the first beginning at 9.45am and the last at 3.30pm. Watson allowed his players a glass of beer or claret for dinner and encouraged them to be sparing with their use of tobacco. The day would be a long one, though, as they would end it with a stroll at 7.30pm, before presumably being told to get an early night.

It is likely that these methods would have felt unusual, even arduous at the time. To convince players of the need to modify their diet and pay such attention to their physical wellbeing would have required a man with a huge personality and charisma.

Tom, therefore, was clearly a moderniser and very much associated with the professionalisation of the game. He may also have influenced the development of football abroad too. Though there is little documentary evidence of his activities overseas, this tantalising line in a *Liverpool Echo* tribute, written after his demise in 1915, is interesting: 'Mr. Watson was in the habit of spending his holiday abroad, and it is not too much to say that he had a distinct influence in popularising the game on the continent.'

Watson himself attributed much of his success as a manager to recruitment. In an article he wrote in 1899, entitled 'Hunting for Men' and published in the *Leicester Chronicle*, he gives an amusing account of the lengths football clubs went to in order to convince not only players to up sticks and move across the country, but also their families. Many of his early attempts to sign players took place in Scotland. However, he claimed to have no preference for Scottish players, pointing out that half his Liverpool team had their roots south of the border. He simply believed they were the best to be found at the time.

When tracking a player, he would often have to employ cunning and subterfuge to outwit the secretaries of the clubs whose players he was 'stealing'. Success, he suggested, hinged on several factors: his friends and allies in Scotland, the owners of Liverpool, who were committed to financing the best football team in the land, and the club chaplain. The latter would be necessary to convince the parents of his targets that Liverpool had their sons' moral and spiritual wellbeing at heart. However, they would occasionally be thwarted in their attempts, as this account suggests: 'Sometimes our experiences were less edifying. The "chaplain" on one occasion had need of all his prayers for his own safety. It was in Glasgow, and we three had made our headquarters at a hotel there while hunting for a celebrated player. Our presence became known to his club, and a plot was laid to entrap us.

'The club secretary himself called at the hotel, pretending he was the player whom we wanted. He was rather shy of coming to close quarters, so we made an appointment to meet him the same night at a house in Govan-hill and settle terms. I thought it cruel hard lines that at the last moment I had a raging attack of toothache. It was a blessing in disguise. I escaped the unpleasant adventure of my two colleagues, who went without me.

'They were attacked in a low part of Glasgow by a mob of footballers, vowing vengeance on the "poachers"; ancient eggs flew right and left, likewise bags of yellow ochre, and more dangerous missiles still, and at last, they had to take refuge in a friendly doorway and knock for admission to the house. Here they passed an anxious time until the arrival of the police, who had been drawn to the spot by the row; half a sovereign rewarded their kindly host, and then, escorted by a large body of Glasgow police, they arrived back at the hotel, not without a parting salute of eggs and ochre from the disappointed mob.

'The "chaplain", I must say, bore a very unclerical appearance. It was rumoured afterwards, at home, that I was the "chaplain" having disguised myself with his clothes; but, as I have said, I was saved – saved by the toothache, probably the only instance on record in which the toothache ever did anybody any good. I would go through it again under the same circumstances.'

The encounter with an angry mob in Glasgow seems to have altered Watson's tactics, and they became even more devious as a result. He continues, 'After that, when in Glasgow, we adopted different tactics. Each of us stayed at a different hotel. The trick was simple enough, but it never failed to work at night. I would then call, in a cab, on my colleagues, pretend to take each of them up in turn, and drive off, followed by a crowd of angry Scots vowing vengeance on the English thieves who were stealing all their best players. When the enemy were out of sight the other two gentlemen set about business unmolested. I engaged the attention of the crowd until it was time to return and "CAPITAL BAGS, OLD MAN", was the news that saluted me when I went to inquire next morning how the ruse had worked.'

Liverpool's fortunes would wax and wane in the early years of the 20th century and the Reds suffered the ignominy of relegation in 1904. This would have come as a huge blow to a team that had won the championship only three years earlier, and we can only marvel at the courage shown by the board in keeping faith in their manager. Their patience would pay dividends as Watson led Liverpool back to the First Division at the first attempt, setting the stage for him to claim Liverpool's second top-tier league title in 1906.

Watson was now the winner of five championships as a manager, at two different clubs. His stock in the game could not have been higher. It would have undoubtedly been a source of great pride then for the

Wadsworth family that one of their own had been picked up by such an esteemed manager.

However, while 'Owd Tom' was an undisputed master of his art, he would not be the only one Walter would meet at Anfield. His journey to greatness had now begun, and he was about to encounter some of the greatest sportsmen in the history of the game. The 21-year-old Wadsworth would soon be rubbing shoulders with the likes of Ephraim Longworth, Bill Lacey and Don McKinlay. However, the friendship he would forge with fellow new arrival Elisha Scott, the Irish goalkeeper, would endure throughout his playing career.

3

Catastrophe and Revolt on the Mersey as Walter and Elisha Arrive at Anfield

WALTER WADSWORTH officially joined Liverpool in April 1912, although the exact date is unknown. He had been playing in the amateur leagues for Ormskirk when he began to draw the attention of Liverpool scouts. This would certainly have been a big moment in his life and for his family too.

Though they seem to have been reasonably well off thanks to his father's business activities, a decision to take up professional football was a risky one. Walter would not earn significant money unless he broke into the first team. That would not come until 1915, when he made his full debut in a 3-0 defeat to Middlesbrough at Ayresome Park. In the intervening years, he would need to combine training with the Reds and work on the docks.

In the same month that Walter signed up, the city found itself caught up in of one of the greatest maritime disasters in history. The RMS *Titanic*, pride of the White Star Line and registered in Liverpool, sank in the Atlantic Ocean over two days between 14 and 15 April. Estimates put the losses at 1,504 souls. Crowds gathered outside the headquarters of the shipping line on James Street, waiting for news.

The very fabric of the city depended on shipping and the sea, with whole communities wrapped up in maritime enterprise, and the impact of such a terrible loss would have affected everyone in Liverpool, having a profound effect on the psyche of the population. For the wealthy shipping merchants and Victorian elite, it was yet another blow to their sense of Britain's unerring march towards progress and enlightenment.

These were already tumultuous times for Liverpool politically and culturally. Three years earlier, in 1909, the city had been ablaze when simmering tensions between Catholic and Protestant communities erupted leading to days of violence and Liverpool being dubbed the 'Belfast of Britain' by the nation's press.

Two years later, in June 1911, industrial disputes involving the city's transport workers led to a strike which brought the city to a standstill. The action involved dockers, railway workers, sailors and other trades, and it continued into summer, culminating in a huge rally to be held on Sunday, 13 August.

Estimates suggest that anything from 85,000 to 100,000 people gathered at St George's Plateau on Lime Street to listen to speeches from the likes of Tom Mann and other speakers from the growing trade union movement. Tensions were high, and the then-home secretary, Winston Churchill, fearing that Liverpool was on the brink of revolution, had dispatched the army to the city, and anchored HMS *Antrim* in the Mersey with its guns trained on the city centre.

The rally had received a permit to go ahead from the local authorities as this letter demonstrates:

> *Dear Sir,*
> *Re Plateau, St Georges Hall*
> *I beg to inform you that your application for the use of the plateau in front of the above building on the afternoon of the 13th of August has been granted for the purpose of a meeting in connection with the Liverpool District Council, and the National Transport Workers Federation, subject to satisfactory arrangements being made with the head constable, and to your being responsible for any damages which may be done to the property of the corporation.*
> *Yours truly,*
> *Thomas Shelmerdine, corporation surveyor*

However, rumours that the constabulary had ordered hundreds of wooden staves of 'unusual length' from a woodworking firm in Birkenhead led to fears among strike organisers that the police were preparing for violence. Subsequent negotiations appear to have been amicable and the rally would go ahead on 13 August. This excerpt from *Memoirs* by Tom Mann, published in 1923, gives an idea of the size and scope of the demonstration: 'A large number of sailors, firemen, ships stewards, cooks, butchers, and bakers, engine men, crane men, tram men, railway workers, mill and warehouse workers, canal men, flat men, and in fact every conceivable branch and section of the transport industry, fell into the procession and marched orderly down London Road.'

Violence appears to have erupted as speakers were calling for an all-out general strike to commence on the Monday, and reports suggest that what followed was a police baton charge, with hundreds knocked to the ground and scores of arrests, including women and the elderly. Some 350 people were injured, and the event became known as 'Bloody Sunday', but things were about to escalate.

Around 3,500 soldiers were now stationed in Liverpool and tensions were running high. On the Tuesday after the rally, prisoners were being transported on Vauxhall Road when a crowd attempted to free them. Soldiers of the 18th Hussars opened fire, wounding 15 protesters, two of them fatally. The victims were John Sutcliffe, a 19-year-old Catholic carter, and Michael Prendergast, a 30-year-old Catholic docker.

Vauxhall Road was situated only three miles from the homes of Walter, Tom and Danny. Their families would have been acutely aware of the troubles. We know that Walter was employed on the waterfront, though it is not known if he took part in any of this activity. It is, however, almost certainly the case that his father's business will have been affected by the strike and resulting turmoil.

Football would have been a release from the troubles of the world, and the opportunities it presented in terms of income, celebrity and travel, including tours overseas, would have been an exciting prospect for all young boys. However, Walter was a modest young man and not drawn to such trappings.

His early years and boyhood were spent at Cowper Street, Bootle. In 1906, when he was 16, the family had moved to Hemer Terrace. In 1911, aged 21, he was still at home with the family, who had moved to Brook Road. Those who knew him well described him as popular, gregarious and a colourful character, well known for his sense of humour and practical jokes.

Walter and Elisha Scott, who arrived later in September 1912, were known to be great friends throughout their playing days. No doubt Walter's personality contributed to the strong bond that formed between them. Both men shared a similar sense of humour and attitude to life and the game.

Walter always spoke of Elisha with affection and they clearly enjoyed each other's company. They could each be brusque and neither suffered fools gladly. If Walter did not want to sign autographs, he would not, and Elisha was not shy about letting people know what he thought of them. Privately, Walter told family members that on the field he and Elisha would always look out for each other, providing cover when necessary. Neither man gave any quarter, and nor did they expect favours.

They had joined a strong squad that included three players of great repute who would also go on to be part of the Untouchables in the 1920s. These were Ephraim Longworth, Donald McKinlay and Bill Lacey. Despite this, there is no evidence that either Scott or the young Wadsworth felt overawed by their surroundings.

Wadsworth's inner confidence and mental toughness came from his tough upbringing and he was certainly not shy; he would frequently be called upon later in his career to give speeches and present awards. But Walter did not seek out attention and was less motivated by fame than he was by the opportunity to be part of a team and compete for honours. As we will see, he was also more than happy to get physical when the occasion called for it, particularly if he perceived he or his team-mates had been treated unjustly and was known to have a strong sense of fair play.

The club Wadsworth and Scott were joining was in rude health financially, having made a profit every season since the turn of the century. Club accounts indicate that at the end of the 1912/13 season they recorded their best set of financial results, with net profits of £5,875 1s. 6d.

Liverpool now owned the ground on which they played. Thanks to a 20-year loan from the Royal Liverpool Friendly Society in 1907, they had successfully purchased Anfield from Sir William Houlding, the son of the club's founder John and chairman of two major businesses, including the theatrical production company Moss' Empires, Ltd. and Houlding's Brewery Company.

The ground had undergone a great deal of development prior to this. The Main Stand, which held 3,000 supporters, had been built in 1906. Designed by architect Archibald Leitch, it had a distinctive red-and-white gable, and may have been modelled on the main stand at Newcastle United's ground St James' Park. Eight years later, the Anfield Road end was built in 1903, from timber and corrugated iron.

However, because of their continued financial stability, the board planned further improvements to the stadium. The cinder paths outside the ground would be concreted over as would the area around the turnstiles. Railings and terracing would be installed on the Kop and in the newly constructed Kemlyn Road stand.

The Kop, which had no roof, had been built in 1906, and had been given its name by a local journalist, Ernest Edwards. Edwards said it reminded him of a hilltop in South Africa during the Boer War, called Spion Kop. Around 300 British soldiers had died trying to take the hill in 1901, and many of them had come from Liverpool.

By the time Walter Wadsworth trod the turf at Anfield for the first time, in 1912, he would have witnessed a stadium utterly transformed from the modest enclosure that stood at the time of his birth. It was now an arena that could compete with the best in the league.

It is intriguing to think that maybe, as he stood on the Anfield turf during those early training sessions, he gazed upon that vast terrace on Walton Breck Road and recalled his days standing there as a supporter. What emotions he would have felt.

Elisha Scott's Liverpool journey had begun two years earlier in 1910. He had been invited to the city at the age of 17 by his brother Billy, who was an Irish international and who kept goal for Everton. Having spent a week at Goodison Park, he would return home after Everton passed on the opportunity to sign him, feeling he was too young. Not to be deterred, Billy continued to look out for opportunities for his young brother, and lobbied fellow Irishman John McKenna to sign him. His efforts paid off and Elisha would join Walter at Anfield.

Scott's start in football could hardly have been less auspicious, graduating as he had from playing as a forward on a patch of wasteland in Belfast with a group of young lads from Lower Broadway. The 'ball' they used was a rolled up bundle of newspaper. It was regulation size, and it beat the empty can of yesteryear, but it would have been in shreds when the game was up.

He had gone on to play for Broadway United in the Irish Junior Alliance before turning out for Linfield. Once described as the 'terror of goalkeepers', he was now uniquely equipped to outwit any centre-forward.

A piece published in the *Belfast Telegraph*, in 1959, tells the story of Elisha's conversion from forward to goalkeeper: 'Elisha – a member of a family of 10 – was born in the Donegall Road. He attended St. Simon's School, and, in his early days played as an inside forward and centre-forward with the 4th Belfast Company of the Boys' Brigade. It was Boys' Brigade football which converted him from an attacker to a goalkeeper. One day he was so annoyed with the keeper on his side that he went up to him and said, "What's the use of us putting the ball into the net, if you are going to let goals in at the other end?"'

At 5ft 8.5in and weighing barely 11st, Scott's physique would not have marked him out for a career between the sticks. However, his agility, goalkeeping brain and decisiveness would see him nicknamed 'The Cat' by supporters. After a single practice match, the board at Anfield made the shock decision to put Scott straight into the first-team setup. He unfortunately injured his wrist, however, and would have to wait until 1 January 1913 to make his debut away to Newcastle United.

According to reports, it was a beautiful spring-like afternoon and 35,000 fans had been drawn out to see the game. Both teams were evenly matched in mid-table but the north-east side took the game to Liverpool, with Newcastle's forwards pummelling the Reds' goal. Try as they might, though, they could not breach Scott's line. The papers declared that 'the fates and Scott were against them'. It was, according to the gentlemen of the press, the 'best display of goalkeeping ever seen at St James' Park'.

A quote from a *Liverpool Echo* reporter declared, 'Hats off to Scott, Liverpool's youthful guardian. His debut was brilliant and a pleasing augury.' Another newspaper clipping eulogised further about the youngster's star performance, 'It will be remembered that Elisha Scott, the 18-year-old custodian, gave a great display for Liverpool against Newcastle United on New Year's Day. The youth created much admiration by reason of his ability to prevent the Newcastle sharpshooters from netting the ball.'

It must have been the most remarkable of debuts because it convinced the Newcastle board to immediately offer a four-figure sum to Liverpool for his services. A bid, said to be £1,000, was turned down forthwith. That would be the first of two reportedly record bids for his services. According to the *Irish News*, in a tribute piece written in 2015, an unnamed club bid £10,000 for him in 1928. These are huge sums of money for the period and are yet more evidence of his brilliance.

The Reds had plans for Elisha, clearly, but this would prove to be his only start of the 1912/13 season, with Ken Campbell returning to the first team for the remainder of the campaign. Elisha made just four appearances the following year but his breakthrough came in 1914/15, when he made 25 appearances in all competitions.

Walter would wait until 1915 for his debut, but both he and Scott would take part in a tour of Scandinavia in May 1914, in which Liverpool played seven games, winning six and drawing the other. Walter is known to have played in four of them and Elisha two. The tour would have been an arduous one, with the team travelling by sea. They would first take the 2.30pm train from Liverpool Central Station to Harwich in Essex on Thursday, 7 May. The journey south would take more than seven hours, with the group arriving with barely 15 minutes to disembark the train and catch the boat to the Hook of Holland.

The team arrived in the Netherlands at five o'clock the following morning and would have had just 18 minutes before they embarked on a train to Hamburg, reaching their destination at 2.47pm. There they would at least be given a few hours to explore or rest before taking the overnight train to Gothenburg, arriving in Sweden on Saturday, 9 May. They will have been travelling for almost 48 hours and though undoubtedly exhausted, the trip would have been a bonding exercise helping to induct both Walter and Elisha into the squad. This is also an indication of how well thought of the pair will have been.

They would remain in Gothenburg until Thursday, 14 May. While there, they played IFK Göteborg, winning 4-1. Half-back Tom Fairfoul's letters home to the *Liverpool Echo* provided supporters at home with insights into the tour. He appears to have been far from impressed with the pitch and the standard of Swedish football.

Fairfoul described the pitch, which was a skating pond in the winter, as being 'covered with gravel and rolled as hard as our toll roads. I may say the look of the pitch caused serious misgivings among our boys, especially the wing players, as a cement cycle track runs right along the touchline, and it is much closer than Aston Villa's used to be.'

He was similarly unimpressed with 'continental football' and claimed, 'Our boys played well within themselves, and without unduly exerting themselves won comfortably.' However, he does seem very taken with the Scandinavian support: 'We had another great reception when coming home, the road being lined for over a mile with spectators, who kept up a continual cheer. It was very flattering to our team, who, needless to say, felt rather proud.'

Then they were off to Stockholm, where they stayed in the Phoenix Hotel. They remained there for several days before departing for Copenhagen for the last leg of the tour. While in the Swedish capital they featured in three games against Djurgården, AIK Stockholm and a Swedish XI, winning 6-2, 3-0 and 8-0, respectively. Fairfoul wrote home after the 8-0 thrashing of the Swedish XI:

'We played our third and last match in Stockholm on Sunday, 17th, against a select Swedish XI. Unfortunately, on this occasion, the stadium was not available owing to a marathon race being on. This, it was feared, might to some extent soil the gate, as the ground on which the game had to be played is situated three miles outside the city. It was therefore a big compliment to Liverpool FC to find 9,000 people (among those present were the two children of the Crown Prince) when they turned out in sweltering heat, more suited to cricket than football.'

The tour was going very well and even the manager would send home a team photograph, writing, 'Everyone has enjoyed himself. Home on Thursday at 2.15pm.'

Before arriving home, Liverpool would play three games in Copenhagen against Kjøbenhavns Boldklub, a Copenhagen Select XI, and a Denmark Select XI. The results were 5-2, 3-3 and 7-1, respectively. On the 3-3 draw, Fairfoul remarked that it was the toughest game of the tour, with injuries playing a part. A crowd of 15,000 watched an enthralling encounter in which – Fairfoul claims – Liverpool were the dominant side but could not break down the opponents' defence. He wrote, 'The Danes, taking courage from our inability to score, became dangerous, mainly through the efforts of their centre-forward, who dribbled finely, beating three of our boys neatly, and finishing with an effort which just scraped the crossbar. This served to show us we would require to play hard to win. Miller had a nice chance to open the scoring, but ballooned the ball over "Spion Kop", the effort causing Tommy himself to smile broadly. It was evident that Lacey wasn't feeling at home in the outside position. He was inclined to work into the centre, and by doing so threw the whole forward line out of gear. Sheldon was doing well, but made a bad mistake when, instead of crossing, he elected to shoot. A cross would have meant a goal here, as Miller was standing unmarked, and could hardly have failed to score.'

The Reds fell behind when an attacker dribbled past three players and scored with a fine shot that drew a huge ovation from the home crowd. That seemed to have spurred the tourists on and Metcalf took a pass from Lacey and unleashed a 25-yard thunderbolt that sailed into the net. The response of the crowd was a little more muted this time, and Fairfoul claimed they 'were not a sporting one'.

After more defensive mishaps, the Danes would go 2-1 up, and Tom has some words for the unnamed scorer, who he claims would do well in English football: 'The Danes were now playing a good game, their centre being a continual source of danger. He had some corkscrew runs which were very clever. His style of play resembles Puddefoot's, of West Ham, very much. This is the second forward we have met who would do well in English football.'

Liverpool would go in at half-time 2-1 down, a rarity indeed on the tour so far, and in the second half they were shocked to find themselves trailing 3-1. The setback seems to have been the wake-up call they needed. Fairfoul describes the moment in his letter home: 'A high ball was shot into Campbell, who punted out to the inside-right, the latter shooting first time and scoring another fine goal. The fat was now in the fire with a vengeance. Our boys realising what was required of them now, began playing something in their old style.'

Liverpool would rescue their pride with goals from Miller and Bill Lacey. The latter's equalising strike was something special according to his team-mate. Fairfoul would go off with 15 minutes remaining thanks to an ankle injury, and though Liverpool were said to have dominated the final stages, even with ten men, they would have to settle for a draw.

Despite the success of the tour, back home Liverpool had become a mid-table team. Neighbours Everton had also failed to build on their success in the inaugural season of the Football League in 1891, having managed just four second-placed finishes since. The Reds had won two league titles between 1892 and 1914. However, crucially, the Blues' 1906 FA Cup Final victory meant they held bragging rights over the Anfield side, the cup being considered by many to be the most prestigious trophy. The Blues would clinch the title in the final league championship campaign before the league was suspended in 1915.

Liverpool's one other chance for glory came in the 1914 FA Cup. They would reach the final for the first time that season and faced Burnley at Crystal Palace on 24 April 1914. Their achievement electrified the city and elevated the club's reputation to elite status.

Sadly, the Reds were beaten 1-0. But reaching the final and playing the game in front of King George V would have captured the imagination of everyone on Merseyside. Their run to that historic final was far from uneventful.

Liverpool began the campaign that year against Barnsley at Anfield and were somewhat lucky to come away with a draw. Having gone a goal up in the first half, they were run ragged in the second. Barnsley levelled in the 70th minute and hit the bar with virtually the last kick of the game. However, Tom Watson's men would get another shot two weeks later at Oakwell and won 1-0 thanks to an 89th-minute winner from Bill Lacey.

After defeating Gillingham 2-0 in the second round at Anfield, Liverpool then needed another replay to see off West Ham. After drawing the first game 1-1, they thrashed the Hammers 5-1 at Anfield. In what was described as a 'slaughter,' 40,000 watched Liverpool brush the Londoners aside with consummate ease. Then came a 2-1 victory over Queens Park Rangers at Anfield, in which the visitors missed a penalty, to set up a semi-final with Aston Villa at White Hart Lane.

The press had Liverpool as clear outsiders to reach the final. Villa were the form side and many felt they would stroll through the tie. This was something that clearly riled Watson. Before the game, he assembled his players in a hotel for lunch. As they finished, he rose to his feet to deliver one of the greatest battle cries the team had ever seen.

Former Liverpool goalkeeper Ken Campbell recalled the events later in an article for the *Weekly News* in 1921. In it he describes Watson's harsh words for the gentlemen of Fleet Street, and by all accounts 'Owd Tom' had turned red in the face, such was his anger. As he finished his speech, Campbell recalls that he thumped the table, causing crockery to jump all over the place, before declaring, 'Never mind boys, I want you to turn out today and show them up. Show them there are more players than Aston Villa in the semi-final.'

His words seemed to have the desired effect and the Reds ran out 2-0 winners. For the first time in their history, they had reached the final of the FA Cup.

The mood in the city would have been incredible as cup final fever took hold. The *Liverpool Echo* captured the excitement under the headline: 'A ROYAL DAY: MERRY SCENES AT THE STATION'. The paper reported that more than 20,000 Liverpudlians made the trip to Crystal Palace by train and coach.

So large were the crowds that 'one of the biggest trains on record' was pressed into service, carrying 1,200 fans. This may have been the first train ever referred to as a 'football special'.

In addition to this, 19 coaches transported what they described as 'the population of a village from Liverpool to London in one swoop'. However, conditions on the train were said to be crammed and uncomfortable, though passengers made up for this by plastering the carriages with red-and-white ribbons and rosettes and placed portraits of the team and their heroes in the windows, and specially produced *Liverpool Echo* badges bearing football battle cries were worn on nearly every hat and buttonhole. There were also suggestions that supporters, just as they do today, would hide away refreshments of a liquid variety in their pockets, ensuring a merry day would be had by all whatever the score.

Liverpool would lose the game 1-0, but events that took place a mere 48 hours before saw the players earn the wrath of their manager and may have affected morale in the camp. Over 50 years after this historic occasion, in 1965, and after another near miss in 1950 when Arsenal would deny the Reds their first taste of victory in the competition, Liverpool would finally secure their first FA Cup. The *Liverpool Echo* reported that five surviving members of the 1914 team had been invited to watch the final against Leeds United. All but Ephraim Longworth, who was too ill to travel, would witness Bill Shankly's team lift the trophy that had eluded them over half a century earlier.

However, it is the headline and opening paragraph of that article that catches the eye most. Under the words 'When Liverpool did a Chelsea at Epping', the local paper goes on to reveal remarkable details of a bust-up that took place in the Liverpool team hotel just days before the 1914 final.

The players and club management had been staying in the Forest Hotel in Epping, London. In the early hours of the morning, a couple of days from the final, team trainer Bill Connell was awoken from his sleep by a loud noise coming from the billiard room below. The paper picks up the story: 'Down in the Forest [Epping] something stirred, and it wasn't the note of a bird, but of several players returning, via a window in the billiard room, in the small hours of the morning.

'They were not given railway tickets and sent home, like Chelsea. They were not even admonished as they re-entered the hotel after their midnight marauding. They were allowed to sleep in peace.'

However, if the players thought they had gotten away with their nocturnal adventures, they would be in for a rude awakening. Watson would serve up the sternest of rebukes for breakfast, leaving none of them in any doubt of how he felt about matters.

'Manager Tom Watson, one of the greatest the club ever had,' the *Echo* continued, 'tore such a large strip off them they would far rather be sent Anfieldwards to escape such a verbal lashing.'

Secrecy around the events was maintained for five decades, and supporters who attended the match never heard of what happened beforehand. The behaviour of the players was certainly not unusual for the time, and purveyors of the modern game will have similar stories to tell but is interesting to note that managers and trainers as far back as 1914 understood the value of discipline and focus as much as their latter-day counterparts and is testament to their professionalism.

Sadly, neither Walter nor Elisha featured in the competition that season, but the men they would have come to know well and who they would play alongside in the future, Longworth, McKinlay and Lacey, did. As a result, Wadsworth and Scott would have looked up to them and respected them greatly.

The final would prove to be Watson's swansong. The man who had led the Reds since 1896 passed away from pneumonia at his home in Priory Road, Anfield, on 6 May 1915 after the conclusion of the 1914/15 season in which the Reds had finished 13th and Everton had won the championship for the first time since 1891. Watson had been at the club for an astonishing 19 years and had overseen 742 games.

He was laid to rest on a warm, sunny afternoon in Liverpool. The May sun beat down on Anfield cemetery as a crowd of hundreds of mourners gathered at a cool spot shaded by trees. On the ground more than 100 wreaths were left by the public, charitable organisations and the world of football. They included tributes from both Liverpool and Everton Football Clubs.

This was a man with no enemies, who was admired by all who knew him, and whose coffin would be carried by the players he led to countless victories. The *Liverpool Echo* captured the event, in sombre tones, on 11 May 1915. Its article listed literally dozens of dignitaries and organisations who were present, and there would have been a huge number of Liverpool supporters there too.

The opening paragraph gives a glimpse of both the popularity of the man and the affection and admiration in which he was held by all in the game: 'A cool corner of Anfield Cemetery had been chosen. The sun's rays shaded his last resting place. "Tom" was buried there. The day was beauteously fine, and the setting of the last act was all peaceful. The whole sports world seemed to be represented. The late manager of the Liverpool Football Club had no enemies and the far-stretching reach of his works – charity being placed No. 1 – was in a measure shown by the representative gathering which attended to pay its last tribute to an esteemed man. The body was borne to its resting-place by old and famed players of the club: Raisbeck, Maurice Parry (in his regimentals), Charles Wilson, Goddard, Ted Doig, Bobbie Robinson, and trainers Fleming and Connell. The following players of the past season were present: – J. Hewitt, T. Fairfoul, K. Campbell, A. Metcalf, D. McKinlay, J. Parkinson, J. Sheldon, R. Terriss, J. Scott, H. Lowe, E. Longworth, E. Scott, P. Bratley, M. McQueen, W. Connell, G. Patterson, and R. Riley.'

Tom had been involved in team affairs just days before his passing and the news would have stunned everyone associated with the club, and in the world of football. In an article that broke the story, the *Liverpool Echo* wrote, in an article entitled '"OWD TOM" WATSON DIES AT HIS HOME', 'Mr Tom Watson – or "Owd Tom" as he was familiarly and affectionately known throughout the whole football world – was perhaps the most popular figure in the association code of professional football.

'All who take any interest in the game know the exceptionally interesting history of the Liverpool club for the past 17 years.

'In that period, it has had its ups and downs, but underlying all was a fine sense of sportsmanship that has overcome most difficulties, both financial and otherwise.

'It was a popular saying that one never knew where Liverpool would be at the close of the season, for the club had a curious habit of finishing either close to the top or near to the bottom of the league competition.

'The Anfielders, thanks in a large measure to Mr Watson's prescience, carried off the first league championship, the second league championship, and the Lancashire League championship.'

Watson was just 56 at the time of his passing and had been planning a trip to the United States in the summer. The press would speculate that he may have been planning to advance the game of football in the United States, had he lived long enough.

The 1914/15 season had been a disappointing one for Liverpool, and it was also mired in controversy. On 2 April – Good Friday – Liverpool travelled to Old Trafford to face Manchester United. Both teams were struggling but United were in a relegation battle.

The bookies had laid odds of 7/1 on United winning 2-0 and stories emerged, even before kick-off, that players from both teams had been seen drinking together before the match. Rumours were rife that they had been discussing plans to fix the game in United's favour. An Old Trafford crowd of 18,000 and the assembled men of the press watched in amazement as many of the players appeared to be going through the motions. United emerged 2-0 winners.

Not all players were in on the fix, however, and there were reports of angry exchanges in the dressing rooms at half-time. We can imagine that Elisha would have been among those in the Reds' camp, remonstrating with those involved in the scam.

With United leading 2-0, Liverpool striker Fred Pagnam, apparently aware of the plot, was determined to wreck it. He almost scored too. Late in the game he rattled the crossbar with a fierce shot, much to the conspirators' anger.

The FA found that seven players from both teams were involved. United's Sandy Turnbull, Enoch West and Arthur Whalley were found guilty. For Liverpool, Jackie Sheldon, Thomas Fairfoul, Bob Purcell and Miller were also found to have been involved.

All received lifetime bans. The clubs escaped punishment as the FA accepted that the players had acted alone. By 1919, all but West had their bans lifted in recognition of their military service, Turnbull was posthumously reinstated, as he had been killed in battle. West would wait until he was 59 before the FA would lift his ban in 1945.

As a result of the scandal, United had escaped the drop at Chelsea's expense. However, the league was expanded for the 1919/20 season to allow them to re-join the First Division. Such controversies had dogged the game in its formative years, though they had been far less common with the professionalisation of football.

However, amazingly, this was not the first time that Liverpool had been embroiled in such a scandal. Just two years earlier, in 1913, the club had been accused of 'lying down' in a game against Chelsea, gifting them a priceless two points and helping them avoid relegation to the Second Division. And, a future Untouchable, Bill Lacey, would be at the centre of the controversy.

Chelsea won 2-1 at Anfield, with Lacey scoring Liverpool's only goal in the first half. Chelsea's two second-half goals came in the 75th and 81st minutes. Several reporters felt Liverpool's performance in the second period amounted to self-sabotage. The accusations, made by one prominent reporter, Henry George Norris in the *Fulham Times*, were reported widely and amplified by the *Daily Express*, which on Monday, 31 March 1913 quoted him verbatim: 'Would that I had stayed away [from the Liverpool and Chelsea game at Liverpool], for I should then have been spared the infliction of witnessing the worst game of football it has ever been my misfortune to see.

'It was early apparent to me what was happening, and the final result of a win for Chelsea by the odd goal in three occasioned no surprise either to me or the many thousands who left the field in disgust. I have no hesitation in saying that many matches played as this one was would effectually kill professional football in this country as surely as professional running and cycling were killed in the olden days.

'I was told by certain of the Chelsea officials that I was talking nonsense and was prejudiced. Was I prejudiced and was I talking nonsense? If I am prejudiced, is the same charge to be levelled at the critic of the Lancashire "*Sporting Chronicle*"?'

This comment was in reference to a report on the Tuesday, which read, 'Liverpool terminated their Easter holiday engagements by one of the worst exhibitions of football during their career in the premier league. They allowed Chelsea to defeat them by the odd goal of three, after a display which must assuredly cause their faithful followers much food for genuine complaint. It was not merely the fact that they were beaten that aroused dissatisfaction, but the manner in which their defeat was brought about that led to universal condemnation of their methods.

'Never before have the Liverpool first team been guilty of such palpable inefficiency as was the case in this game, and Chelsea's success was due not to their superiority, but to the pandering of their opponents, who practically added to their own discomfiture by their crude unintelligence and utterly feeble efforts.'

Several other papers seem to have picked up on Liverpool's unusually lacklustre display and Norris, though stopping short of accusing the team of outright cheating, asks some pointed questions about their apparent lack of effort. His insinuations were taken seriously by the leaders of the game and a special commission of the Football League Management Committee was established to make enquiries and the then-Liverpool chairman and president of the Football League, John McKenna, was required to make a statement.

In a sign of just how seriously the club took the accusations, McKenna also gave an interview to *Echo* reporter 'Bee'. His comments reveal that the club had indeed conducted its own internal enquiry and had been assured by the players that they had given their best. Despite their protestations, Bill Lacey, Tom Gracie and Jack Parkinson were left out of the following game against Manchester United, when Liverpool also lost, 2-0.

However, the Liverpool directors appeared keen to reassure journalists and perhaps the Football League that they were not dropped because of their conduct in the game against Chelsea, but to protect them from the crowd, who may have been influenced by negative press reporting. Writing in the *Echo*, 'Bee' had this to say: 'It was significant that the Reds' attack on Saturday contained but one member of the attack that played against Chelsea. I have reason to believe that certain forwards were not dropped because of their want of form, but because the directors feared the crowd might become restive. The effect of the game played on Monday was seen on Saturday, when the crowd was unusually small for an attractive match.'

It may well have been the case that the club was seeking to protect its forwards, and the three men were again selected for all three of Liverpool's remaining fixtures that season. It seems that Liverpool's collapse in form during the 1912/13 season predated the game against Chelsea and they would lose two of their final four matches. Inconsistency had dogged them all season, and they had finished 12th in the table. Regardless of how 'offended' Mr Norris and some of his colleagues had apparently been about the Reds' performance against the Londoners, accusations that they had deliberately thrown the game seem far-fetched.

McKenna, a man trusted and respected throughout football, was emphatic in his declaration that the matter must be fully investigated by the Football League. For him, the very honour of the sport was at stake. On 31 March he told the *Echo*, 'In the interest of the game, and of the clubs concerned, I shall at once ask the Management Committee to inquire into the grave charges made by Mr Norris. I am determined that the obnoxious matter shall be sifted to the bottom.

'Faked matches have been absent from football in recent years, and this is well, for a greater death-blow to the popular game than players "lying down" cannot be found.'

Notts County, who were along with Chelsea battling to preserve their First Division status, had also lodged a complaint and irrespective of McKenna's own position on the matter, an inquiry was unavoidable. It took place on Friday, 11 April 1913 with McKenna representing Liverpool and lasted three and a half hours. A statement issued afterwards by the Football Association read, 'The Commission is satisfied that no inducement was offered to the Liverpool players to influence the result of the match. Indeed, Mr Norris assured the Commission that he did not suggest any corrupt or ulterior motive. There is evidence that the form displayed by the Liverpool players was unsatisfactory, but the Commission is satisfied that the allegation that they did not desire to win the match is unfounded.'

Norris, whose extensive commentary had fuelled the whole controversy, was more circumspect after the inquiry and seemed a little chastened by the whole affair. He would admit to the *Derby Daily Telegraph* that he had been 'indiscreet in giving publicity to the Football Association and the Football League'.

The following season, 1913/14, Liverpool slumped to 16th in the table. In truth, after their league title victory in 1906, the club had been treading water in the league. The FA Cup Final of 1914 had marked a high point in an otherwise mediocre spell. Had he lived long enough, it is entirely possible that Tom Watson could have masterminded a rebirth. The spine of the team that would eventually become the Untouchables had been assembled under his reign.

Don McKinlay, who would go on to captain that championship-winning side, had signed in 1910 along with Ephraim Longworth who would become a stalwart of the club and an England international. Watson had already added youthful quality such as Wadsworth, Scott, Lacey and goal machine Harry Chambers who all joined before his death in May 1915. Scott would later be acclaimed as the greatest goalkeeper of his generation.

All these men would be integral to the success of the 1920s. We will never know what impact they would have made between 1914 and

1919, or whether peace would have facilitated the likes of Tom Bromilow and Danny Shone to join their local team much earlier than they did. Sadly, the war would put their development and the progress of the club on hold.

Despite the objections of many within football, the outbreak of hostilities in July 1914 failed to prevent the game struggling on for one more season. Some argued that this was in poor taste for something as frivolous as football to continue while war raged on the Continent. As news of losses filtered home those calls would grow. The editor's notes page in a joint Everton and Liverpool programme produced for the Merseyside derby on 3 October 1914 sheds light on this debate: 'The first month of another football season has passed away, and the game is likely to continue. We should say that the past four weeks have been the most momentous that have ever occurred in the history of football. Opponents of the winter pastime have been pleased to level their gibes and sneers at players and spectators alike; they have seized upon the opportunity afforded to them by this wretched war to sling forth their abusive epithets, and draw invidious comparisons to suit their miserable mood.'

These are strong words for an official club programme and compared to their modern-day equivalents could even be considered refreshingly honest. Clearly, in the early stages of the war, with the idea that it would 'all be over by Christmas' still prevalent, the people surrounding the club saw the game as a welcome release from the tensions associated with the conflict, as evidenced by this line: 'Thank goodness there is a football match to take our minds away from war and its woeful work.'

The editor goes on to decry those who would have them 'wear fiddle-faced masks' – a saying that described an individual wearing a miserable expression – and pointed to the very large sums of money raised from crowds attending games and donated to the war effort. The author concludes that opponents of football were guilty of 'irresponsible blatancy and flapdoodle', which essentially means 'talking obvious nonsense'. How much more poetic language was in those days.

Despite this strenuous defence of football, the league would be suspended for the remainder of the war once the 1914/15 campaign was concluded. Walter Wadsworth and several other players including

McKinlay, Longworth, Lacey and Scott remained on the home front. In the case of Walter, this was likely to be due to the prominence given to his work at the port of Liverpool with his father's business. Lacey and Scott were both Irish and exempt from being called up until 1918. Neither McKinlay nor Longworth served in the war and both played a significant number of wartime games for the club.

However, the Liverpool career of Harry Chambers had barely got under way before he would find himself on the battlefields of Europe. He would serve with distinction and pay a price for his efforts. However he would return to Anfield after the war along with several veterans, including Bromilow and Shone among others, who would reinforce the Liverpool ranks and help lead the club to hitherto unparalleled success.

Part Two

The Untouchables at War

4

Private Tom Bromilow: from Flanders Fields to Anfield

He shall not hear
the bittern cry
In the wild sky
where he is lain

Lance Corporal Francis Ledwidge (1887–1917)

IN A sea of mud, under a clag of gas and rain, men cower in trenches carved in the earth by shovels carried on backs that ached for home. The stench of the fallen, who have been swallowed by the land, drowned, or cut down by shrapnel and bullets sprayed by an unseen foe, mixed with the sickening reek of chlorine and filled their nostrils, curdling their bellies.

There is no birdsong to greet the rising sun, just a chorus of ordinance filling the air then, like monstrous peels of thunder, bombs land, shaking the ground and obliterating their targets. It threatens to disappear underfoot, carrying men, their horses and their instruments of war away from this hell through corrupted soil and on to a suffocating death. Yet this is merely a presage, the softening up of those designated as foe by distant politicians and generals. Soon the jarring sound of whistles will ring out across the lines, trembling hands will fix bayonets and with a shot of rum in their stomachs, men who have yet to truly live will throw themselves into a hail of death.

This is the Ypres Salient, an area of the Western Front during the First World War that takes in and surrounds the Belgian village of Passchendaele. The date is 26 October and amid this terror is Private 5231, Thomas George Bromilow, of The King's (Liverpool) Regiment. Tom, and many thousands of British soldiers, charged across no-man's land to the north of Passchendaele in support of Canadian forces, who would attack and ultimately take a heavily defended ridge overlooking the village.

Tom's brothers, John and William, had also enlisted during the First World War. William, like Tom, served with The King's (Liverpool) Regiment and in the Machine Gun Corps, and John also saw active service in the European theatre.

This campaign in Ypres was part of a series of battles that had begun in July 1917 and had raged for three months, turning the landscape into a killing field of craters filled with toxic sludge. It was ostensibly fought to open the way for the Allies to capture a submarine base on the Belgian coast. However, the Allied command seems to have abandoned this aim and continued to conduct the offensive for no other reason than to tie the German army up and whittle away their resources, at huge cost to their own numbers.

Conditions on the field of battle were appalling. Men, heavily laden with weapons and kit and creeping along planks of wood, or duck boards, laid across the treacherous terrain, risked slipping or being blown off their feet by the concussive blasts of falling bombs, ending their lives by being slowly swallowed by the earth.

Those who commanded them to their deaths judged this sacrifice worthwhile in the context of a deliberate strategy of attrition or what became known as the 'wearing war'. This tactic, developed by Field Marshal Douglas Haig, was predicated on the fact that Allied forces were more numerous than their German counterparts and that even colossal losses could be tolerated, because the enemy would eventually run out of men with which to fight.

A year earlier, one of the costliest battles in military history had taken place. The Somme offensive in France had a casualty rate that topped one million, including 300,000 dead. Around 200,000 French soldiers and half a million Germans were also killed, injured, or missing. During that three-month period Britain sustained 420,000 casualties, including 125,000 dead. Politicians and the public had been repulsed and were understandably wary of a repeat on the Western Front.

So, with losses again mounting at Passchendaele, Haig was challenged by Prime Minister David Lloyd George during a meeting of the war cabinet late in 1917. The field marshal was reminded of the losses at the Somme and was left in no doubt as to the government's grave concern about the already grim list of casualties Haig responded that the casualty rate at the Somme had been no more than he had anticipated. Another general at the meeting suggested that the loss of half a million men would be a price worth paying to rid Belgium of the Germans.

Estimates vary, but by the end of Passchendaele the list of those killed and injured would number in the region of 560,000. The Allies accounted for around 300,000 of these with the Germans sustaining some 260,000 casualties. In the immediate aftermath, both sides would declare it as a military victory. Yet the scars left on families across the world and on men like Private Tom Bromilow and so many more are incalculable.

For Bromilow, who had turned 23 barely three weeks earlier, the horrific scenes surrounding him would have represented a terrible awakening. It was all a far cry from that sunny day in September 1914 when he had enlisted with the King's Regiment, which was headquartered in Liverpool. In fact, such was the enthusiasm to enlist at the outset of the war that the regiment numbered 49 battalions and consisted of 100,000 men.

However, it is not the case as some suggest that Tom joined as part of the four battalions of Liverpool Pals regiments recruited by Lord Darby at the behest of Lord Kitchener. These consisted of groups of men who had worked alongside each other in factories, offices or who had been school-mates. Some 200 of them would be killed and 300 more injured or captured in a single day during the battle of the Somme in 1916.

The Pals had enlisted at the same headquarters of the King's Regiment in St Anne's Street, Liverpool, in August 1914. Tom Bromilow had instead joined the second line of the 5th Battalion of the King's Regiment a month later, on 10 September, and would be trained as a rifleman.

It is not known what drove him at the age of 20 to enlist. Maybe he was one of the many young men who feared being sent a white feather, a symbol of cowardice. Or perhaps he felt it his patriotic duty, or was he seduced by the promises of recruitment campaigns and dreaming of adventures on foreign fields?

Tom was born in the Kirkdale area of Liverpool to John and Alice Bromilow on 7 October 1894. He was their seventh child. John was a blacksmith, a trade that meant his income would have been double that of an unskilled labourer. This may have meant the Bromilow family were better off than some. However, with so many mouths to feed, life would have undoubtedly been challenging for them.

Tom, the youngest of the brood, showed no signs of wanting to follow in his father's footsteps, however. From an early age he showed a keen interest in football, which by now was being played regularly across the city. He played for Fonthill Street Council School and later represented the Unity Presbyterian and West Dingle teams.

The game was becoming increasingly professionalised during Tom's formative years, though it is hard to imagine him thinking that this could provide anything like a decent income. So, in 1911, around the time of his 17th birthday, he would take up a position as a clerk to a shipping company in Liverpool. Gaining employment in this area suggests that he had benefitted from his schooling and was an articulate and intelligent young man, something that is also evidenced by the many newspaper columns he penned later in life.

Still, he never lost his love for football. It was later suggested by *Liverpool Echo* journalist 'Bee' that Bromilow honed his skills playing the sport in the early years of his army career. However, a letter to the *Liverpool Echo* dated 7 October 1932 challenges this. A gentleman intriguingly named Mr W. Derby from West Derby, who claims to be a former team-mate of Bromilow in pre-war amateur football, contradicts the legendary *Echo* sportswriter's assertion. He writes, 'Just a few lines, hoping I'm not intruding: but as a keen reader of your splendid notes I was interested in Tom Bromilow. Who gave you that stuff about tom [sic] learning his football around army camps? You can believe me as one who has played amateur football for 20 years with Kirkdale FC, that Bromilow played left-half and also outside-left. He knew how to play before he ever went into the army. Also, Tommy got his first (gold medal) championship with Kirkdale.'

The claims made in this note are substantiated by an obscure piece dated 7 August 1962 in the *Liverpool Echo* congratulating a Mr and Mrs Tom Brown of 23 Brisbane Street, Kirkdale, who were celebrating their golden wedding anniversary. The article continues, 'Mr Brown will be remembered by football old-timers for the part he played in starting the old Central Combination league of which he was an official for 25 years.

'In the early 1900s he was secretary for a team called Ferndale which later became known as Kirkdale. One of the players for this team was a certain Tom Bromilow who, when World War I broke out, joined the forces.

'After demob this young player returned to play for Kirkdale but it was not for long. Tom Brown recommended him to Liverpool FC.'

An earlier article, written in 1915, indicates that Kirkdale were something of a rising star in amateur football on Merseyside. They had won the Central League championship that year, and the local press refer to them as 'a nursery team for future stars'.

It is therefore clear that as well as working as a shipping clerk after leaving school, Tom was also a footballer of some repute in the amateur leagues on Merseyside. He may well have honed his skills in the army prior to being deployed to the Western Front, but he certainly did not learn how to play the game in the forces, as was later claimed during his Liverpool career.

The fact that Tom was such an enthusiast for the game, means he may have attended matches at Anfield or even Goodison. If so, he would undoubtedly have been exposed to collections outside the respective stadiums, attempting to raise funds for the war effort. He would also have seen recruitment posters adorning the walls of buildings and shop windows around the ground.

It is known that the war cabinet saw football grounds as fertile territory for raising funds for the war effort as well as encouraging players and supporters to enlist. In addition, local newspapers across the country seemed only too happy to support their cause.

The *Liverpool Echo*, dated 3 September, just weeks before Tom Bromilow enlisted with the King's Regiment, carried a photograph of the Kop at Anfield beneath the headline 'THE SPION KOP ARMY AT ANFIELD'. The text below the image states, 'A section of the crowd watching the Liverpool and Bolton match last night. There is room for some of them in the ranks.'

These efforts, focused on football grounds, were ramped up throughout the early months of the war. A report of a conference between Lord Darby and the Liverpool clubs in mid-December appears in the *Manchester Courier*, dated 15 December 1914, and describes a scheme that sought to recruit players and fans alike to the army: 'It was decided to put into operation an attractive form for recruiting the followers of football for reserve battalions at the two big matches on Christmas Day and Boxing Day.

'The scheme, which has the approval of Lord Kitchener, is for the presentation of post-cards to those playing in and attending the matches who are eligible for the Army, on which they are requested to signify their desire to serve, or to state reasons for not doing so. In this way, Lord Darby explained, a proper census of the position in regard to football followers would be obtained, and accusations of lack of patriotism in this connection dealt with.

'Lord Darby added that would-be recruits would register their names, and would be duly attested and medically examined at such a time as would avoid interference with their civil occupations. They would not be called up without due notice, and players would be given facilities to continue their engagements on Saturdays.

'The scheme was readily approved by the football club representatives, who promised it every assistance.'

These postcards were indeed circulated at Anfield and Goodison and many players indicated their willingness to enlist if required. Both Walter Wadsworth and Elisha Scott were among them.

The early days of Tom Bromilow's military service could not have been further removed from the horrors of Flanders. Those arriving at their training base in Liverpool did so in all manner of clothing and it must have been near impossible to imaging the reality of the battles that lay ahead.

This extract from *The History of the 2/6th (Rifle) Battalion 'The King's' (Liverpool Regiment) 1914–1919*, written by Capt. C.E. Wurtzburg, M.C., references Tom's 5th Battalion and gives an indication of the life of a newly enlisted man in Liverpool in September 1914: 'Those early days are amusing to look back upon. We came daily to the drill-shed for training in every form of costume that can be imagined – some men in everyday clothes of a clerk, some in shooting coats and grey trousers, others in khaki bought at their own expense, and so on. Bowler hats were early discouraged, but except for that there were no restrictions as to dress.

'Little by little khaki began to appear and our regulation black puttees, though the regimental "walking out" uniforms had for some time to be used as a temporary arrangement, which made us look a motley crowd.

'"Bugles" were soon formed, and behind these we marched gaily to the Old Farm Field in Sefton Park for drill, and to Allerton or Arrowe Hall for field days. In those early irresponsible days life proceeded easily.'

Men would attend the medical officer for inoculations, marched through the city's streets and presented for inspections but kit and equipment, at least in the early days, was in short supply. It was during these days, while stationed in bases in Liverpool, Blackpool, Canterbury, Aldershot, and finally Woking in Surrey, where Tom may have found time to play football and other sports amid the scheduled training, which included 'arms drill (with 20 old D.P. rifles circulated in turn), outposts, guards, musketry (including miniature range practice), route marching, and physical training. The foundations were also laid of the scout and signal sections.'

Tom moved from Liverpool to Blackpool on 10 November 1914 and was billeted in the streets at North Shore, where the men stayed at guest houses and were paid a subsistence allowance. The officers, meanwhile, stayed at Stretton Private Hotel on the front. From this point on preparations became much more serious, with the recruits mustering in the early hours for parades in the freezing weather along the waterfront, and hours of drill on the beach or marches up and down the bleak windy slopes of Norbreck Hill.

These drills took place every day except Sunday, while evenings were filled with lectures and a degree of free time to enjoy 'the local attractions'. There was even a chance for some, if not all the men, to enjoy Christmas leave before being moved south. January brought some hardships as training intensified and recruits were issued with rifles. Though, as there were no slings available, they were provided with string instead.

On 10 January the battalion marched to Garstang and back, a journey of 33¾ miles, and on 1 February they embarked on an arduous route march to Liverpool and back. The first leg took them to Preston, where they stayed overnight before continuing to Ormskirk in the rain. Tom and his comrades enjoyed a joyous reception on arriving in the town. Then it was on to Liverpool's Exchange Flags, where they were allowed some free time in the city before the return trip to Blackpool the next day.

In all they had managed a 100-mile round trip with few casualties, some of whom had succumbed to ill-fitting boots. By now Tom would be in fine shape and ready for his battalion's move to Canterbury on 8 February 1915, to replace the 1/6th. They would travel to their new homes in requisitioned civilian vehicles. There Private Bromilow would join the 171st Brigade of the 57th Division.

Conditions at Canterbury were harsher than at Blackpool, with two or three men to a billet, and Tom would now be relying on army rations. This led to some men being marched to Margate to lessen the cramped conditions. Records seem to indicate that the battalion behaved themselves and were well received by locals in the town.

It was here that Tom would finally have been given a rifle that he was able to fire, as opposed to the ornamental gun he had sported in Blackpool. He was slowly being transformed into a fighting soldier and his days of school, amateur football and memories of his relatively sedentary occupation as a shipping clerk just a year or two earlier will have seemed like they belonged to another world.

The section of the battalion stationed at Margate were now in a zone of potential invasion, and as such were charged with the town's defence. This meant they would be regularly subjected to practice exercises and on occasion they would be called into action by reports of an imminent attack, which often proved false. Captain Wurtzburg describes one such incident: 'Alarms, practice or otherwise, occurred at most inconvenient moments with most unpleasant frequency. Many are the stories connected with these alarms, but lack of space prevents their narration. Easter Monday morning, in particular, saw us marching hurriedly to Broadstairs at 5.30am, where the remainder of the Brigade met us from Canterbury. This was believed to have been a genuine alarm, but it ended in nothing. Zeppelins were the only form of enemy we saw, and they dropped no bombs on Margate while we were there.'

Despite these drills involving a degree of jeopardy, it is hard to escape the huge contrast with these preparations and what lay in store for the men once they were shipped overseas. This point is reinforced by the following passage from Captain Wurtzburg's history of the battalion: 'If we had been worked hard at Margate, we had certainly had a good time. Sea bathing, concerts, Sunday afternoons on the promenade with our band playing in the Oval, and other pleasurable forms of recreation abounded. Mention must also be made of two most successful singing competitions organized under the auspices of the Mayor and Corporation, for which the proprietors of the Winter Gardens very generously provided their magnificent hall free of charge.'

Tom's military training amid these pleasant surroundings and entertaining distractions, including football and cricket, continued until July 1916. However, there were regular Zeppelin scares, which would on one occasion keep the unit on high alert for a week, as well as rumours of imminent deployment overseas. All of this would begin to ramp up the tension and some men would become impatient to join the fight, while others would undoubtedly grow more anxious. Claims by commanding officers, however, that morale remained high, may have overlooked the inner thoughts and natural anxieties experienced by the men.

Captain Wurtzburg wrote, 'The continued rumours of early foreign service, however, still buoyed us up, in spite of their failure to materialise, and it speaks wonders for the battalion that they endured two and a half years of training in England, with every kind of alteration in policy, without losing to any extent their cheerfulness and their keenness.'

The cheerful and almost stoic disposition of the British soldier during the First World War is referred to in several texts, with many historians suggesting it owed more to a form of coping that manifested itself in gallows humour, which would become increasingly prevalent in the trenches of the Western Front. This is perhaps epitomised by the marching songs employed by men entering battle, such as this one:

What's the use of worrying?
It never was worthwhile,
So pack up your troubles in your old kit-bag,
And smile, smile, smile

In her book, *Letters from the Trenches: The First World War by Those Who Were There*, Jacqueline Wadsworth relates a family story which perhaps most graphically illustrates the way in which soldiers dealt with the unimaginable terror of war: 'On the rare occasions when my grandfather, Edwin Wood, spoke about his time in the trenches, he told this story. Every morning he and his friends would pass a dead man's arm sticking out through the trench wall, and each morning they would shake its hand, "All right mate?" One hundred years later this may sound rather disrespectful, but for the men who lived through those grim times, what better way of coping than by allowing themselves an ironic smile?'

Spending his days on Margate promenade, bathing in the sea or attending concerts at the Winter Gardens, Tom would surely have had no conception of what lay ahead. His cheery resignation to his present conditions would have given him no insight into the trauma he would learn to adjust to, nor how he would be transformed mentally and physically in the years that lay ahead.

The summer of 1916 brought a switch to Bourley, Aldershot, before a further move in September took them to Woking. The unit spent another Christmas billeted and wondering what lay in store for them before they were finally mobilised for war in February 1917 and heading to France in the same month. This is how one of Tom's officers reflected on their imminent deployment: 'With what high hopes we set off on our journey! Now at last we felt that the final stage in our education had been reached. Aldershot and Salisbury Plain were the universities of the military student, whence he was launched into the vortex of war complete with all the necessary knowledge. That we had now at last been admitted to this select academy must mean that our days in England were strictly numbered. Alas for our hopes!'

By 26 October 1917, Tom's battalion, the 2/5th of the King's (Liverpool) Regiment, were in the thick of the battle for Passchendaele. He would endure the fighting for a month. We have no letters from him that describe his experiences and his family remember no stories relating to this particular conflict. However, this letter home from Private G. Giggins, No. 32750, 62 Machine Gun Company, cited in Lyn MacDonald's *Passchendaele: The Story of the Third Battle of Ypres 1917* and written a month before Tom arrived, gives some insight into what lay in wait for him: 'Well, the front-line dead – a lot of people won't like this – they're simply dead. You can't do much about them. In most of the attacks, if they were killed they just had to lie there until they disappeared under the mud. That was the reason we had so many missing. When a fellow gets hit by a splinter or shell, or even a bullet, he collapses at the knees and usually falls face forward because of the weight on his back, which means you've only got to have a few inches of mud and he drowns in the mud.

'I was right behind the lines one day at Tor Top, going down a track towards Zillebeke, and I saw a haversack, a very good haversack, just lying there half in the mud. Now a machine-gunner can always do with a haversack because ours get very dirty and oily from carrying tripods. So I tried to pick the haversack up and it was attached to a dead body. That was the sort of thing you saw all the time. The thing was that you couldn't do anything for the dead. It's surprising how heavy a man is when he's dead, and if you are being pushed back, or even if you were just going out of the line, you had enough to carry with guns and ammunition. The most important thing is to get the wounded back, because they *do* stand a chance.'

It is hard to understand how the human psyche can withstand such trauma, keep moving forward and continue to fight. Of course, many would quite understandably succumb to what we now call post-traumatic stress disorder, but what the army referred to as nervous cases or the shell-shocked. These men would shake violently, and mumble incoherently. Their comrades would describe them as 'stark raving going mad' and shamefully some would brand them cowards; some were shot.

Men like Tom Bromilow, and it must be said those in the German ranks too, came through this living hell thanks to a combination of extraordinary bravery, the human survival instinct and pure luck. Tales of German machine gunners chaining themselves to their guns to prevent themselves from fleeing in terror, and Allied soldiers risking life and limb to drag the wounded from the mud, are plentiful, as are stories of men launching themselves at enemy trenches and capturing them from shell-shocked and bewildered enemy soldiers, who had endured days of artillery barrage.

However, for every one of these events, there are those of sheer luck. Men talked and wrote of seeing the comrade in front, behind or standing next to them being killed. The difference between life and death was measured in seconds and millimetres at Ypres. For the average soldier witnessing such scenes in Flanders, it was often a case of, 'There but for the grace of God go I.'

The Ridge at Passchendaele would eventually be taken, despite incredible losses to the Allied ranks. The futility of such sacrifice for such a small patch of land is underscored by Haig's decision to effectively abandon the battle and divert troops to battles in Italy and France. In truth this had always been about wearing the enemy down, regardless of the losses to his own ranks.

Writing years later, Lloyd George, as prime minister a man who had the power to stop the offensive at any point between July and November 1917 but who chose not to, would write, 'Passchendaele was indeed one of the greatest disasters of the war … No soldier of any intelligence now defends this senseless campaign.'

At some point after the end of Ypres, Tom changed battalion and joined the 2/6th. With this came a change in service number to 202310. He was listed as sick on 8 May 1918 in Captain Wurtzburg's history of the King's Regiment but was not discharged. Given the horrendous sanitary conditions on the front, coupled with the fact that gas such as mustard and chlorine were frequently used, it would not have been surprising for him to have succumbed to illness.

However, given that he was not sent home to England, we can be relatively confident that he recovered from his illness and returned to his regiment. This makes it highly likely that he would have seen further action during the subsequent battles at the Drocourt-Quéant Line on 2 September 1918, Canal du Nord between 27 September and 1 October

1918, Cambrai between 8 and 10 October 1918, the occupation of Lille and the final advance into Artois during the final weeks of the First World War.

Frustratingly, many records pertaining to the conduct of Tom's battalion and the war in general have since been lost. This makes it hard for us to speak with absolute certainty about Private Bromilow's movements during these key operations. We have been unable to identify any letters written by him and he appears, like so many who served with him, to have chosen to speak little of his time in the armed services after his return home.

However, Tom's family do recall a story often retold among relatives of how his unit had found themselves outnumbered by German troops, and how he had needed to hide in a bombed-out building to evade capture. We are unable to verify this but given his extensive involvement in several decisive battles during the Hundred Days Offensive towards the end of the war, it cannot be discounted.

Bromilow's battalion ended the war in France, at Faubourg de Fives, Lille, on Armistice Day (11 November 1918). According to Tom's Medal Rolls Index Card, he was awarded the Victory and British War Medals, both of which were commonly awarded to military personnel who fought in the First World War. In all, the King's Regiment would receive 58 battle honours, including six Victoria Crosses, and lost some 15,000 men.

Tom would return home after demobilisation in 1919, apparently fit and healthy and remarkably ready to put his experiences behind him and resume his career in football. As we will see, his decision to approach Liverpool Football Club secretary George Patterson and personally request a trial would prove to be a fruitful one for both club and player.

5

Wounded on the Western Front: Private Danny Shone's Battle for Survival

IT IS 18 May 1918, and a train laden with casualties from the Western Front rolls into the station at the small and beautiful seaside town of Étretat. Among the many casualties on board is a badly wounded soldier, Private Danny Shone of the 1st Battalion of the Sherwood Foresters, service number 109094.

Danny's war, though brief having only arrived in France a little over a month earlier, was over. Danny is in a great deal of distress and has sustained a gunshot wound to his abdomen. He now faced a more personal battle, this time for his life.

The town is located on the French Channel coast and its citizens have by now become accustomed to such scenes. During the darkest days of the Somme offensive, they had witnessed hundreds of soldiers lying wounded in the streets or being transported on horse-drawn carts to their final place of rest.

The British Expeditionary Force's General Hospital No. 1, located in the town, had become so full that tents were erected outside to deal with the constant stream of injured and dying servicemen, and it would eventually annexe a nearby hotel to create more space. In the final year of the war, the hospital at Étretat had become so depleted of medics, who had been killed or injured, that it recruited nurses to train as anaesthetists.

Canadian nurses referred to the practice of administering anaesthesia as 'slinging the slumber juice', and an extract from the diary of an

Australian nurse who volunteered shows how eager they were to fill in the gaps and help the wounded. On 10 November 1917, six months before Danny arrived at the hospital, Sister Elsie Tranter wrote, 'Fritzie has been doing so much damage lately to medical officers that the supply of them now is not equal to the demand and many more are needed to cope with the ever-increasing work. There is a scheme afoot for army nurses to be trained as anaesthetists to free medical officers for medical and surgical work. To this end, 250 volunteers have been called for from among all the nurses on service.'

Waiting outside the station in May 1918 was a fleet of British Red Cross ambulances and dozens of female drivers who were referred to as 'British Chaufferettes', ready to transport Danny at once to the hospital. The lightly wounded would walk along the road to the town centre, while buses would transport those unable to make the journey. The ambulances were reserved for the most heavily wounded.

Private Shone would have endured an uncomfortable trip and may have been administered morphia to control his pain. While he may have felt relief at being transported away from the front, he would have been aware of the serious nature of his wounds and was possibly fearful for his life. We can imagine him reflecting upon the path his life had taken and wondering whether he would ever see England and his family again.

Danny was born on 22 May 1899 in the Edge Hill area of Liverpool, meaning he was just four days short of his 19th birthday when he was wounded in battle. His parents were Ellen and Daniel Shone, and Danny had seven siblings: Peter, John (who sadly did not survive infancy), Ellen, Sarah, Edward, Elizabeth and William.

Daniel was employed as a master brick maker at the time of his son's birth and the family lived at 1 Freeman Street, Edge Hill, off Earle Road. Freeman Street consisted of typical 19th-century terraced housing and it ran between Earle Road and Spekeland Road in the Toxteth area of the city.

By 1911, the family home appears to have expanded, now taking in 1-3 Freeman Street, and they now owned and ran a general store which sold groceries and household goods. They had acquired the house next door from John Phease, a carpenter and joiner aged 29, and his wife Elizabeth.

A door was installed downstairs to link the two houses, which now boasted nine rooms, more than enough for the expanded family. Danny's father, now 49, had now quit brick making and was running the grocery store with his wife Nell, who was 42. Young Danny, aged 11, was still at school along with his younger siblings Elizabeth (9) and William (6). As for Danny's older brothers, Peter (22) helped out in the store while Edward (20) was an asphalt labourer, and his sister Ellen (14) was apprentice to a dress maker.

The front room of 3 Freeman Street became known as the 'men's parlour', and women and children were prohibited from entering. Life appears to have been a stable and happy one for Danny. His parents were well regarded in the area, often running lines of credit for customers whose income would have been precarious. However, there is evidence of some drama in 1904, which involved his father and his uncles being accused of engaging in illegal gambling.

On a spring afternoon in May 1904, at the age of 42, Daniel, his 45-year-old greengrocer brother Peter, and an associate, 38-year-old baker Charles Matthews, found themselves in front of Liverpool Assizes (courts). They were formally charged with having, as the occupiers of St James' Hall, James Street, Garston, or as persons using the same, unlawfully kept the premises for the purpose of betting.

Fortunately for the family's honour they were all acquitted, with the magistrate convinced that the group were engaged in nothing more than casual betting at their social club, suggesting the possibility that the local constabulary had been a little overzealous. In any case the Shone family appear to have put this behind them. Like many young men in working-class cities across the country, Danny soon developed an interest in sport. He was a keen cricketer and won medals playing the game, but football soon came to dominate.

A player called Shone appears in a line-up for St Ives in a piece dated 3 April 1914 and Danny did go on to carve out a successful amateur career with Earle FC in the South Liverpool Amateur Alliance. Clearly a promising youth player, he would soon attract the interest of Liverpool scouts, and his family believe he signed amateur papers for the club at the age of 15 in 1914. Sadly, all record of this has not survived the intervening years during which the club routinely purged its files and records.

The Anfield side had only a first team and reserve side until 1921, so there would have been no youth setup for him to join. It is possible that he trained with the reserves, a practice that survived until the 1960s. He may even have played with them but owing to the absence of official documentation this can't be confirmed. Whatever the arrangement with Tom Watson's Liverpool was, the outbreak of war in Europe appears to have put a temporary halt to any developing Anfield career.

With the eventual suspension of the Football League, any interest in him from Liverpool appears to have fizzled out, and he returned to Earle FC. According to newspaper and league records at the time he was something of a prolific striker in amateur football, and during the 1916/17 season he scored 53 goals, a record that was not beaten until 1935.

At some point he gained employment for local ship builders Grayson's of Garston as a shipwright. However, it has been claimed that the company were more interested in him as a footballer, and as such he would simply clock on and clock off apparently without doing much work in between. Danny, it seemed, was living every young man's dream.

The arrangement would have allowed him to spend much of his time training with and playing for the firm's football team, who competed in the West Cheshire League, while earning a workman's wage. It is hard to imagine a life more removed from the horrors of the Western Front. Therefore, as he lay in the back of that ambulance in Étretat, France, in 1918, his sense of disbelief and despair must have been overwhelming.

Danny's journey to the front line began on 30 April 1917 when he enlisted with the 5th Manchester Regiment, under the terms of the 1916 Military Service Act. He was aged just 17 years, 11 months and eight days. He would play football for the regimental team before being deployed overseas.

The British Army had realised by 1916 that their strategy of attrition, which had led to a huge volume of largely anticipated and planned for casualties, meant they could no longer rely on voluntary recruits. Even though over one million had joined up by January 1915, this supply could not match the demand as tens of thousands were killed, injured or captured. The problem had been further compounded by an understandable decline in voluntary recruits as news of casualties filtered home, the collapse of the French Army and later Russia's withdrawal from the war.

The Military Service Act therefore imposed conscription on all single men aged between 18 and 41, but exempted the medically unfit, clergymen, teachers and certain classes of industrial worker. A second Act passed in May 1916 extended conscription to married men. Despite protests involving a crowd of 200,000 at Trafalgar Square, and widespread opposition, a further 1.1 million were conscripted by 1917.

Danny initially posted to the 5th Manchesters in May 1917; a Territorial Force battalion headquartered at Wigan. He was given the service number 55940 and sent for training – most likely with the 71st or 67th Training Reserve Battalions. These were based at Ripon (71st) or at the Altcar Training Camp in Hightown, Merseyside (67th).

This would have felt like a frantic time for Private Shone with little time to think as he came to terms with his new life as a soldier. He appears to have been on the move a lot after initial training. He was posted to the 5th (Reserve) Battalion of the Manchester Regiment on 27 November 1917, then to Scarborough before proceeding to Folkestone on 30 March 1918.

The following day, Danny's battalion consisting of around 250 men, supplemented by a further 100 from the Lancashire Fusiliers, arrived in Boulogne. He would have then been assigned to the Manchester Infantry Base Depot (MIBD) at Étaples, where on 4 April he was transferred to the 1st Battalion Notts and Derby Regiment (1/Sherwoods), and given the new service number 109094. Private Danny Shone was now deemed ready for active service and would soon be deployed to the battlefield.

The Germans had launched their spring offensive along the Western Front only a matter of weeks earlier, on 21 March. The bombardment endured by the British defensive lines was said to be the fiercest of the war. The Germans would target an area covering 150 miles, launching 1.1 million shells in five hours.

By the end of the first day, the British had lost 7,512 dead and 10,000 wounded, and the Germans had broken through the Allied defences in several places. It was feared that they could advance all the way to the ports within seven days. This prompted Field Marshal Sir Douglas Haig, on 11 April, to issue an order stating, 'With our backs to the wall and believing in the justice of our cause, each one of us must fight on to the end.'

It was into this terrifying theatre of destruction that Danny was placed. His battalion moved on 12 April and joined the front line at Villers-Bretonneux a week later and there they would remain until 23 April, when they were relieved and marched to reserve billets in Blangy-Tronville, a small town in the Somme region of France. However, their respite was to prove short-lived.

In the early hours of the following day, the Germans launched a frontal assault, under cover of mist and smoke and using tanks for the first time. They successfully broke through the Allied lines at Villers-Bretonneux by 9.30am. With barely any time to rest, Danny's battalion were immediately placed under the temporary command of the 23rd Infantry Brigade and thrust into a counter-offensive attack at 10pm.

Three days of bloody combat ensued and eventually the German attack was repelled, but at a terrible cost as 234 men were either killed, wounded or injured, some of whom Danny will surely have known well. Then, exhausted both physically and mentally, the battalion was apparently afforded some time to regroup before being moved up to the front line to help relieve the 1st Worcestershire Regiment. These trenches would come under intense bombardment ten days later, as the Germans mounted an offensive that led to the third battle of Aisne.

Troop movements were complex at this stage of the war, and with heavy losses men were deployed to fill gaps wherever necessary. They arrived on 17 May and began the hazardous process of relief, which involved men moving around in the open and consequently exposed to sniper fire. The weather during the day had been blisteringly hot, and the men would have been carrying kit that weighed up to 32kg. In the evening, however, temperatures had dropped offering some relief. Nevertheless, the operation, which was not completed until 3.45am on 18 May, would have been laborious and exhausting.

In the final hours, with manoeuvres almost complete, the battalion took enemy fire and Danny was hit. After little over a month in the field of battle, and having come through Villers-Bretonneux, he now lay in the dirt having sustained a potentially mortal gunshot wound to his abdomen. Soldiers faced with such injuries with potentially mortal wounds would often ask those attending to them to pass messages to loved ones back at home, and Danny would have been fearful for his life and acutely aware that he may not see family in Liverpool or play football again.

His fear would have been justified as penetrating injuries to the abdomen were grave. Aside from the risk of massive blood loss, there was also the danger of infection and sepsis as well as obstruction of the bowel later. In 1915, battlefield surgeons did not expect to operate on such wounds. It was felt that such difficult surgery was not possible in the field. In early battles, such as the Boer War in South Africa, the mortality rate from such wounds was extremely high. However, by the final stages of this war, improved methods of evacuation to military hospitals away from the line and advances in anaesthesia meant that Private Shone at least had a fighting chance.

However, he faced a desperate race against the clock. Many wounds were heavily contaminated with the filth and mud of the battlefield. Fellow soldiers carried a small first aid kit that contained dressings and they may have used water to irrigate his wounds. However, if Danny were to stand any chance of survival his fate rested on several factors and time was of the essence.

In the first instance, he needed to be evacuated to a clearing station, which required removal from the line by stretcher bearers. This was a process loaded with jeopardy, and without pain relief it was incredibly uncomfortable. Stretcher parties did carry morphine preparation for those who were in a great deal of discomfort and who could not keep still or quiet during their transport. Although it was custom not to fire on soldiers tending to the wounded, this practice was often forgone in the closing stages of the war, and those attempting to rescue men from the trenches risked being gunned down or blown up. There are numerous cases of this happening during the battle of Passchendaele, for example.

Danny's arrival at the dressing station would have led to a swift decision that he needed to be transported immediately to a hospital where surgery could be performed. His wounds would have been cleaned with sodium hypochlorite solution and dressed using dried sphagnum, or 'bog moss'. This had much better absorbent properties than cotton wool, combatted sepsis and slowed down bleeding.

Men who made it to an operating theatre in under six hours stood the best chance of survival, so he would have spent little time at this dressing centre before being whisked away and placed on the train. The distance from Aisne near Paris to the General Hospital No. 1 in Étretat is around 326km (202 miles) and the journey may well have been an uncomfortable one, with plenty of time to contemplate the seriousness of his predicament. This meant his survival depended on the fine margins of the skill, speedy decision-making and bravery of many people working in unison.

After successfully undergoing surgery, Danny recovered sufficiently to be posted to the 5th (Reserve) Battalion of the Notts and Derby Regiment to continue his recovery and receive treatment. The subsequent battle of Aisne would cost the Allies 137,000 casualties; however, Danny's war was now over.

Elsewhere, the war would take a decisive turn. By September, the Allies had made significant advances. From August onwards they would win a series of battles and took tens of thousands of prisoners in what became known as the Hundred Days Offensive. This saw them progress to the Hindenburg Line, a series of concrete, steel and barbed wire fortifications that spanned a section of the Western Front.

We know that Tom Bromilow's battalion was involved in the Battle of Cambrai, a decisive victory that broke through the line in October. Germany was losing men and supplies and in addition had lost support from Bulgaria, who signed a separate Armistice in late September. The entry of the United States into the war, at a rate of 10,000 per day, bringing manpower and oil supplies, gave the Allies a significant advantage.

With news of Germany's imminent defeat spreading through the ranks, dissent grew, and fearing mutinies, Admiral Reinhard Scheer and General Erich Ludendorff attempted to launch a last desperate offensive to 'restore the valour of the German navy'. However, revolution had erupted in the north of the country, which included revolt of the sailors. In short, the German navy refused to set sail and the uprisings spread to the whole country. The German Republic was declared on 9 November 1918, which led to the abdication of the Kaiser. The newly installed German government then surrendered.

The Armistice with the Allies was signed on 11 November 1918, and Danny was subsequently discharged under Paragraph 392 of King's Regulations Category XVI – no longer physically fit for war service – three days later. He was awarded the Victory and British medals.

Having been declared to have a 60 per cent disability due to wounds sustained in battle, he would receive a war pension effective from 15 November. Today, we understand that people exposed to such trauma are at great risk of psychological illness. It would have been understandable had Danny experienced mental health issues as a result of his service. However, his family can recall no examples of him sharing his feelings, and he rarely discussed his time overseas with them. As we know, this was not unusual for retuning servicemen.

Prior to the First World War, there was little understanding of such issues and no treatment. However, owing to the sheer volume of combatants involved in the conflict, it would quickly become apparent that as well as causing terrible physical injuries, war damaged minds too. Over 600,000 German servicemen were treated for 'nervous' diseases during the four years of war. The UK recorded 80,000 cases of 'war neuroses' between 1914 and 1918, and up to 200,000 veterans received pensions for war-related nervous disorders after their return home.

During fighting, soldiers described the effects of trauma as 'shell-shock', believing symptoms were caused by exposure to artillery bombardment. As early as 1915, army hospitals became inundated with soldiers requiring treatment for 'wounded minds'. Effects included tremors, blurred vision and fits. Yet despite it being a widespread condition observed all along the front, men experiencing the condition were often accused of moral failings and weaknesses, with some soldiers even being accused of cowardice.

Even after war, men reported symptoms such as nightmares, hyper-vigilance and tremors. It had previously been believed that a healthy soldier who was well trained and integrated into a unit with high morale was resistant to psychological pressures. And, although it was recognised that exceptional events could lead to breakdown in a healthy soldier, a full recovery was expected once he had been removed to a place of safety. These attitudes, even among the men themselves, led to stigma and a fear of being branded a coward or weak, leading to many men suffering their demons in silence long after the war.

We will never know if Danny Shone was one of those poor souls. He was undoubtedly a healthy young man at the time of his deployment, but his frequent movements between battalions during his relatively short involvement in the war made it difficult to fully integrate and form close bonds. Meanwhile, his overall lack of experience in battle may also have increased his risk of post-traumatic stress.

From the available evidence we can only say that he eventually returned to England at the end of hostilities, his physical wounds healed (according to his bio in a 1928 West Ham programme, Danny had also sustained wounds to his arms, though these can't be verified) and showing no outward signs of battle stress. He was apparently simply ready to make the most of the rest of his life. He would return to Grayson's of Garston where he continued to distinguish himself as a fine footballer. In the coming chapters we will see that despite all he endured in that brief spell at the front, he recovered sufficiently to carve out a very successful football career. That is perhaps the most remarkable aspect of his story.

6

The Home Front

AT THE outbreak of war in 1914, Liverpool had established itself as the maritime capital of Britain. Its waterfront could now rival that of any major European port. The Mersey Docks and Harbour Board (1907) and the iconic Liver Buildings (1911) had been completed and the construction of the Cunard Building, which would complete the city's so-called Three Graces, was under way.

The livelihoods of the people of Liverpool depended heavily on the sea and on trade with the rest of the world. The Mersey was so significant to the people who dwelled on its banks that when war was declared 12,000 men enlisted to do battle at sea. It is said that between 1914 and 1918, every single battleship had Liverpudlians on board.

On 31 August 1914 queues of men desperate to enlist in the army had developed at St George's Hall on Lime Street. Once the scene of labour unrest and protest, the vast plateaux at the heart of the city had become the scene of mass recruitment of men keen to fight for 'King and Empire'. A thousand of them had joined up by mid-morning. Many of these men would form the Pals battalions of the King's (Liverpool) Regiment, and thousands more would sign up, although 3,000 of them would not return home.

The idea of empire and colonialism rightly offends many today, but it is important to understand the psyche of people living in Britain in the early decades of the 20th century. The nation had become accustomed to its country's role on the world stage, and the idea that the British had the right to 'rule the waves' would have infected every newspaper read by the masses and taught as a birth right in classrooms and reinforced from the pulpit.

We know that even during their leisure time, workers attending football matches would have been the subject of recruitment campaigns and appeals to patriotism. Meanwhile, the excesses and atrocities committed by the empire would doubtless have been obscured or even hidden from view.

Many of these recruits would have been eager to serve, considering it their duty. Attitudes towards those who did not sign up were sometimes harsh and accusations of cowardice were not uncommon. Aged 23 at the outbreak of war, Walter is thought to have joined his father's coal merchant business, supplying ships of the Mersey, when the Football League was suspended. He also worked as a stevedore, an occupation deemed vital to the war effort. This meant Walter wouldn't be drafted.

However, despite this reprieve, we know that he did sign a pledge card issued as part of the Lord Darby scheme and discussed earlier. Therefore, we can say without doubt that he was not a conscientious objector. However, it is known that Walter's older brother Arthur, also a footballer, did serve in the forces during the war. He was captured and spent more than two years in a German prisoner of war camp.

Prior to the suspension of the Football League, Walter was already attracting attention as a footballer of some promise. His career was clearly just getting started when war broke out. A report in the *Liverpool Echo* on 20 January 1916 refers to his attributes: 'This tall young fellow is one of the few locals capable of keeping his place without a "back scratcher", and the day is not far distant when he should figure regularly in a senior side.'

He would make just one appearance in the 1914/15 season, in a 3-0 defeat to Middlesbrough. However, he would feature regularly during the war years, when he made 114 appearances and scored nine goals. The best though was yet to come, and Walter would play 241 times for the Reds. The title-winning seasons were clearly a highlight but on a personal level he would be proud of his significant contribution to both championships. In 1922, he made 42 appearances and followed that up with an impressive 41 starts in 1923.

Other Reds players who were not called up included Ephraim Longworth, Donald McKinlay and John Bamber who were 26, 23 and 19, respectively when war broke out.

Longworth was born on 2 October 1887 in Halliwell, Bolton. His parents were James and Jane, and he was one of seven children. Ephraim had three brothers – Vincent, William and John – and three sisters – Esther, Mary and Sarah. The family lived at various addresses in the town until 1911, including 19 Osborne Grove and 262 Oxford Grove.

By 1910, Ephraim had become a married man, having tied the knot with bride Florence at St Augustine's Church in Tonge Moor, Bolton. The couple then moved to 53 Hanwell Street, Anfield. And the 1911 Census records his occupation as 'Footballer, Liverpool Football Club'.

He had already made his first appearance for the Reds in September 1910, a 2-0 defeat to Sheffield United at Bramall Lane. A report of the game in a joint Everton/Liverpool programme reflects that Longworth had a 'fair' game, and suggests that he 'promises to come on, for he can both kick and tackle'.

In truth, Ephraim was a player with a considerable football pedigree long before he joined Tom Watson's Liverpool. Starting his career at Chorley Road Congregationals in 1904, he moved to Bolton St Luke's two years later, and turned out for Halliwell Rovers and Hyde between 1906 and 1907. He moved to Bolton Wanderers for the 1907/08 season before transferring to Leyton where he spent two seasons between 1908 and 1910.

During the 1909/10 season Liverpool had conceded 57 goals and finished in second place behind Aston Villa, who had a superior goal average and were five points clear. Watson was keen to improve his team's defensive qualities. Using his extensive contacts, he asked former Liverpool player Michael Griffin, who was now playing for Crystal Palace, for a recommendation on the best defender in the Southern League. Griffin put forward Ephraim Longworth. The fee was not known but reports at the time suggest Watson persuaded the board to part with a record sum.

Ephraim also featured in Liverpool's first FA Cup Final at Crystal Palace, which saw the team fall to a 1-0 defeat to Burnley in 1914. All this meant that by the time war broke out, Longworth was already a man and a player with great maturity and experience.

With football suspended in England between 1915 and 1919, regional league competitions were set up in place of the Football League and FA Cup . Although many games took place during this period, appearances in these tournaments do not count in players' official records.

With teams depleted because of players going off to fight, managers would face the arduous task of combing the country to pull together enough men to compete. As a result, players would often guest for different teams throughout the war.

Ephraim Longworth played 121 times for Liverpool between 1915 and 1919, scoring three goals. Amazingly these turned out to be his only goals for the Reds. He would go on to enjoy an incredible 18 years at the club he also captained, and in addition to his two league championship medals he was also capped for England five times. Having made his international debut at 32 years of age, he would become one of only a handful of Liverpool players to captain his country, when taking the armband against Belgium on 21 May 1921, aged 33 years and 231 days.

Scottish league football continued during the war, with authorities' principal aim being the maintenance of public morale. They did, however, suspend the Scottish Cup for five years. Yet despite this, Donald McKinlay seems to have resisted the urge to return to his homeland during the hostilities. Instead, he would feature in 136 wartime games for the Reds, scoring 24 times.

His surname is often spelt MacKinlay, and he is even known to have signed his autograph using this spelling. However, examination of his birth certificate demonstrates that McKinlay is the correct spelling. Donald was born to parents Angus and Mary in Old Monkland Western in Lanark, Scotland, on 25 July 1891.

By 1901 the family had moved to 22 Pitt Street, Cambuslang. Young Donald played football for Newton Swifts between 1905 and 1908, then spent a season at Rutherglen Woodburn before moving to Newton Villa in 1909. Watson brought him to Anfield in January 1910, and in 1911 he is recorded on the census as a boarder at 140 Walton Breck Road.

McKinlay was now lodging with fellow Liverpool player John McConnell, and the head of the household was Billy Dunlop, who was a tobacconist and newsagent but had previously enjoyed great local acclaim as a title winner with the Reds in the 1900/01 and 1905/06 seasons. Interestingly, this address would also belong to the future 1960s Liverpool legend Peter Thompson, who would own a garage on the site.

McKinlay played 435 times for the Reds, scoring 35 goals. As we will discuss later, he also took over the captaincy in January 1922 from Longworth.

John 'Jack' Bamber had joined Liverpool on 4 December 1915 and had probably been brought to the club by George Patterson, who had assumed secretary duties following the death of Tom Watson. Born in Peasley Cross, St Helens, in 1895, John had played amateur football for St Helens Recreation, Heywood, St Helens Town, and Alexandra Victoria before moving to Anfield.

John featured in 118 of the club's wartime games between 1916 and 1919, scoring eight times. He may have escaped the call-up due to his occupation. He worked in the glass-making industry in St Helens, but it is difficult to be certain about that. Men could also claim ineligibility for service via a military tribunal if they were of poor health or due to family hardship. There is no evidence to suggest either of these was the case with John.

Bamber's best seasons for the Reds came in 1919/20 and 1920/21, in which he featured 28 and 33 times, respectively. However, he seems to have been incredibly unfortunate at the start of 1921/22, when he developed appendicitis after the opening game. By the time he had recovered, his place had been taken by Jock McNab. He made just eight appearances that season, and when the Reds retained the title a season later, he had featured just four times.

Life during the war years would have been difficult and families lived with the constant fear of receiving news that they had lost a loved one in combat. The war also contributed to major changes in British society, and amplified tensions that had been present for many years. Liverpool felt the effects of this alongside other major cities. The absence of so many men, now fighting in Europe, meant that many more women entered the workforce. They worked the land and took up vacant places left behind by men in factories. Many of them carried out dangerous work in munitions factories. Across the UK, these 'Munitionettes' numbered some 950,000. Women also carried out important work in government departments, the post office, public transport, served as police officers, as well as being clerks in business and working in childcare.

Liverpool had boasted a thriving women's suffrage movement since 1894, when the Liverpool Women's Suffrage Society (LWS) had been founded by Edith Bright, Lydia Allen Booth and Nessie Stewart-Brown. They set up headquarters in Lord Street and became affiliated with the National Union of Women's Suffrage Societies (NUWSS) in 1898. They agitated for reform and held meetings in cafés, gave talks, held poetry reading and dance recitals throughout the city.

These, however, were women from prominent families in the city and their membership would distance themselves from more radical working-class suffrage societies such as Women's Social and Political Union (WSPU), which was a more militant organisation campaigning for women's right to vote from 1903 to 1918. Led by Emmeline Pankhurst and her daughters Christabel and Sylvia, they became known as Suffragettes and advocated civil disobedience and direct action.

The more moderate LWS was led by Eleanor Rathbone, a member of Liverpool's prominent Rathbone family, from 1897. The organisation set up several campaign shops in the city during the 1910 elections. The LWS later merged with the Liverpool Women's Citizens Association in 1919 after a fall-out with the national union.

The war and the changing role of women in society, coupled with the strenuous campaigning of these women's rights groups, played a significant role in securing the Representation of the People Act in 1918, which gave the vote to tax-paying women over the age of 30. Liverpool's women played a significant role in the fight, many of them resorting to radical tactics which meant they faced imprisonment in Walton Gaol. Hunger strikes were common, with many being force-fed. Universal suffrage was not achieved, however, until 1928.

Life seems to have moved on in Liverpool during the war, even football carried on in some sort of fashion, and societal tensions were coming to the fore. In his book, *The Morbid Age: Britain Between the Wars*, Richard Overy describes how the confidence and faith of the Victorian elite in the inevitability of societal progress was slowly being eroded during the First World War and subsequent events. News of the carnage on the Western Front and the economic and social upheavals that followed would fuel the sense, at least among the most influential commentators, that civilised society was on the brink of collapse. Elements of this mood prevailed throughout the 1920s and it is reflected in much of the literature and political discourse of the time.

This gives us something of an insight into what it would have felt like to live through these times, how events and environment would have shaped the attitudes and values of the people, and perhaps why, faced with this sense of impending doom, many like the men who became the Untouchables decided to live life to its fullest, and embrace whatever opportunities came their way. This is a theme picked up by Martin Pugh's history of 1920s society, *We Danced All Night*.

Between 1914 and 1918 the people of Liverpool would have been spared the horrors of air raids endured by their descendants in 1940. However, they will have lived with the ever-present threat of Zeppelin raids, and Germany's U-boat campaign, which wreaked havoc on British shipping and claimed the lives of many thousands of seamen, would have had special significance in a port city like Liverpool.

The aim of the U-boat campaign was to target the Allies' trade routes and it was principally fought around the British Isles, and the Mediterranean. Britain relied heavily on imported food and raw materials for the war effort. Germany was in a similar situation and both sides attempted to blockade each other's ports and cut off supplies.

The Royal Navy blockade of Germany during this period led to widespread starvation and food queues, a fact that was hidden from the British public. While the German U-boat campaign failed to have the same impact on British cities like Liverpool, it had a disastrous repercussion on shipping.

In the Atlantic alone, 5,000 ships, or nearly 13 million tonnes, were lost. However, one event during this campaign would devastate the tightly knit communities living around the docks in Liverpool. The sinking of the RMS *Lusitania* on 7 May 1915 off the coast of Kinsale in Southern Ireland had a profound effect on the city. German U-boat *U-20* had torpedoed the passenger liner, which had 1,959 people on board, killing 1,191 passengers and crew.

A further 405 crew members were killed, many of whom were from Liverpool. The sinking caused outrage among the community and there were riots across the city and in London. Germany claimed the attack was legitimate, as the ship was carrying munitions. However, the British and Americans, who had lost 128 citizens in the attack, declared it illegal. The sinking probably began a process that ultimately led to the United States joining the war.

By the end of the war, U-boat losses were having a devastating effect on their crews. Hostilities were coming to an end and a prerequisite of the Armistice was the surrender of these submarines. On 24 October 1918, all German U-boats were ordered back to base and the Allies ordered that they be broken up or surrendered to them. In November, over 160 surrendered at Harwich in Essex. Several ended up in Liverpool, and one of them, *U-534*, survives today at Woodside Ferry Terminal.

Aside from the horrors of the war, and the daily grind of making ends meet, Scousers were presented with plenty of diversions, particularly in the city's thriving entertainment industry. Examination of Everton/Liverpool joint matchday programmes and the *Liverpool Echo* pages between 1915 and 1918 reveals countless adverts for evenings out, including a 'Kostume Komedy' performed by Roger Dun's 'Nyte-Lytes', and a 'Go as You Please Competition' at Picton Hall on William Brown Street. The Empire Theatre on Lime Street and the Olympia on West Derby Road also appear to have done a roaring trade.

For Liverpool's Irish contingent, as well as growing concerns regarding the conflict in Europe, news from home added another dimension. On Easter Monday, 24 April 1916, a group of Irish nationalists launched an uprising against the British and attempted to establish an Irish Republic.

Rebellion was planned across Ireland, but the centre of the unrest was in Dublin. Around 1,500 rebels took control of key buildings within the city, including the General Post Office, and clashed with British soldiers. The rebels found great sympathy in Liverpool, with its large Irish population, and a group called the Liverpool Irish Volunteers was immediately formed. They numbered approximately 50 young men and women who travelled to Dublin to take part in the rebellion. These were a mix of people who were born in the city or who had moved to the city from Ireland.

According to an exhibition at the Liverpool Museum, they were from varying occupations and social classes, ranging from teachers and journalists to clerks and dockers, all united by their commitment to Irish independence. Their role in the Easter Rising was significant, and it is believed that it was a Liverpool man, Joe Gleeson, who raised the Republican flag over the General Post Office.

After a week of struggle the insurrection was eventually suppressed, and around 2,600 people were dead or injured. The British forces interred and executed 16 of the rebellion's leaders, an act which martyred the men and swung Irish opinion behind the rebels and the cause of independence.

Liverpool's prominent Irishmen, Bill Lacey, a Catholic, and Elisha Scott, a Protestant, were great friends and remained so throughout their careers. Both men returned home to Ireland during the war but frequently changed teams, and Lacey featured for the Reds as a wartime guest. Bill had been released by the club, allowing him to ply his trade on both sides of the Irish Sea.

Ireland's football leagues disbanded in 1915, effectively forcing their teams into amateur status. Players' wages were cut to £1 per week. The same happened in Scotland, and then in England. Playing as an amateur at least had the benefit of allowing the players to move around, and Lacey took advantage of this. At one point he was playing for two Irish sides. The trip between Belfast and Liverpool is a short one, so appearing 'cross-channel', as one newspaper termed it, would be easy.

An article in the *Liverpool Echo*, dated 27 October 1915, gives an insight into these movements, and confirms that Lacey was regarded as leaving the club during the war. It reads, 'There's good news for Liverpool FC followers. They will be delighted to hear that William Lacey has decided to return to this city, and that he will be playing in the home match v. Manchester United next Saturday, at Anfield, the directors having chosen him last night at their selection meeting.

'Lacey is a popular player wherever he goes, and the loss of so good a half-back has been felt by the Liverpool club. This is the time of the prodigal's return, however; and after last Saturday's reunion at Everton, when Parker and Harrison resumed with their old club, Lacey has "rejoined his regiment", as it were.

'The Irishman has had a number of rumours around his name in recent weeks, Belfast United being his objective, it was said. This is the new Irish club, you know, that is bidding high for well-known players. Although Lacey was consigned to Belfast United, he turned out eventually with his old team, which is now controlled by Val Harris – Dublin Shelbourne, the club. Certain it is that the Anfield spectators will be in full force on Saturday in view of the special treat afforded, and readers may now realise why I ventured to suggest yesterday that Saturday's gate would be a record for the Anfield ground.'

A healthy crowd of 18,000 did indeed turn out to see Lacey in the game against United, a game in which Elisha kept goal. Sadly, the Reds lost 3-0.

Bill was born in Enniscorthy, Ireland on 20 September 1889. His parents were John and Eliza, and he was baptised two days after his birth by a Reverend Rossiter at the Cathedral of St Aidan, Enniscorthy. His godparents were listed as William Doyle and Bridgett Copeland.

Bill's early football career took him to Shelbourne (1906–08), before he travelled to Merseyside to play for Everton between 1908 and 1912. At Goodison, Lacey was part of the team that finished runners-up in the First Division in 1909. He left the Blues midway through the 1911/12 season to sign for Liverpool for a fee of £150.

At Everton and Liverpool, Bill forged a great friendship with Scotsman Tom Gracie. The pair moved to Anfield together as part of the same deal. Tom left the Reds in 1914 after playing 33 games and scoring five goals. He would return to Scotland to play for Heart of Midlothian, finishing the 1914/15 season as Scottish football's top scorer with 29 goals, and his team would miss out on the title to Celtic by four points.

Tragically Tom, who had enlisted in the army at the outbreak of war, had now developed leukaemia. He died on 23 October 1915. Bill felt the loss of his friend very deeply, and to this day the Lacey family have a photograph of Gracie among his treasured belongings.

Before the outbreak of war, Bill had already played for Liverpool on 112 occasions, notching 20 goals. In the inter-war years he featured again for Shelbourne and turned out for Belfast United and Linfield. He would re-sign for Liverpool after the war and went on to feature a further 148 times for the club, scoring nine times. During the two title-winning seasons, in 1922 and 1923, Lacey featured in 43 and 34 games, respectively.

Elisha Scott had made 30 appearances for Liverpool before the war broke out, and in the 1914/15 season he seems to have made the breakthrough with 25 first-team starts. His performances were so impressive that he seemed certain to displace the Reds' regular keeper, Ken Campbell who was aged 20.

As with his other team-mates, Elisha would have to accept that his career was now on hold, and he would content himself with 15 appearances for Liverpool during the war years, before he returned home to Ireland for much of the conflict. There, he would play for Belfast Celtic, a team he would later manage after he left Anfield. The team won the Irish Cup in back-to-back seasons, in 1917 and 1918.

Football players were now on amateur terms, enabling them to move freely to Irish and Scottish leagues. With the changes to their contractual arrangements brought about by the suspension of the professional game came a reduction in wage. So naturally these men looked to move around; they needed to find games to play but the need to earn a wage would have been more pressing.

Players such as Lacey and Scott, and as we will see later, Harry Chambers, were able to move freely to adjacent leagues. Irish football was now a tempting prospect, and transfers to Ireland would prove mutually beneficial. For the clubs, obtaining players of this calibre would no doubt be something of a coup.

With gate receipts dropping, such high-profile names were sure to attract big crowds. For the men who made the move, there would be an opportunity to continue the sport they loved while also earning a decent living. A report in *Sport (Dublin)*, as early as Saturday, 13 October 1915, suggests that attempts by the Irish FA to impose a maximum £1 per game limit on players' wages was proving fruitless, with clubs frequently in breach.

Meanwhile, on 15 March 1915, the *Northern Whig* and *Sunderland Daily Echo and Shipping Gazette* both reported that the Football League had issued new rules placing limits on players' wages and even prohibiting clubs from paying players during the suspension of football, with any such payments being deemed illegal and punishable under rule 12 of the Football League.

Players like Bill Lacey found themselves in great demand in Ireland and Lacey would tell one journalist that he 'relished the prospect of playing for whatever club he pleased'. However, he would still first need to seek approval from the English FA before signing on at both Shelbourne and Belfast United. Reports written at the time suggest the FA were unhappy at the prospect of losing players to Irish football.

In a piece written on 4 November 1916, in *Sport (Dublin)*, one scribe describes the FA as 'guileless' for requiring Bill to explain his reasons for leaving England: 'Could the guileless FA explain to Lacey how he could pay board, lodgings, and buy clothes, and have pocket money to live in England, and play football "for nothing" for Liverpool.'

The same report also carries a reference to Elisha Scott playing for Belfast Celtic 'in defiance of the English authorities'. However, the Irish FA remained steadfast in its support of players like Bill and Elisha and despite several letters from the English described by officials as 'autocratic' and 'cheeky', Scott and Lacey were left to earn a living in Ireland without sanction.

7

Tales of Gallantry and Redemption

AS BRITONS struggled to come to terms with news from the battlefields of Europe, while living life as best they could, the likes of Harry Chambers, Cyril Gilhespy, Richard 'Dick' Forshaw and Jock McNab would endure extraordinary trials of endurance before returning home to play their part in Liverpool's resurgence.

Harry, born in Willington Quay, North Tyneside, to parents Elizabeth and James on 17 November 1896, and christened Henry Chambers, had joined the club in May 1915. He had enjoyed a spell at Willington United Methodists in 1912/13, and two seasons at North Shields Athletic between 1913 and 1915.

Henry grew up with one sibling, his brother Benjamin. The 1901 Census has the family living at 11 Keelmans Row, Willington Quay. James worked as a shipyard riveter, most likely with the Tyne Iron Shipyard. His son would also find employment there before the war and then football took over.

By 1911 the Chambers family were living at nearby 18 Headlam Street, in a two-roomed house. Conditions would have been cramped, as the census of that year records that a Margaret Chambers (listed as a lodger) was now living with the family.

At some point in his life, people began referring to Henry as Harry, and he also acquired the nickname 'Sharkey'. His interest in football developed early on and newspapers would later refer to him as 'bow-legged and pigeon-toed', afflictions that never prevented him from becoming a prolific goalscorer in amateur football and later as a professional with the Reds.

His arrival at Anfield owed as much to his barefaced cheek as it did to his incredible talent, given that he does not appear to have been scouted by the club. Having already enlisted with the Northumberland Fusiliers, on 12 January 1915 and while on temporary leave, Harry is said to have simply knocked on Tom Watson's door and asked for a trial.

It is not known what he was doing on Merseyside and why he chose Liverpool. Perhaps it was Watson's reputation and association with north-east football that tempted him to travel to Anfield. Whatever the reason, Liverpool can be thankful that he made the trip, and three months later he became Watson's final signing for the club.

However, within a matter of months the suspension of football in England would place Harry's career on hold. His military records list him as Private Chambers, service number 33940, and reveal that he had joined the 3rd (Reserve) Battalion of the Northumberland Fusiliers, which had formed on 4 August 1914. The Fusiliers were stationed at Newcastle upon Tyne before moving to East Boldon. They were a feeder battalion for units on the front line, which were becoming badly depleted by the growing list of casualties. As part of this process Harry would later move to the 12th (Service) Battalion.

By 19 January 1917 we find Harry on the battlefields of France and arriving by train at a military hospital in Lapugnoy. There he was treated for an undiagnosed fever overnight and returned to service at Carnières the following day.

Harry's battalion were involved in heavy action during 1917, including an attack on the German 3rd Army at Hénin-sur-Cojeul and Croisilles on 2 April and the battles of Arras, which also took place along the Hindenburg Line. These engagements were particularly fierce as the Allies attempted to break through enemy lines, and the combined Allied casualties and losses numbered 158,000.

Private Chambers came through it all and by the winter he was almost certainly involved in action at Passchendaele. His records show that on 20 November Harry was discharged with a gunshot wound. The site of his injury is not stated. For his service, he was awarded the Victory and British medals and the War Badge.

He would convalesce in Ireland after the war and featured for Belfast Distillery and Glentoran, before heading back to Merseyside to feature in two wartime games for Liverpool, in the latter stages of the Lancashire Senior Cup (renamed Lancashire Section Subsidiary Competition). The Reds had reached the semi-final of the competition and on 24 May 1919 they faced Blackpool at Bloomfield Road. They won by a single goal scored by John Miller, but the victory was not without controversy.

Blackpool director Albert Hargreaves, himself a qualified referee, was overheard complaining to the referee, a Mr Alderston, about his performance and had seemingly amplified Blackpool supporters' claims that their team had been denied a clear penalty in the final minutes of the game. He was eventually escorted away after the home crowd invaded the pitch. He would avoid sanction by the authorities but a large crowd that had hung around after the match would only disperse after an appeal from the club's board members. Liverpool's victory then set up a clash with Oldham Athletic in the final at Old Trafford.

That game took place on 31 May and goals from the brother of Walter Wadsworth, Harold, Harry Lewis and Miller sealed a 3-0 victory and the cup for Liverpool. For his part, Chambers had done enough in the two games to convince Liverpool that he had a bright future with the club. He also caught the eye of the press, who declared that the Reds had a 'genuine star in their ranks'.

He was officially re-signed later that year. An article in the *Daily Mirror*, dated 13 September 1919, reported the happy news that Chambers, who would become known as 'Smiler' despite being virtually toothless or maybe because of that fact, had returned to Anfield after his service in Greece. Despite his injuries, he would recover sufficiently to feature 339 times for the club, scoring 151 times.

Another veteran of the First World War who eventually found his way to Anfield was Harry Beadles. Born in Llanllwchaiarn, Newtown, Wales, in 1897, Harry was a contemporary and team-mate of Danny Shone as the pair played together at Grayson's of Garston. He later served in Gallipoli, earning several honours.

According to evidence uncovered by Welsh football historian Ken Davies, Harry and two of his elder brothers, Ewart and Ernie, enlisted in the 1st/7th Royal Welsh Fusiliers (later part of the 53rd Division) at the outbreak of war. While Ewart and Ernie were of age Harry was only 16 years old. Apparently feeling a deep sense of duty and a desire to serve alongside his siblings, Harry was initially enlisted as a bugle boy while the regiment was undergoing training at home.

By August 1915, the brothers had been sent to Gallipoli, landing at Suvla Bay, and Harry appears to have become a rifleman. He would serve on the front line despite his tender age, but his lack of maturity did not prevent him from performing acts of extreme gallantry.

In one particularly fierce exchange on the front lines, Harry was lying face down in the soil and praying the next bullet or shell did not have his name on it. As he looked around himself, he noticed a wounded Serbian officer trapped in no-man's land. With ordinance detonating all around them and the terrifying whistle of bullets overhead, he would have been forgiven for freezing on the spot or retreating into the cover of the trenches. Instead, he kept moving, despite both his cap and epaulettes being shot off by enemy fire, and hauled the stricken officer to safety. The officer, presumably badly shaken, immediately took down his rescuer's name, assuring Harry that his valour would be recognised later. He would be as good as his word, as Private Harry Beadles was awarded the Medal of Miloš Obilić and the Star of Karageorge.

Sadly, Harry's brother Ernest was less fortunate, sustaining a wound to the foot in 1918. Though a relatively minor injury, it proved to be fatal. Soldiers would often succumb to such wounds, which would become infected and eventually overwhelm them. At the end of the war Harry returned to his hometown and played for Newtown FC in 1919, before returning to Grayson's of Garston. He eventually signed for Liverpool in 1921 along with Danny Shone. Sadly for Harry, he managed only 18 appearances and six goals before leaving the club in 1924.

Another veteran who played a relatively minor role at Anfield during the rise of the Untouchables was Cyril Gilhespy. Cyril was born on 18 February 1898 in Bournmoor, Chester-le-Street, County Durham, and named Thomas William Cyril Gilhespy. He was raised by his father Francis and mother Mary. Francis worked initially as a gamekeeper before later finding employment in the mines.

Cyril was one of four children, having two brothers, Francis and Richard, and a sister, Annie. He was a keen amateur footballer, turning out for local teams Chester-le-Street and Fencehouses. But, on 7 March 1917, at the age of 19, he would enlist in the Royal Navy. According to his military records Cyril was small in stature, measuring 5ft 6.5in in height with a 36in chest. He had brown hair and grey/blue eyes. He had been employed as a grocer before signing up.

He was posted to the recommissioned HMS *Furious* on 15 March 1918 and sailed out of Portsmouth. This was a ship with something of an illustrious naval history. It had been refitted to enable it to embark aircraft and launch them on operations behind enemy lines. It was the world's first aircraft carrier. The ship's main mission in 1917, however, was patrolling the North Sea on anti-Zeppelin manoeuvres.

Between 15 March and Cyril's final day in service, 15 February 1919, he was involved in the famed Tondern raid on 19 July 1918. During the raid, seven of the *Furious*'s Sopwith Camel aircraft successfully destroyed two Zeppelins and their sheds at Tondern, Denmark. This was a major strategic blow to Germany as their Zeppelin airships had been involved in strategic bombing raids on Britain.

Holding the rank of Ordinary Seaman, Thomas William Cyril Gilhespy, service number J. 68281, was awarded the British War Medal and the Victory Medal for his naval services during the war. At the end of hostilities, Cyril enjoyed a successful season with Sunderland before joining Liverpool in 1921 for £250.

Signed as an outside-right, he faced an uphill battle to get into the first team owing to the form of Bill Lacey. Sadly Cyril would manage just 19 First Division games for Liverpool, scoring three goals before leaving for Blackburn Rovers in 1925. Cyril managed just two appearances in the 1921/22 title-winning season, filling in for the injured Lacey, which was not enough to earn him a medal. However, he did appear on ten occasions as the team retained the championship in 1923, making him a bona fide Untouchable, but it still would not be enough to earn him a medal.

Earlier, on 8 October 1918, the 1st and 3rd British Armies were involved in a deadly battle at the Hindenburg Line, action that formed part of a wider series of battles known as the Hundred Days Offensive.

Amid the assault was Private Dick Forshaw, a man whose goals would later help Liverpool to achieve back-to-back league titles in 1922 and 1923.

Forshaw was born on 20 August 1895 in Preston and joined the 1/12th Loyal North Lancashire Regiment at the age of 23, under the terms of the Military Services Act 1918. He would sustain wounds during an engagement with German forces in and around the French city of Cambrai between 8 and 10 October 1918. The offensive involved 324 tanks, closely supported by infantry and aircraft, and the resultant Allied victory led to the capture of over 10,000 prisoners and 200 guns. Dick was one of 12,000 casualties sustained by Allied forces during the engagement.

Fortunately, Forshaw recovered fully from his injuries and officially signed for Liverpool on 31 July 1919. He went on to play 288 games for the Reds, scoring 123 goals. Forshaw had played for Gateshead St Vincent, Nottingham Forest and Middlesbrough as a wartime guest. He also turned out for Liverpool on two occasions. Forshaw was also an ever-present in the 1921/22 and 1922/23 championship seasons, scoring 20 goals in both campaigns.

Around the time that Dick was sustaining his wounds at Cambrai, another future Liverpool legend was already four years into his war and also fighting along the Hindenburg Line. He was perhaps the most colourful of the Great War veterans, who would go on to capture the imaginations of Kopites in the 1920s, and his name was John 'Jock' McNab.

Born in the village of Cleland, near Motherwell in Lanarkshire, on 16 April 1894, he was one of four children. The family, consisting of John, his parents David and Lizzie, who were both born in Ireland, his sister Martha and brothers James, David and Samuel, lived at 92 Primrose Place.

It is known that Jock developed an interest in football early on, and he would play for Bellshill Athletic in the junior leagues for several years. However, in a somewhat voluminous ode to Jock McNab published in 1919, there is more than a hint of the young McNab's misspent youth. Indeed, if the erstwhile poet, William Noon is to be believed, the outbreak of war may well have been the making of the man.

Jock McNab

Of little use in life was he, the loafer the name he got
Some said he was a ne'er do well, a low and drunken sot
Hind prison bars they locked him, for many a weary day
But punishment had no effect, he kept on his wicked way

Still, there was one who cared for him always kind and true
Frequently gave him pardon for the wrong he fell into
And often said if he's quit the drinking and quit the public-house
Her husband would be a gentleman, as good as any and douce

When war broke out and the bugles note with pipers' music blent
The ne'er-do-well he heard it too, and knew what the message meant
And straight away went with the raw recruits donned the raiment brown
Bravely marched with the soldiers away from the native town

In course of time, they safely reached the gun-set shores of France
Where merry Frenchmen cheered them danced
When they spied the lads in their tartan-dress headed by Jock McNab
(six-feet-one in stockings, and fists like an iron grab)

Like Lords of the land they were feted – brandy, roast and cake
But Jock McNab was teetotal – never a drop would take
He kept his word to Lizzie 'No more liquor for me.
Darling when I return again, a different bloke I'll be'

The winter died and the young spring wind sang 'neath the cherry tree
The white flakes vanished from the soil, and new blooms graced the tea
On the Western Front the cannon boomed, and many a tent did shake
For days and months the wild Huns tried our line of steel to break

Many a daring deed was done throughout the day and night
And many a soul we knew and loved gaed doon in Freedom's fight
But there was great glee round the campfire when the men had learned
That Jock McNab was promoted, had honour and glory earned

Calm was the hour when the king strode forth in the light of the morning sun
And gracefully pinned on Jock's broad breast the medal he'd nobly won
For capturing the enemy guns in the heat of the glory strife
For shooting three big Germans and saving his comrades life

Now Jock McNab is a sergeant and wears the grand M.C.
Every officer likes him – he's the pride of the company
When Lizzie heard the joyful news, she laughed and leapt for joy
And soon the whole of the village was praising her gallant boy

Last week Jock got a lengthy note – he guessed from whom it came
And as he read he chuckled, then his face turned red as flame:

For these were the words that Lizzie wrote:
'A mother proud is me, another young Jock McNab has come and a soldier too he'll be.'

William Noon, *Fife Free Press, and Kirkcaldy Guardian*, 10 February 1919

Clearly, we cannot be certain how much licence this balladeer took with McNab's story, and it is impossible to ascertain whether the characterisation of him as something of a tearaway is fair. However, an examination of his military records confirms his service, his bravery and the fact that he was promoted to the rank of sergeant.

Jock appears to have enlisted with the Highland Light Infantry, 9th (Glasgow Highland) Battalion before the outbreak of war, in April 1913. His service number was 330251. Perhaps he enlisted as many still do, due to a lack of opportunities or to gain some structure and discipline in life. If the poet Noon is to be believed, he certainly needed it.

The battalion was headquartered at Greendyke Street, Glasgow, and when war broke out in August 1914 he was immediately mobilised and moved to Dunfermline on defence duties. They were then deployed to France on 5 November 1914, where the battalion was split up and joined the 5th Brigade, 2nd Division and 23rd Division. The paucity of military records for this time makes it difficult to identify which one Jock joined, but it is known that they saw action during winter operations through to 1915.

In May 1915, Jock found himself caught up in the battle of Festubert, which took place in the Artois region of France. As he took up position on the front line, the Allies launched a five-day bombardment of the German lines involving 433 pieces of artillery firing around 100,000 shells. The sound would have been horrific, even for the Allied troops waiting to join the fray. The fighting that followed was fierce and the 2nd and 7th Divisions sustained heavy casualties and had to be withdrawn.

Festubert was eventually captured on 25 May at great cost. In total, British, Canadian and French casualties amounted to some 123,906 men, with the Germans losing 73,072. The Allies gained barely two miles of land.

Later that year, Jock saw further action in the battle of Loos, the first military operation in which the British used poison gas and the largest battle of 1915. Again, the Allies suffered major casualties numbering 59,247.

During this battle McNab fought alongside troops from India. Curiously, in an obituary in the *Wishaw Press* in 1949, there is mention of Jock being a 'one-time heavyweight boxing champion of India'. We have been unable to verify this or locate him in India. It is likely that those records no longer exist. However, we do know that he retained an interest in the sport throughout his life.

Jock was in the corner for Lancashire boxer Peter Kane during the British and Commonwealth title fight with Jackie Paterson at Hampden in 1943. Kane fought many times in Liverpool and this is likely where McNab came to know him. Kane was already the world flyweight champion, but the bout in Scotland would prove one fight too many. He was knocked out within 61 seconds of the start of the first round.

After the horrors of the battle of Loos, Jock's division would transfer to the command of the General Headquarters in January 1916. He would go on to see action at the Somme, the Arras offensive, actions on the Hindenburg Line and would have been in the same arena as future team-mate Tom Bromilow in the Third Battle of Ypres.

By now Jock was a battle-hardened soldier who had seen things, and endured hardships few of us could ever imagine. He was finally discharged from services due to wounds sustained on 21 December 1918. He would be awarded the Victory and British War medals, the Military Medal for Gallantry and the Silver War Badge, awarded to those who were honourably discharged due to wounds or sickness during the First World War.

Several sources confirm Jock's heroism. His name appears in a list of men recommended for honours in an article published on 11 October 1916 in the *London Gazette*, and he is listed on a 'Roll of Individuals entitled to the Victory Medal and British War Medal granted under army orders 301 and 206 of 1919', found on the Great War Forum, which suggests that his heroic deeds took place in France prior to June 1916.

There is therefore a weight of evidence, both documentary and in popular verse, to suggest that the fabled ruffian and drunkard of Cleland grew into an officer and a gentleman of distinction during his service in the First World War. Jock was clearly already a hero to his comrades long before he joined the Anfield band of brothers.

However, as war had been raging in Europe, and stars of the future battled for survival, Merseyside football seemed oblivious to the fact that it had lost a great figure from the past. In 1917 a man who had played a significant role in the creation of both Everton and Liverpool, William Edward Morton Barclay, passed away in tragic circumstances. After giving so much to the city and helping to build both clubs, he appears to have died in relative obscurity.

A paragraph in the *Liverpool Echo* on 31 January 1917 reports the 'suicide during temporary insanity' of a 60-year-old munitions storekeeper who resided in Upper Beau Street. He had injuries to his forearm, there was a razor next to him and a note, addressed to a friend, spoke of his intention to end his life.

The newspaper suggested he 'had once been in a better position'. This was a case of monumental understatement. Barclay was said to have been plagued with headaches, so severe that he apparently saw suicide as the only way out. It is possible that working with munitions such as TNT may have contributed to his illness; nevertheless, for such a prominent figure in the club's history to die in such circumstances and without recognition is troubling.

Barclay had now joined his old friend John Houlding, who had passed away in 1902 at his new home in France. That left only John McKenna as the last surviving member of the trio of Liverpool FC's founding fathers. His tenure at the club would survive the war, but he would not remain at Anfield to witness the Untouchables reach their zenith.

The old guard, who had given so much in the creation of the city's newest football club, would each give way to the new. The world had been changed by the war, and its people were entering new era of uncertainty in which faith in the old order had been severely undermined. We will, however, see that the foundations laid at Anfield by Houlding, Barclay and McKenna would prove strong enough to carry the next generation to glory.

Liverpool Football Club had not only survived its fiery birth, but it had also thrived. What came next was nothing short of sporting alchemy. With a dash of former heroes, a sprinkling of battle-hardened veterans and one mercurial manager, Anfield emerged from its tumultuous adolescence to take the football world by storm.

Part Three

The Untouchables Assemble

8

War Is Over but a New Foe Stalks the Land as Football Finally Returns

THE END of the war would see Tom Bromilow and Danny Shone return to their native Liverpool in 1919. It would not take them long to rediscover their old passion, football, and soon they would find themselves at Anfield. There, they would join fellow veteran Harry Chambers, and Jock McNab and Dick Forshaw. Meanwhile, Elisha Scott – who was now married and the father of a baby son – and Bill Lacey were returning from Irish football to join up with John Bamber, Walter Wadsworth and stalwart Ephraim Longworth, all of whom had remained at home throughout the war years.

Writing in the *Liverpool Echo*, the legendary reporter Ernest Edwards, whose work appeared under the pseudonym 'Bee', commented somewhat comedically on how the Wadsworth clan reported for duty on 24 January 1919: 'The return of the brothers Wadsworth who have been on the sick-list, is worth a special note. The younger member poisoned his foot, and Walter has been "boiling" over with indignation! Charles, another brother, is helping the reserves, and the eldest brother, himself an old footballer, would like to play again, but is left a bit too weak after two and a half years in Germany.'

Harold had signed from Tranmere in January 1918 and would not turn professional until May 1919. He seems to have presented for duty with a slight foot injury and, judging by Bee's reference to Walter's temperament, the defender had by now already established his reputation as a no-nonsense sort. Charles made his debut for the reserves in November 1918 and featured in several games for the Reds' second string, including a 5-0 drubbing of Garswood Hall in the Lancashire Combination League, on 3 January 1919. However, he never managed the step up to the first team.

Just five days after that piece, Walter became a married man, having wed Elsie Dora Marshall at Holy Trinity Church on Walton Breck Road. He was 28 years old.

The war had been a deeply troubling time for Walter and his family, not least because his elder brother, Arthur, had been captured at one of the battles at Passchendaele. This is the brother referred to in Bee's piece above.

Arthur Wadsworth had been a talented player in his own right before the war. However, he was captured in action on the European front and spent more than two years in a prisoner of war camp. The scars of his experiences meant he would not follow his brothers into the professional game.

Research carried out by Jacqueline Wadsworth gives a vivid account of Arthur's life, and reveals that Walter's elder brother took a very different path to his younger siblings. He had emigrated to Canada at some point between 1911 and 1914 and enlisted with the Canadian Expeditionary Force (CEF) in 1915 seeing active service in Europe during the First World War.

Arthur was transported to England aboard the troopship SS *Lapland* on 9 November 1915, and his military records show that he was assigned from 'B' Company to the Pioneer Section stationed in the village of Bramshott, Hampshire. He seems to have struggled with a condition called lumbago, or sciatica, which causes severe back pain, and in January 1916 he was hospitalised for 12 days with the condition.

His recovery would see him transferred to the Canadian Mounted Rifles (CMR) and dispatched to France. However, conditions on the battlefield meant that all six regiments of the CMR were dismounted and converted to infantry. Arthur's campaign at Ypres lasted for barely two months, and he is reported missing between 2 and 5 June 1919.

His battalion had been defending positions along the 3rd Canadian Division's front, when the Germans launched their assault at the outset of the Battle of Mont Sorrel. They were overrun, and 557 of its 692 members were killed, wounded, or captured. That represented 80 per cent of their ranks. Arthur was among those captured but mercifully was not killed.

Jacqueline Wadsworth's research of prisoner of war records has revealed that he spent time at three German camps: Dülmen and Minden in 1916, then Sennelager from February 1917 until his eventual release in 1918. He arrived back in England at Ripon in Yorkshire in December 1918, and was later transported from Rhyl to the Canadian city of Winnipeg, Manitoba, some time after March 1919.

Walter had always been close to each of his brothers, and news that Arthur had been reported missing was clearly extremely distressing for him and the family. His safe return, however brief, must have been a huge relief. The brother's strong bond is confirmed also by the fact that Charles was best man at Walter's wedding and the eldest sibling, Frederick, moved in with Walter's family after his own wife died, and Walter's son, Bill, remembers that all of the brothers looked up to Walter.

The war had devastated an entire continent, robbing Europe of its youth and destroying its infrastructure. Things could never be the same again. The collapse of Tzarist Russia and the emergence of the Soviet Union sent convulsions across the continent. At home, the British ruling class had already tasted rebellion in Ireland, and a movement that would lead to independence for the south of the country and partition of the north at the outset of the 1920s.

As tens of thousands of men returned home from Europe to face the same old struggles, and mothers and fathers anxiously awaited news about lost sons, some of whom would never be found, the old order was beginning to look very fragile. Liverpool, still a significant city in the British empire, became something of a microcosm of the whirlwind of unrest blowing through Europe.

The city's council wards would see Irish nationalist councillors elected along with those representing both the Protestant and Catholic traditions. Meanwhile labour politics was growing in strength an in the years after the war, the city would witness the rise of the left, with the Communist Party organising several rallies and even a bank robbery to raise funds for the cause.

By 1922, a local Communist Party activist, Jack Nield, had won the St Annes ward council seat with 57 per cent of the vote. Liverpool was fertile ground for revolutionary ideas. Even without the consequences of the war, mass unemployment, poverty pay, dreadful housing conditions and the challenges of public health gave communists and socialists many causes to rally behind. However, as the battlefields fell silent and broken men and crumpled souls trudged home, a new foe would stalk the land, the so-called 'Spanish Flu'.

This strain of influenza was so virulent it would lead to the worst pandemic, in terms of mortality, in the history of the world. By the time the virus burnt itself out, anywhere from 50 to 100 million people across the globe had perished, many more than had been taken by war. The virus struck in waves with the highest peak occurring between March 1918 and April 1919, and its victims were not the very young or the elderly and infirm but people in the prime of their lives, those aged between 25 and 35.

Liverpool, a major port, was already vulnerable to the pandemic. With thousands returning home from Europe and other disease-affected areas across the globe, the city would be hit hard by several waves of the virus.

Chris Jones, a retired university lecturer from Liverpool, has carried out a study of how newspapers like the *Liverpool Echo* covered the pandemic after the war. In his paper, 'Whistling in the Dark', he describes how the local paper began reporting cases of a 'mystery disease' and a 'wartime epidemic' as early as May and June 1918. 'In the early days of the epidemic, speculation about its cause was rife,' explained Chris, 'with the local press musing that anything from consumption of bacon from America contaminated with borax preservative, to poison gas ingested on the battlefield.'

Others believed, in contradiction with the views of expert medical opinion, that the 1918 fashion of women wearing much flimsier blouses than previous generations had contributed to the higher female mortality rate, and the garments were dubbed 'pneumonia blouses'. This was the name given to blouses thought to be flimsy by 1918 standards. A poem published in the *Liverpool Echo* on 26 October advised women to dress up warm to beat the flu:

Though ne'er flu free before
You'd be so they profess
By wearing rather more
And baring rather less

Naturally talk of cures was rife, with claims that eating Spanish onions could eradicate the pandemic appearing in gossip columns, while others suggested taking quinine. The latter advice led to stock of the drug running perilously low by October 1918. Others argued that imbibing stimulants, mainly alcohol, could stave off the killer disease and by 1919 a glass of whiskey was being described as 'the best remedy' in an article in the *Liverpool Echo*. This led to nurses in Runcorn trawling pubs in the town armed with medical certificates and pleading for supplies of the spirit.

By late 1918, public gatherings in places like cinemas and theatres were being limited and Sunday schools were being closed, much to the ire of business owners and church leaders. The first advice to wear masks in public came in February 1919, with some people even resorting to soaking their face coverings in creosote, a tar-like preservative which was thought to have antiseptic properties.

The local press was filled with advertisements exhorting readers to buy 'germ destroying medicines', which went by the name of Karsote or Jackson's Bronkerchief liquid, while sales of Bovril went into the stratosphere leading to shortages and panic-buying of the product. Amid all of this many of the city's women struggled with the ramifications of war and disease while in many cases raising children alone. The *Liverpool Echo*, in an article entitled 'The Hope of the Nation', argued, 'The unmarried mother must be helped and protected,' referring to this as 'a matter of national urgency'.

It was against this backdrop of social upheaval, economic crisis and a gathering public health catastrophe that the footballing authorities got ready to resume the sport. And despite the restrictions on theatre- and cinema-goers, it seems football grounds were able to welcome supporters in their tens of thousands. Liverpool's opening game of the 1919/20 season, a 3-1 away victory over Bradford City at Valley Parade, was watched by 25,000 people. The following two home fixtures would draw crowds of 12,000 and 30,000 respectively.

Tom Bromilow was demobilised from the army in 1919 and returned home immediately to Liverpool. Though stories of how he had developed his skills as a footballer in the army persisted throughout the 1920s, we now know that prior to enlisting he had already established his reputation as a fine local footballer for several teams. This passage from the *Derby Daily Telegraph* on 2 April 1921, which appears to have an incomplete knowledge of Tom's amateur football record, is typical: 'Tom Bromilow, the clever Liverpool and international half-back, graduated to Anfield by way of the Union Presbyterian FC and West Bathgate, though, like a good many present-day players it took a war and army football fully to develop his skill. He is a real Merseysider and the best of his career is that he did not cost the Liverpool club a penny.'

Bromilow had, however, been on the radar of Liverpool's scouts long before he served in the military, while playing for his local team Kirkdale. Nevertheless, had he not taken matters into his own hands, his career at Anfield may never have got off the ground.

In 1919 Tom, who was approaching 24 years of age, walked into Anfield, knocked on the door, and asked for a trial. He was still in uniform. Club secretary George Patterson decided that it was worth looking at him. Much later, he would describe Bromilow as 'the luckiest signing I ever made'. He explained, 'His signature was obtained in the strangest manner. He came to the ground in uniform during the war and asked for a game. I asked George Fleming, who was in charge of the second team then, how he was fixed and he said he could do with another player. Bromilow played at outside-right and was an instant success.'

Here, Patterson's recollections may be somewhat blurred by the passage of time. We know that Tom did not return home until after November 1918 and therefore his meeting with Bromilow couldn't have taken place 'during the war'. It is also known that as well as seeking the views of Fleming, Patterson also requested the opinion of Tom's former manager at Kirkdale, Tom Brown, who gave him the highest possible recommendation.

Bromilow signed for Liverpool officially as soon as he was demobilised from the army. He would make his full debut at the age of 25 on 25 October 1919, and featured in a 2-1 victory over Burnley, a team he would go on to manage. Tom seems to have given a great account of himself, with a club programme later saying, 'Quite a good impression was created by the local lad Bromilow at right half-back; it was asking a great deal of him to place him against such a clever pair as Lindsay and Mosscrop, but he came out of the ordeal with distinct credit.'

James Lindsay was an experienced inside-forward from Scotland. Eddie Mosscrop was an England international, born in Southport, who had the distinction of being part of the Burnley side who beat Liverpool in the 1914 FA Cup Final. For Tom, with little experience as a pro, to face them and come out on top was quite an achievement. Writing later about his trial match for the Reds, *Athletic News* had this to say on 7 March 1921: 'Bromilow is highly intelligent, and in the trial game showed, as always, power of anticipation and a rare gift in the bestowal of the ball. In no situation did he ever seem at a loss as to what he should do. There is a bright future for Bromilow.'

Patterson had given a future Liverpool captain and England international his debut. He would go on to feature 23 times for the Reds that season and would become a darling of the supporters and a mainstay of the team for many years to come.

Bromilow played on both the right and left side of central defence, forming a formidable partnership with Walter Wadsworth. However, at 5ft 9.5in and weighing 11st 4lb, Tom would have to rely on his footballing brain and guile to outwit his opponents. Early reports of his performances paint a picture of a cultured centre-half who was great with the ball at his feet. However, the key was the partnership he struck up with Wadsworth, and how their contrasting styles complemented each other.

Consider this from *Athletic News* in 1921, for example: 'Wadsworth was a vigil destructive agent primarily, but in this game he also provided his forwards with repeated chances of forging ahead. Bromilow was more dainty in his methods but eminently efficient.'

Tom, writing in *Topical Times* in 1938, gives a description of Walter's style that betrays his admiration for the man and the player. In it he describes Wadsworth in these terms: 'A bundle of muscle and bone. He gave and received knocks with a smile. Nothing disturbed him. He was a tremendous worker and a keen tackler.'

The men were clearly friends on and off the field, holding each other in high regard. And theirs was a combination that served Liverpool well as they developed into a great championship-winning team. In a season review, published in *Athletic News* in 1922, the journal had this to say of Liverpool's back line, which by then also included another player with whom Tom and Walter had forged a strong bond, Jock McNab: 'The half-backs have presented contrasts, but they have all proved valuable in their different styles. The artist has been Tom Bromilow. It has been said repeatedly that team managers have found left half-backs the most difficult position on the field to fill to their satisfaction.

'That idea arrived before the famine in centre-forwards. We make no comparisons, but Bromilow is a player of the McWilliam type – that is to say, he achieves his purposes by footwork and the exercise of ingenuity.

'Walter Wadsworth is an intervener, a breaker-up of combination, with a more robust method. With Bamber stricken by appendicitis McNab has been most often seen at right half-back, and he has been very resolute. A footballer of his possibilities will probably become more refined.

'As a line these men have been very effective in their dual capacity.'

Jock had signed for Liverpool in November 1919 from Scottish side Bellshill Athletic. He made his debut in a goalless draw with Manchester United at Anfield on New Year's Day 1920. It was one of only two appearances that season with the second coming just two days later, a 3-2 defeat away to Sheffield United. He made only one appearance during 1920/21, having been kept out of the team by John Bamber.

However, when Bamber needed surgery for appendicitis early in the 1921/22 title-winning season, and his deputy, Francis Checkland, failed to take full advantage, McNab seized his chance. He missed just four games in the reminder of that campaign and earned himself a championship medal in the process.

While Wadsworth and McNab were recognised for the efficacy of their defensive attributes throughout the 1920s, Bromilow is described as an 'artiste to the fingertips', a player who could both stop and start attacks, and one of the most cultured defenders in the country. The *Derby Daily Telegraph* would later claim that he was one of the finest corner takers in the game, writing on 3 September 1926, 'Yet another international, but just a dapper little fellow who has to rely purely upon craft and cunning for his success. [He] is purely Liverpool bred and born, and learned the game with such junior clubs as Union Presbyterians and West Dingle. His footwork in tackles is remarkable for the accurate timing he shows, while he is one of those halves who must feed his forwards after he has come out of a struggle with the opposition.'

Another match report in the same paper, written after a game against Portsmouth in 1928, summed up his abilities as a player: 'Though on the small side so far as weight and muscular strength are concerned, he is wonderfully effective and artistic in all he does. Has been in league football since 1919, and has reached international rank. No half could play the ball with greater effect.'

Bromilow would go on to serve Liverpool for 11 years, captaining the side during the 1928/29 season. Clearly a pivotal player for the club during his time at Anfield, his contribution to the team is lauded in a *Liverpool Echo* retrospective, published in 2011. In it, Tom is described as the brains of the outfit, and there is more than a suggestion of his local superstar status. However, the regard in which he is held in the national press suggests his prominence and celebrity went much further than Merseyside.

Off the field, Bromilow's opinions were frequently sought on all manner of issues. He was a deep thinker about the game, something that marked him out for management later in his career. He was also something of a celebrity, having been sought by advertisers for health-related products such as the mysteriously named Phosferine. One poster, dated 1920 and carrying a picture of Bromilow in action, featured this quote from the player: 'Weakness and exhaustion of any description can be successfully opposed by the employment of Phosferine – it is a great stimulant to the nerves.'

Not quite as catchy as Kevin Keegan's Brut advert in the 1970s, or the Nivea adverts that feature Liverpool's current crop, but perhaps we should rethink who we consider to be our first 'superstar player'. The date of the advertisement suggests that his celebrity status had been earned very early in his Liverpool career.

The press regularly sought out Tom's thoughts on the game in general and he wrote many columns for newspapers during his playing days, including one while on a club tour in Italy. His views on the quality of the Italian game were far from flattering.

In another, much later, he would seem ahead of his time, calling for the introduction of a second referee. It is little wonder that in 1927 the *Rugby Advertiser* described him as 'the deep-thinking half-back of Liverpool'.

In trawling through the records and archived newspaper articles, we begin to get a picture of a footballer who was held in the highest regard in the English game; a man hugely popular among supporters and admired by reporters and fellow professionals alike. It is not hard to understand why. This is a local lad from modest beginnings, who served his country in wartime, and who played football at local and international level. Tom was capped five times for England.

The man who gave him his break at Anfield, George Stanley Patterson, was made of very different stuff. Born on 23 April 1887, to parents Adam and Gertrude, Patterson had a good start in life. The family lived at addresses on Wynnstay Street and Arnold Street in Toxteth. George was christened at St Philemon Church in nearby Admiral Street. In the 1920s this was a relatively affluent area of the city, inhabited by those with better incomes and status.

The young Patterson therefore seems to have had a comfortable upbringing. With Adam being a 'Master Mariner', the family would have enjoyed a reasonable income compared to most. However, it is likely that Adam would have been away at sea during George's upbringing. George enjoyed football and played for local teams Marine and Orrell.

He arrived at Anfield at the age of 21, in 1908, and obtained a back-office job at the club. His talents for administration were immediately recognised and this would be the beginning of a long career at Liverpool. Within three years, George was living as a boarder at 50 Malvern Road, near to Newsham Park in the Tuebrook area of the city. The 1911 Census records that he was a clerk under the employment of Liverpool Football Club.

Patterson would learn from the very best and his career as an administrator would see him rub shoulders with Tom Watson and John McKenna, men who had overseen the growth of football on Merseyside. He must have also earned the respect of the board as the club would frequently turn to George in times of need, most notably after the death of Watson in 1915.

This contradicts contemporary portrayals of Patterson, which paint him as something of an accident-prone character, and latter-day authors have even sought to downplay his role at the club. While there are some comical references to his clumsiness – he once walked into a tree and injured himself severely – there is also a reference by reporter 'Bee', writing in the *Liverpool Echo*, to his unsuitability for military service: 'I am glad that Mr George Patterson has been appointed secretary of Liverpool FC. He is a practical man, unobtrusive, and shows wisdom with pen and in football matters. He is following one of the best in the late Tom Watson, but has been well schooled, and will make good. In his football days he played a deal of football with Orrell and other clubs, but from an army point of view his big frame is useless – he has an extraordinary number of wriggling bones that have been broken. Here's to him!'

That may not seem much by way of a ringing endorsement, though the emphasis on Patterson's administrative skills may be telling. Given that his appointment coincided with the suspension of the Football League after the outbreak of war, Patterson's steady pair of hands will have been appealing to the board. He was a man who could keep the ship afloat until the conclusion of hostilities, a task he was almost tailor made to do.

During the war years Patterson dealt admirably with many challenges, not least of which involved the paucity of available players. With some stationed overseas and others stationed in barracks across the country, he brought talented youth players through the ranks and even persuaded a former Liverpool legend, Arthur Goddard, back to the club as a guest.

And 1919 would prove to be a big year indeed for Patterson. With the war over, he had taken charge of the Liverpool team in his official capacity of club secretary at the start of the new football season in August. Just two months earlier, he had married Minnie Wilson at St Philip's Church in the Litherland area of Merseyside. Their daughter, Vera Gertrude, was born on 29 August 1919. The family were now living in Marlsford Street, not far from where George had been lodging in 1911.

However, Patterson's managerial record during his 18 official games from August to December 1919 was less than impressive. He won only seven games, losing nine and drawing two. His last match in charge was a 1-0 victory over Middlesbrough at Anfield, in which Harry Chambers would grab the winner. The win did little to lift the spirits, however. The Reds were languishing in 18th in the table and relegation was a very real prospect, which seems to have persuaded the board to replace George at the helm.

It is notable though that the club did not dispense with his services altogether, with Patterson instead returning to the boardroom. It is therefore possible, even likely, that he would have had a hand in the appointment of his successor, David Ashworth, who the club tempted away from Stockport County in December 1919.

Patterson's Liverpool was in many ways the antithesis of the team that would blossom under Ashworth. Despite featuring many of the names who would go on to earn the honorific Untouchables title, including Walter Wadsworth, Donald McKinlay, Bill Lacey and Harry Chambers, in the opening months of the 1919/20 season Liverpool were painfully inconsistent.

Missing from the line-up for many of the opening games was club captain Ephraim Longworth, a veteran of the 1914 FA Cup Final, though his return to the team on 11 October did little to arrest the slump. By this point Liverpool were in free-fall.

Among players who came into the team towards the end of Patterson's brief reign was the younger brother of Walter Wadsworth, Harold. Born in 1898, Harold found his way to Anfield via St Matthew's and Tranmere Rovers. The pair featured alongside each other on five occasions during the 1919/20 season.

Walter often referred to his brother as 'our kid', a fact that was not lost on the Anfield crowd who upon seeing the youngster bombing down the wing would shout, 'Go on, our kid!' It is said that if any opposition player kicked Harold too hard, the Kop would be in uproar, shouting in the direction of his older brother, 'Get him, Waddy!'

Perhaps one of the most notable of the games in which the brothers competed was the Merseyside derby at Anfield on 27 December 1919. Liverpool ran out 3-1 winners in what was David Ashworth's fourth match in charge, and the victory would have been keenly celebrated in the pubs around Anfield long into the night as it was the Reds' first win over Everton on home soil since 1899.

Not surprisingly a record attendance for the season, with over 49,000 supporters turning out to see the game, meant that Anfield was full to bursting. The crowd must have been much larger than this as by kick-off it had spilled out of the stands and had lined the entire perimeter of the pitch. Despite this, according to a match report in the *Liverpool Mercury*, the supporters were well behaved and never interfered with play.

The game got under way in high winds, with gusts so strong that in the fifth minute an attempted clearance by Everton's goalkeeper Tommy Fern was blown straight back at him and was immediately intercepted by Birkenhead-born Harry Lewis, who unleashed a fierce shot. Fern dived the length of the goal but could not keep the ball out.

Liverpool, kicking to the Anfield Road end in the first half, sensed blood, and with fierce gusts at their backs they took full advantage. Ten minutes later they were two goals to the good thanks to Scotland's Tom Miller, who ghosted through the middle of Everton's defence to bury the ball past a despairing Fern. Liverpool were in the ascendency but an injury to veteran Bob Pursell, who had joined the club from Queen's Park in 1911, took the wind out the their sails. With no substitutes allowed, the team was simply reshuffled with Purcell moved to outside-right. However, despite seeing the game out, he was of little use there and could barely move.

Everton managed a few attacks but Liverpool's defence, superbly marshalled by Longworth and with Walter Wadsworth acting as destroyer, held firm. Miller would then add his second and the Reds' third thanks to an assist from 'our kid' himself, Harold Wadsworth. The *Liverpool Mercury* records that the goal owed much to 'clever work' by Walter's younger sibling. Imagine the raucous joy in the stands as Liverpool, after years of pain at the hands of their bitterest rivals, went 3-0 up.

Everton did rally and debutant Bobby Parker scored a late consolation goal from a corner in the 83rd minute. However, it was too little, too late and Liverpool, who had effectively been playing with ten men for much of the game, ran out worthy winners.

Liverpool enjoyed something of a resurgence under Ashworth's stewardship in the second half of the season, winning 12 of their remaining 19 matches and finishing in fourth place, just a point behind Chelsea in third. It was quite an achievement given the club had been flirting with relegation back in December 1919.

During that run, the Reds faced back-to-back games against Manchester City in the spring of 1920. Liverpool had now moved up to third place, and already Ashworth had started to put his stamp on things. His players won the first of the double encounter, at Anfield, by a single goal, with Harry Chambers netting on the stroke of half-time. However, it was the game at Hyde Road seven days later that would have lived longest in the memories of the players, especially Walter Wadsworth.

The game was attended by King George V, and it is believed that this was the first time a reigning monarch had attended a football fixture outside of the capital. The King had attended the Grand National steeplechase at Aintree in Liverpool the day before. He had watched in heavy rain as Irish horse Troytown, ridden by a well-known Welshman Jack Anthony, stormed home to victory by some 12 lengths.

After the race, the King decided he would like to take in a football game and made the trip to Manchester to see City take on Liverpool. According to reports, the monarch, who had been accompanied on his journey by a local alderman named To Fox, was treated to a 41-glass salute by a crowd of men stood outside the Didsbury Hotel as his car sped past. He would have no doubt found that to be the most amusing aside to the day's proceedings, but then he was yet to encounter Bootle's Walter Wadsworth.

With around 40,000 people crammed into the stadium, the rain pelted the players as they lined up to greet the King. Cold and wet, and standing in what looks like a mud bath, Wadsworth stretched out a hand as the monarch walked by. The pair pause, and in a photograph of the incident a smile can be seen flashing across the player's lips, as he asks cheekily, 'You wouldn't have a hip flask in your pocket would you, your majesty? If you do, could you give me a drop?'

It was a moment of irreverence typical of Walter, and it appears the King saw the funny side. The Reds fought through the mud and the rain, and in the 20th minute, they won a penalty. Chambers dispatched

Tom Bromilow (front row on the right) at Fonthill Street Council School. Photo courtesy of the Bromilow family and restored by ANT-OGRAPHY via Facebook.

A 12–13-year-old Tom Bromilow pictured in 1906/7 (second row far right). This would be either the Unity Presbyterian or West Dingle team.

Liverpool FC 1913/14. With war about to bring professional football to a temporary close, this team features several Untouchables, including Donald McKinlay, Elisha Scott, Ephraim Longworth 2nd row and Bill Lacey 3rd row, 2nd from the end on the right. It also features George Patterson on the left with the straw boater hat, and trainer William Connell right with flat cap. Photo courtesy of the Wadsworth family.

Tom Bromilow (left) and his brothers off to war. Photo courtesy of the Bromilow family.

Harry Beadles in military uniform. Photo courtesy of the Beadles family.

This 1916 Liverpool team features, Standing L-R: Edward Askew Bainbridge (Director), unidentified player, Ephraim Longworth, Elisha Scott, Arthur Goddard, Wilfred Watson, George Patterson. Seated L-R: Norman Bradley, Ernest Pinkney, Fred Pagnam, William Banks, James Middlehurst, Donald McKinlay. Photo courtesy of Adrian Killen and colourised by ANT-OGRAPHY via Facebook.

Colourised image of Bill Lacey, courtesy of the Lacey family. Colourised by ANT-OGRAPHY via Facebook.

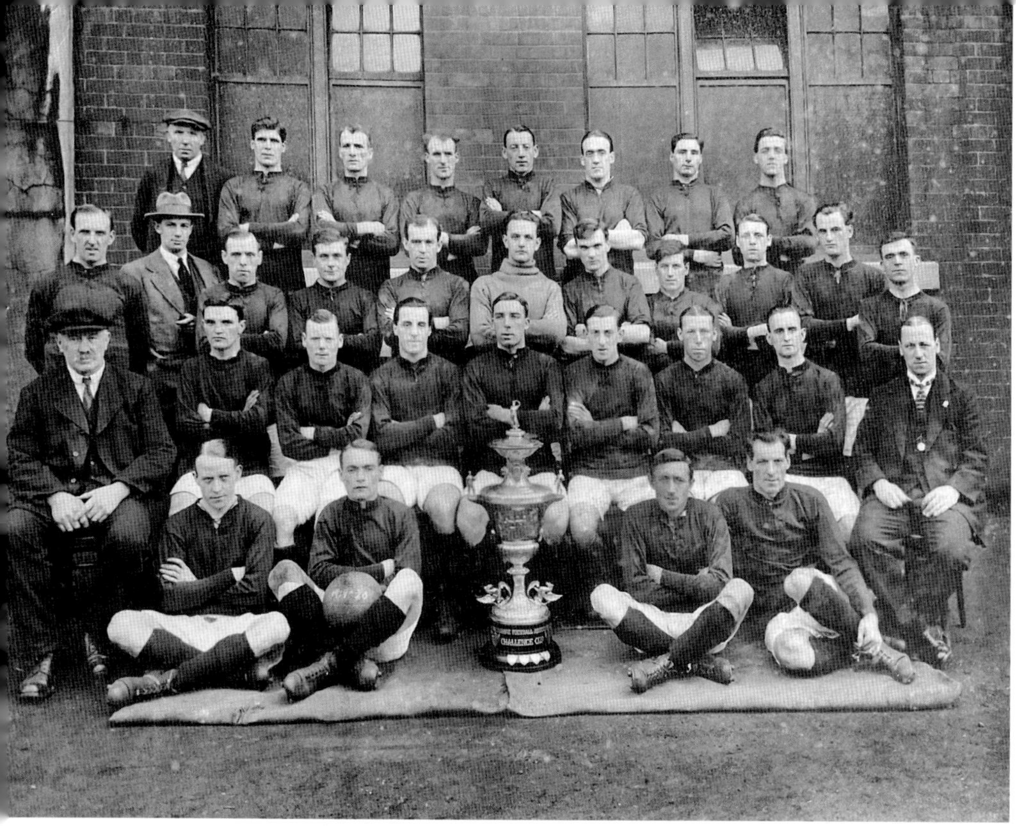

Liverpool FC Lancashire Cup Winners 1919. Photo courtesy of Wadsworth family and restored by ANT-OGRAPHY via Facebook.

Liverpool FC 3 May 1919, a benefit match against Tranmere Rovers in aid of former player and war veteran, Ralph Holden. Ralph had lost his leg in WWI. £15 was raised from auctioning of a bag of sugar and a smoking pipe, and 5,000 people attended. Tranmere won 2-0. Photo courtesy of the Wadsworth family and has been restored by ANT-OGRAPHY via Facebook.

Walter Wadsworth meets King George V before a game against Manchester City at Hyde Road in 1920. Walter jokingly asks the King if he has a bottle of whiskey in his pocket. Photo courtesy of the Wadsworth family.

Sports Gazette *clipping dated 3 March 1921, shows Dick Forshaw, Fred Hopkin, Tommy Lucas, Elisha Scott, Bill Lacey, and Tom Bromilow in their alternate away kit, at Ayresome Park prior to facing Middlesbrough. Photo courtesy of Tom Neal.*

Tom Bromilow training with the ball in front of a roofless Kop. Photo courtesy of the Bromilow family.

Elisha Scott stretches to save a shot in training. Note the Kop with no roof or sides behind him. Photo courtesy of Liverpool FC.

Picture taken before Tom Bromilow's England debut at Ninian Park, a British Championship game against Wales, 14 March 1921. Standing L-R: George Wilson, John Bamber, Warney Cresswell, Bert Coleman, Jack Silcock, Tom Bromilow. Seated L-R: Sam Chedgzoy, Bob Kelly, Charlie Buchan, Harry Chambers, Alf Quantrill. Photo courtesy of the Bromilow family.

Elisha Scott chats to Scotland captain Jimmy Gordon before an international between Ireland and Scotland. Photo courtesy of Liverpool FC.

Harry Beadles captains the Welsh national team against Scotland in 1925. Photo courtesy of the Beadles family.

Elisha Scott in action for Ireland at Windsor Park. Photo courtesy of Liverpool FC.

England v The North Trial Match at Burnley, played 28 February 1921. Selectors used this and a previous match, to select the England team for games against Wales (Tom Bromilow's debut) and Scotland. The North won 6-1. Standing L-R: John Bamber, Warney Cresswell, Jack Mew, Jack Silcock, George Wilson, Tom Bromilow. Seated L-R: Sam Chedgzoy, Bill Kirton, Charlie Buchan, Harry Chambers, Tommy Urwin. Photo courtesy of the Bromilow family.

David Ashworth lines up his men at the corner of the Main Stand and Anfield Road end. From left to right, David Ashworth, Donald McKinlay, Walter Wadsworth, Jock McNab, Bill Lacey, Fred Hopkin, Harry Lewis, and Tom Bromilow. Photo courtesy of Jacqueline Wadsworth and Mark Platt.

Liverpool squad 1922/23 pictured in the directors' box at Anfield. Photo courtesy of the Lacey family. Restored by ANT-OGRAPHY via Facebook.

A staged photo at the corner flag located in the corner of the Main Stand and Anfield Road end, shows Liverpool player pretending to play golf. Bill Lacey attempts to putt, as Jock McNab holds the flag. Crouching is Fred Hopkin, while from left to right Walter Wadsworth, Harry Lewis and Donald McKinlay appear to be enjoying the joke. Photo courtesy of Jacqueline Wadsworth and Mark Platt. Restored by ANT-OGRAPHY via Facebook.

The Liverpool squad pictured in front of the Spion Kop 1921/22. Photo courtesy of the Bromilow family. Restored and colourised by ANT-OGRAPHY via Facebook.

Undated picture, circa 1922, shows Bill Lacey, Danny Shone, Harry Chambers, Harry Lewis, Harry Beadles, and Fred Hopkin, on the pitch at Anfield prior to a training session. Photo courtesy of the Lacey family. Restored and colourised by ANT-OGRAPHY via Facebook.

Donald McKinlay and Walter Wadsworth lead out the team at Anfield. Bringing up the rear are Harry Lewis, Harry Chambers and Bill Lacey just emerging from the tunnel. Photo courtesy of the Lacey family. Restored by ANT-OGRAPHY via Facebook.

Elisha Scott dives in the mud at Ayresome Park in a match against Middlesbrough, as Sam Speakman of Liverpool (stripes) and Middlesbrough's Walter Tinsley look on. Photo courtesy of Liverpool FC.

Liverpool FC pre-season tour of Italy, 1922. L-R David Ashworth, Dick Forshaw, Tom Bromilow and George Patterson, pose in front of Lake Maggiore, along with some of the directors, including Tom Crompton (seated centre) and Walter Henry Cartwright (seated right). Photo courtesy of the Bromilow family.

Elisha Scott clears following a Dixie Dean shot, as England face Ireland in a Home International Championship at Goodison Park, October 1928. Photo courtesy of Liverpool FC.

Elisha Scott (Right) and Tom Bromilow (Left) shepherd the ball to safety in a match at Anfield, 1920s. Photo courtesy of Liverpool FC.

Elisha thwarts the Tottenham attack as Jock McNab looks on. Photo courtesy of Liverpool FC.

A trio of Liverpool defenders (left to right) Walter Wadsworth, Tommy Lucas, and Jock McNab looking on as Elisha Scott punches the ball clear. Photo courtesy of Liverpool FC.

Walter Wadsworth looks on anxiously as Elisha deals with a cross into the box. Photo courtesy of Liverpool FC.

Elisha Scott wrestled to the ground at Anfield, as Ephraim Longworth and Jock McNab look on. Photo courtesy of Liverpool FC.

Tom Bromilow in action. Photo courtesy of the Bromilow family. Restored by ANT-OGRAPHY via Facebook.

From the celebration dinner at the Adelphi Hotel in 1922. This copy belonged to Harry Beadles. Courtesy of Rob Gower.

Informal photo of the 1922 league champions grappling with their trophy, taken at Anfield. This picture was taken by the Liverpool Echo and used in a competition entitled 'Find Smiler' [Harry Chambers]. Harry can be seen bottom left hiding between John Bamber's legs. Photo courtesy of the Bromilow family. Restored by ANT-OGRAPHY via Facebook.

Walter Wadsworth in action at Anfield. Photo courtesy of the Wadsworth family. Restored by ANT-OGRAPHY via Facebook.

Liverpool directors, players and guests at their dinner to commemorate the 1922 championship at the Adelphi Hotel, Liverpool. Courtesy of Rob Gower.

Danny Shone's 1922 gold pocket watch, presented to him by the club as a member of the 1922 league title-winning side. Photo courtesy of Doug Barlow, Paul Shone Barlow, and Peter Barlow.

Jock McNab, unidentified gentleman, Harry Chambers, Elisha Scott, and another unidentified gentleman admire the championship trophy, unceremoniously placed on a chair pitch side. Photo courtesy of Liverpool FC.

The case for the defence (L-R) Jock McNab, Walter Wadsworth, John Bamber, Tom Bromilow. Photo courtesy of the Wadsworth family.

Liverpool's forward line (L-R) Bill Lacey, Dick Forshaw, Dick Johnson, Harry Chambers and Fred Hopkin. Photo Courtesy of Adrian Killen.

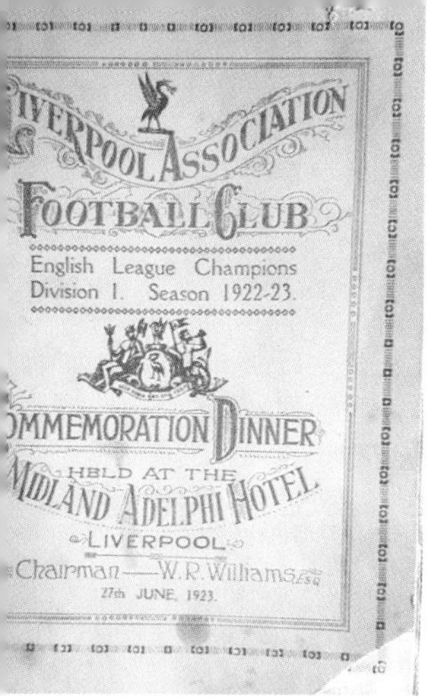

From the celebration dinner at the Adelphi Hotel in 1923. Courtesy of Rob Gower.

Jack Hayes, Liverpool's first Labour MP (Edge Hill) guides the Liverpool players and directors on a tour of the Houses of Parliament, December 1927. The club made history as the first non-international football team to be invited to a reception by the Lord Mayor of London at Mansion House, with Jack Hayes presenting them to the Lord Mayor. Photo courtesy of Liverpool FC.

Harry Chambers, Dick Johnson, and Fred Hopkin each wait in line as Elisha Scott drinks from a water fountain in London during a visit to the capital circa 1924. Photo courtesy of Liverpool FC. Restored by ANT-OGRAPHY via Facebook.

The Untouchables arrive on their 'Chara', Blackpool 1922. Photo courtesy of Liverpool FC.

The Untouchables on the Mersey Ferry. Photo courtesy of Liverpool FC. Restored by Anthony Winson.

'Hats off to training' Jock McNab and 'The Untouchables' board the train to Cleveleys for a training camp by the sea. Photo courtesy of Liverpool FC.

the ball into the net, and it looked like a repeat of the previous week's victory at Anfield was on the cards.

Sadly, though, the Reds laboured in the second half and City rallied. A brace from Horace Barnes in the 60th and 75th minutes took the points for the Manchester club. However, as the Liverpool players trudged off the pitch at full time, there would be a surprise waiting for them in the dressing room. The King, after hearing Wadsworth's pleas, had dispatched a crate of whiskey to the away dressing room.

Footballers in general were now growing in confidence and beginning to assert their power as 'entertainers' and men who generated a great deal of wealth for their clubs and the game in general. By way of evidence, one report in the *Football Echo* dated Saturday, 3 April 1920, stated that a crowd of 28,000 watching Liverpool beat Derby County 3-0 had generated some £2,000 in gate receipts, a sum that was twice Derby's transfer budget.

It appears that some of Liverpool's players were now part of a movement that sought to establish a players' union and achieve recognition from the FA. These were important figures in the game and would have wielded considerable influence. Elisha Scott and Kenneth Campbell kept goal for Ireland and Scotland respectively, Bill Lacey captained the Irish team and Ephraim Longworth made his international debut for England on 10 April 1920 against Scotland.

For Elisha, the honour of representing Ireland was considerable. The following extract from an interview he gave to the *Manitoba Free Press* in 1939 gives ample evidence of just how much it meant to the young Scott:

'In 1919, football recommenced after being stopped by the war. But in my opinion there was a far more important happening in the football world. The Irish selectors found a young broth of a boy playing goalie for Liverpool and decided that no other should represent them in the Victory International against Scotland.

'That same broth of a boy was Elisha Scott, and never will I forget the day I learned that the Emerald Isle was requiring the services of myself. I was playing, as I say, with the Liverpool club, and when the manager came to me one morning and told me that I was wanted by the Old Country to play against the Scots, at Ibrox Park, I wagged my head very wisely and said, "The other leg is better far for pulling, it's got bells on."

'It took the manager half an hour of powerful argument and much waving of official notes before I could believe that such great honour had come to the same boy.'

Sadly, for Elisha, the Scots ran out 2-1 winners in the first of two games, which was played at Glasgow's Celtic Park. This is how Scott recalls the day and the match:

'The journey to Scotland took, I believe, about eight hours, but Elisha Scott thought it was a hundred hours. The nearer I got to Glasgow the further I wished I was away. I was as nervous as a sheep on the way to the butcher, and felt very much like the sheep would.

'The first of that game was too rapid for me. I stopped one or two easy pots and began to feel like a goalie at last. Then some spalpeen ousted the rules inside the area and Andy Wilson, the Scots' centre, came up to take the free pot.

'I believe he scored. I don't know. The referee said so, the crowd said so, and next day's paper said so, and therefore he must have done. But I never saw that ball go past.'

It was clearly a rude awakening for the youngster, but Scott would see his team equalise and vowed that the Scottish would not get past him again. Alas, this was to be an international baptism of fire: 'Soon after that the lads took the ball to the Scots and gave them a spot of running to do. Billy Halligan, the Hull City laddie, gave the ball a thundering kick, and I had the pleasant sensation of seeing my Scots' counterpart fish the ball from where all the good shots go to.

'Hurrah, I thought. One each, and they don't come through here while there's a breath in my body. They didn't either, for although they scored another goal I had no breath in my body when they did it. Donaldson, the outside-right, who used to play with Bolton Wanderers, sent in a centre. It was rising quickly and the wind was bringing it in. With that touch of the Irish which makes the whole world grin, I dashed out of the citadel and grabbed the ball.

'A flashing thought of congratulation struck me just a split-second before a flashing body hit me in the ribs and I sat upside the net with the ball in my lap. The second goal was also the property of Andy Wilson.

'It was a very subdued Elisha Scott that returned to Liverpool that day, and I felt sure that never again would I play for my country. You can judge my surprise therefore when I was told that I had to play in the return match at Windsor Park, Belfast – these were Victory Internationals, you understand.'

By all accounts, the return match in Belfast was something of a feisty affair, and the Scots would be entering a cauldron of partisan Irish support. This description by Scott of an encounter with a young Irishman before the game tells its own story: 'The crowd at Belfast was after my own heart, and the good old brogue came kindly back to my ears. The cheers which rent the air when "we" took the field were as sweet music.

'I remember very distinctly a remark made to me by a bonny boy from the hills. The boy was dressed up in traditional Irish costume. His cheeks were somewhat rosy, more by acquaintance with the potsheen than with fresh air, and in his hand he wore, or grew, as we say, a shillelagh.

'This potent weapon he handed down to me with a profound observation, "If they git so close to be lolke danger give 'em a kiss wi' the ould magic wand and they'll trouble divil agin."

'I was tempted to slip the easy stick up my jersey, but refs are sometimes rather finicky.'

The game would end goalless with the Irish missing a penalty. Elisha said that it broke his heart. However, after tasting the nerves of an international debut and the fire of such a partisan atmosphere, nothing could ever phase Elisha Scott again. It was an experience he carried with him throughout his career.

The passion and fervour associated with football, and adulation that followed players like Scott, would undoubtedly have strengthened their negotiating positions when it came to talking contracts and wages. This new almost adversarial relationship between players and the authorities was pinpointed in a report in the *Football Echo* dated 24 April 1920, which called the moves to form a union a 'players' offensive' and discussed how Irish players were formulating a demand for a minimum wage of £3 per week.

Articles relating to these developments seem suspicious of the moves and almost seem to bemoan the popular support enjoyed by the players from 'contemporary onlookers' (supporters) who seemed to feel that players should be treated fairly and generously, while others argued that directors treated them 'like a regimental sergeant-major does with the conscript recruit'. Commentators, no doubt briefed by members of the footballing establishment, stressed the need for clubs to prune wage bills at times of financial hardship.

The extent to which the Liverpool playing staff engaged with this movement is unclear. Nevertheless, it does not seem to have affected performances on the pitch. The team had now achieved some much-needed consistency, and the club was now moving in the right direction.

Ashworth had also guided the Reds to the fourth round of the FA Cup and to the final of the Lancashire Senior Cup on 5 May 1920. Following a tense game which ended 1-1 after extra time the trophy was shared. Liverpool's new manager was off to a great start. With the likes of Longworth and Lacey recapturing their pre-war verve, and Walter Wadsworth, Tom Bromilow, John Bamber and Don McKinlay coming into their own, Ashworth had also brought Elisha Scott into the team on 26 February 1920, and in doing so he had provided newcomers Forshaw, Johnson and Chambers with the most solid of rearguards on which to build their reputations.

Elisha had missed out on much of the 1919/20 season as he had been recovering from surgery for a varicocele, which is an enlarged testicular vein. His return in the spring of 1920 would see Ken Campbell, who had been between the sticks up to that point, transferred to Partick Thistle within a matter of weeks.

With the spine of a great team now in place, the stage was set. The Reds inched forward in the 1920/21 season, finishing fourth, and just eight points behind champions Burnley. However, things were destined to get much better for the Anfield faithful.

9

David Ashworth, His Captain, and the 1920s Boot Room

IN DECEMBER 1919, with the newly resumed Football League hurtling headlong into the Christmas fixture list, all was not right at Anfield. The team were struggling and despite being well regarded by the board, the players and the supporters, George Patterson had realised his time as manager was nearing its end. A 1-0 home victory over Middlesbrough did little to change his mind.

The club had already begun their search for a replacement, and no doubt Patterson would have been involved in recruiting his successor. The 'chosen one' would be the highly respected and well-liked manager of Stockport County, David Ashworth.

The *Liverpool Echo* reported the capture of Ashworth as something of a coup, on 17 December 1919: 'Mr David Ashworth, secretary and manager of the Stockport County Football Club, has accepted the offer of team's manager to the Liverpool FC.

'At a meeting of the directors of the Stockport club, held last night, Mr Ashworth's resignation was received with profound regret.

'Mr Ashworth, who is a well-known and highly respected figure in the football world, has during his several years' connection with the County rendered valuable work. Previously Mr Ashworth was with Oldham Athletic.'

Another report in the *Hull Daily Mail*, dated 18 December 1919, heralded his arrival at Anfield with this: 'The secretary and manager of the Stockport County Football Club, Mr David Ashworth, has accepted an appointment with the Liverpool club.

'Mr Ashworth is well known in the football world and has been with Stockport County for six years. Previous to taking over the position at Edgeley Park, he was for eight years in charge of Oldham Athletic. During his stay there the Athletic rose from the Lancashire Combination to the Second League, and to the First League.'

David George Ashworth was born in the borough of Fylde, a little over 50 miles from Liverpool and close to the coastline at Blackpool, on 2 June 1867. He appears to have had something of a curious upbringing, living at various addresses around Blackpool, separate from parents William and Maria and their three other children, who were living in the Market Inn Hotel, where they were publicans.

David married his sweetheart Annie Whittaker in Newchurch-in-Rossendale in 1891. The newlyweds moved into 3 Booth Street in the Lancashire mill town of Waterfoot, between Rawtenstall and Bacup, an area well known for its shoemaking history. They would live there for 20 years, with Annie's father William and her sister Hannah. The 1901 Census records that David, now in his early 30s, was working as a slipper machinist.

Annie gave birth to the couple's only child, Nellie, in 1906. By now David had developed a keen interest in football and had taken to refereeing games, initially in the thriving amateur leagues. However, he soon progressed to officiating league fixtures.

In a report in the *Sheffield Daily Telegraph* on 6 August 1904 he was listed as the referee of the upcoming Second Division season opener between Liverpool and Burton United on 1 September 1904. The Reds would triumph 2-0 thanks to two first-half goals from Bobby Robinson and would go on to earn promotion as champions in 1905.

Just two years after his stint as referee at Anfield, Ashworth would move into football management with Oldham Athletic as the first person to take the role at the club. He would remain there for eight years, seemingly developing a strong bond with the town and the club. The move would also be a lucrative one for David and his young family, and the 1911 Census records have them living at 45 Mitchell Street, Oldham, a large house with four bedrooms.

After years of moving from one house to another and sharing with extended family, it appears Ashworth was now finally settled and in a home that would have seemed palatial in comparison with the accommodation he was accustomed to. However, as we will see later, Ashworth's nomadic upbringing left him with a wanderlust he could never shake off.

Oldham, who had previously gone by the name of Pine Villa FC until 1899, had just won election to the Football League. Ashworth would lead his newly promoted team to the First Division at the end of the 1909/10 season. In doing so he had overseen something of a boom time for the club, with one local report dated 29 August 1910 eulogising, 'Oldham Athletic's promotion to the First Division will naturally increase the interest in their performances. They have a well-balanced team, and it is quite evident that they mean to leave no stone unturned in their efforts to retain the position they have won.

'The players are confident of being able to give a good account of themselves and, remembering their wonderful performances in the latter half of the season, one is inclined to think this confidence amply justified.

'That the club will receive greater public support than formerly is certain, and in view of this, the ground has been improved, and will now hold comfortably 45,000 spectators. The bottom bank has been raised, the stands renovated, and the dressing accommodation considerably extended.'

Oldham would finish a creditable seventh during their first season in the top tier and even managed to beat Tom Watson's Liverpool 3-1 at Boundary Park on 3 December 1910. However, fortunes started to fluctuate after that, with the club narrowly avoiding relegation in 1912, before stabilising in ninth in 1913 and fourth in 1914. After a meteoric rise, Ashworth was beginning to get itchy feet, and would leave Oldham for Stockport shortly before the outbreak of the First World War.

David remained there throughout the war, and according to the *Manchester Evening News*, in an article dated 1 October 1914, he was a member of a sub-committee of managers responsible for organising military training for footballers. Interestingly, neither Liverpool nor Everton participated in the scheme, as they had organised their own. Anfield had even erected a rifle range to allow players target practice.

Ashworth was apparently something of an eccentric character, an aspect to his personality that many found endearing. According to the Twitter account OAFC Memories, he would curl his moustache, fashioned into a fine point either side of his mouth, upwards or downwards dependant on the team's results, and he would follow games by charging up and down the stand at Boundary Park to keep tabs on the action.

In a later incident, while he was manager at Anfield, Ashworth snatched a player from under the noses of Everton in somewhat comical circumstances. Writing in the *Liverpool Echo*, on Thursday, 11 October 1928, Ernest 'Bee' Edwards recalled the moment, which had occurred when Ashworth had attended a match at Goodison Park.

Describing it as 'the biggest football joke of the century', 'Bee' tells how the Blues were trialling a player they wished to sign. Unfortunately for them, Ashworth also liked the look of him, and proceeded to borrow a 'signing form from the Everton club and promptly signed the player Everton were about to sign'. Though the famed *Echo* columnist acknowledged the affrontery and the 'bitterness' that ensued, he claimed to now remember the occasion with a chuckle. Sadly, the name of the player is not revealed.

Football did continue in a fashion during the war and Ashworth's Stockport would be pitted against Tom Watson's Liverpool, in the Lancashire Section Principal Tournament, on 9 October 1915. The *Liverpool Echo* featured this preview the day beforehand: 'We recall Liverpool beating Stockport 3-0 in a cup tie recently; we remember the "Snow Saturday" – who can say offhand the date of that vile day? It was on 11 January 1913, and vividly the minds tell us afresh that Stockport that day surprised everyone by their ability to plough through the snow-slushed ground.

'This season, however, Stockport, under the "cute" guide of Davie Ashworth – the man who made Oldham at cheap rates of payment – have been creating surprise and, as stated earlier in the week, have done so well that a lying rumour has been connected with the old club's name.

'They have beaten Rochdale 2-0 and Preston 5-0, beat Stoke and, better still, drew at Burnley. That is sufficient recommendation for Anfield followers. They'll go to Liverpool's match tomorrow in thousands to see this new-framed and clever side.

'The start, take note, Mr Spectator – is still at 3.30pm, and the band of the 8th Irish Regiment will wile [sic] away the time of your waiting on the Kop or elsewhere.'

Liverpool would win the game 2-1, but this summary illustrates that Ashworth was by now a manager of some repute. However, it is the familiar use of 'Davie' that catches the eye, suggesting he was also a popular and engaging figure.

It is therefore little surprise then, that when it became clear that Patterson was more suited to the administrative side of the game, the Anfield hierarchy turned their attentions to Ashworth. And they seemed utterly delighted to get their man, and it appears the feeling was mutual. A *Liverpool Echo* account of the annual general meeting of the club, published on 24 June 1920, reported, 'The chairman eulogised the services of their new manager, Mr David Ashworth, who, in reply, said he knew no better board of directors and no more loyal players.'

In truth, Ashworth loved a 'project', to coin a more modern phrase. In Liverpool, he would have seen a once great club punching well below its weight, and the chance to build something special was deeply appealing to him. After all, he had done similar jobs at both Oldham and Stockport.

With Ashworth, there is a sense of someone always searching for the next challenge and not comfortable settling anywhere too long. The one exception is Oldham, where he spent the best part of a decade. Oldham had been good to David, and his role as manager had provided him with the means to support his wife and raise their only daughter. Annie and Nellie had continued to live in the town, despite his move to Stockport and then Liverpool. It is therefore possible that this shaped his decision to leave Liverpool and return to Athletic midway through the 1922/23 season. However, as we will see, when it comes to Ashworth, things are rarely straightforward.

Ashworth inherited the nucleus of a great team. Liverpool already had the building blocks of future success in place. Many of the mainstays of the team that would go on to earn the title 'Untouchable' were already at the club. He would also be blessed with a talented and loyal backroom staff in William Connell, Charlie Wilson and Joe Hewitt.

These three men were already stalwarts of the club and steeped in football and were a group of loyal lieutenants who ensured the players were well drilled and prepared to implement Ashworth's plans on the pitch.

William 'Billy' Connell had been the chief trainer at Anfield throughout the war years and would continue under Ashworth's charge. He retired and was succeeded by Wilson in 1928 having spent 25 years in the club's service. Billy joined in 1903, and his loyalty and contribution was rewarded in 1924 with a testimonial game against Rangers, which Liverpool lost 2-0.

Born William Downing Connell, in Heaton Norris, Stockport, on 8 May 1863, he was the son of a blacksmith, John Connell, and mother Martha. His siblings were Herbert, Allat and Bertha.

At the age of 20 he married Miranda Chandley on 18 May 1883, in St Peter's Church, Levenshulme. The couple lived at two addresses, 10 and 70 Lloyd Street in Heaton Norris, Stockport, between 1883 and 1903. Billy's occupation is recorded in census documents during this period as 'Hatter' and 'Felt Hat Blacker'.

However, Connell had developed a passion for football and alongside his day job had taken up the role of trainer at Stockport County, working alongside Charlie Wilson. The two men were good friends and Wilson would recommend Billy to Liverpool. After arriving at Anfield, he quickly developed a considerable reputation in the game.

He and Miranda lived at 27 Clapham Road, Anfield, where they raised their four children, and at this point the 1911 Census records Billy's occupation as a 'Trainer of Professional Footballers'. Now earning a living from the game, his stock was such that several commercial brands sought his endorsement.

In 1904 he was featured in a newspaper advert for a product called Zam Buk, an ointment for cuts and bruises, and later in 1914 an advert for Bovril, a beef-flavoured drink, which appeared before the club's appearance in the FA Cup Final, carried a quote from Connell:

'During the training of the team for the "English Cup" competition, they have consistently taken "Bovril", which they have found gives them great staying powers. W Connell, Trainer.'

His continued contribution after being replaced by Wilson was recognised in the *Liverpool Echo*, who after the club had retained the title for the first time, in 1923, wrote:

'Liverpool's fine consistency both this year and last pays silent tribute to their silent trainer.'

Furthermore, a letter to the *Echo*, penned in 1925 by a local referee in the amateur Zingari League, Charles Taylor, joined in a chorus of praise for Connell, who he claimed was and 'an expert in manipulating tired muscles'.

Wilson was a former Liverpool player and a key member of the 1900/01 championship-winning team. He had joined the Reds from Stockport in 1897 and played 92 times, rubbing shoulders with great players like Alex Raisbeck and Sam Raybould. He was therefore something of living legend at Anfield, with a reputation as a talented defender and something of a student of the game.

Charles James Wilson was born on 22 April 1873 in Sutton, Prescot, Lancashire. His parents were Charles James and Elizabeth. He had one sibling, Eliza, born in 1874, who tragically died well before her second birthday in 1876. Wilson's father was employed as a 'Stationary Engine Driver' and there is reference to Charlie being employed as a mechanic, before football took over his life.

Tragically, his playing career was blighted by a horrific injury which saw him break his leg in the first minute of a game against Middlesbrough on 28 February 1903. Legend has it that Wilson had dreamed he would suffer a break the night before. Whether this is true or not, the injury put him out of the team for eight months and he would manage just nine appearances afterwards. Wilson played his last game in 1905 and his playing contract expired in 1907. He stayed on among the backroom staff at Anfield until his eventual retirement in 1939.

During the war, Charlie continued to work at the club, while claiming that he spent his leisure time 'filling shells with Ernest Peake, and training lady footballers'. At the end of the war, his services were retained, and in 1922 the club would award him the sum of £500 in lieu of a benefit match.

Wilson's capture from Stockport was something of a coup, and it is thought that the promise of a lump sum of £100 had been enough to stave off interest from Manchester City and seal his move to Anfield.

This cannot be officially confirmed, but journalist, author and oral historian Stephen F. Kelly recalls a conversation with Charlie's son, Doug, who suggested that the money, though promised, was never forthcoming. Doug's insights also revealed something of Charlie's deep connection to the club, his apparent influence behind the scenes and provides an insight into the role of manager and trainers in the 1920s: 'Doug always insisted that it was really Charlie who was the manager in the '20s and '30s,' said Stephen. 'He was called "coach" but really he was the man on the field dealing with the players on a daily basis.

'He won a championship medal with the 1900/01 side, and one for the 1905/06 championship, despite not featuring at all that season. Throughout his life he always wore the medal on a chain tucked into his waistcoat. You can spot the chain in lots of photos of him.'

There is undoubtedly some merit in Charlie's assertions. Ashworth's role was not on the training pitch. He would have been liaising with the board, involved in scouting and recruitment, and organising off-the-pitch matters. It is likely that the manager would have had input into tactics and formation, while the training staff would have drilled the players on a day-to-day basis, forming a string relationships, puting an arm around some, while giving others a much-needed kick. Stephen F. Kelly agrees that Charlie deserves greater recognition and highlights his role in training the players and developing tactics:

'Charlie Wilson must be one of the most underrated people in the history of Liverpool Football Club. Ostensibly a centre-half, in his playing days, he was very much a utility player who could play anywhere in defence. Few others have served Liverpool as long as he did.

'He made his debut in March 1898 and played 26 times during the 1900/01 season as Liverpool clinched their first title. In 1905 he helped Liverpool win the Second Division title, after which he turned to helping the club as a scout and was there as Liverpool clinched their second title in 1906.

'By the time the club won their back-to-back titles in the early 1920s Wilson had risen from scout to trainer and then to coach, a position in those days more akin to what we would understand as manager. Tom

Watson and David Ashworth were officially known as "manager" during this period but neither of them had ever played professional football; they were more administrators with the daily role of looking after the players and tactics the responsibility of the coach.

'And it was Wilson who was coach as Liverpool clinched consecutive league titles between 1921 and 1923. He remained with the club until the outbreak of war, and he can be spotted on every team photo throughout the 1920s and '30s, sporting his gold chain hanging out of his waistcoat pocket. And on the chain was his league championship medal for the 1900/01 season, such was his love of Liverpool. Maybe one day Wilson will become more recognised for his service and appreciated as one of the club's greatest servants.'

It is certainly dangerous to appraise the role of these men through a modern lens. What we call manager now bears little relationship to the role in the 1920s. Indeed, even as late as 1959, the board at Anfield were picking the team, while the likes of Phil Taylor and his backroom team focused on training and coaching the players.

However, it is also difficult to ignore the impact of Ashworth on the club after his arrival. The evidence in terms of results is undeniable as they are in stark contrast to those achieved under the administration of Patterson. Clearly the role of 'manager' or 'secretary' set the tone at a football club and provided leadership and vision.

Liverpool Football Club was transformed after Ashworth's arrival, and the team appeared more balanced and consistent than it had under Patterson. As with all good leaders, his true skill may well have been in identifying talented people, listening to them, and giving them the space and resource to do their jobs to the best of their ability.

The club's greatest managers of the modern era have all shared this trait: Bill Shankly, Bob Paisley, Joe Fagan and even Jürgen Klopp. They each surrounded themselves with people who were loyal and who addressed gaps in their own skill sets. If the attention Ashworth received for the upturn in results irked the likes of Wilson, who saw themselves doing the important work on the training pitch, that is understandable. However, it is possible to recognise the contributions made by all these men. The adage, 'success has many fathers' seems apt here.

Moreover, Ashworth, had been a referee, loved football, which he had played in the Rossendale amateur leagues, and he understood not just the rules of the game, but its ebb and flow. That contrasted starkly with George Patterson's approach, which favoured the business and secretarial side of the game.

It is important here to emphasise that Ashworth, like Patterson before him, would have had to marry the needs of the administrative and commercial side of the club with those of overseeing first-team affairs. His natural leanings lay in the direction of the latter, but with Liverpool's back-office operation being a little light in terms of manpower, there would have been much to occupy his attention in terms of the organisation of the club's activities. In this sense, having capable men such as Charlie Wilson and Billy Connell around must have been a great help to him.

Therefore, rather than trying to sort out who deserves most credit for Liverpool's rise in the early 1920s, it is probably more realistic to think of it in terms of a coming together of a great team behind the team, and a group of people with the combined skills and attributes creating real synergy.

Indeed, Ashworth's appointment made the board aware of the need for someone to manage the first team. Matt McQueen, who took over from Ashworth had been designated as players' manager. The club would scrap this when appointing Patterson as secretary-manager. However, they would return to this idea in 1936 with the appointment of George Kay to the newly created role of team manager, allowing Patterson to concentrate on his secretarial duties. A *Liverpool Echo* special report detailed the move on 6 August 1936, writing:

'Let me explain the position. Liverpool FC have never been overstocked in the office or secretarial section, and the directors felt it wise to give Mr George Patterson the single task of secretary, assisted as usual by Mr J. Rouse. They decided to appoint a team manager and that is the newly created post.'

This suggests that rather than seeing the manager or secretary as nothing more than administrator, the club had previously expected the manager to take on all aspects of the running of the club and the first team, something they were aware was too much. Their repeated attempts to modify the role suggest as much. A further evolution would take place in 1959, with Bill Shankly taking an even greater degree of control over team selection, tactics and transfers, which would become a model they would eventually stick with.

Whatever the nature of Wilson's feelings about his role and his relationship with Ashworth, there is no doubt he felt a great affinity with Liverpool and his pride in both the 1901 and 1906 title wins is obvious. That the club would award him a medal for the 1906 championship perhaps suggests that despite him no longer playing, his influence behind the scenes remained significant.

Charlie spent 42 years at Anfield, as player, trainer and coach. He is therefore one of the great unsung heroes of the pre-Second World War era. Undoubtedly, he would have had a pivotal role in helping to mastermind the club's historic back-to-back titles in 1922 and 1923.

Making up the triumvirate of staff who would support Ashworth as he sought to rebuild the club was Joe Hewitt. Born in Chester on 3 May 1881 to parents Joseph – an engine driver – and Emma, Joe had four brothers: Charles, George, John and William.

A keen footballer in his youth, Hewitt played at inside-left for the St Paul's school team, Chester Boys and Newtown Rangers. He then transferred to Chester Locos, following the formation of the Chester and District League, before returning to Newtown after one season, helping them to the league title. His efforts saw him picked up by Sunderland where he enjoyed three seasons before Liverpool snapped him up for £150 in 1904.

In March 1907, events off the field exposed Joe and his family to significant trauma. He was living in Finchley Road, Anfield, when in the early hours of the morning he heard a terrific banging at his front door. Tragically, a neighbour, Sarah Ann Sweeney, who lived next door at number 12, was getting out of bed when her nightdress caught fire on a candle.

A report in the *Dundee Courier* describes how Joe had tried desperately and in vain to save his neighbour's life. Though he managed to douse the flames, the poor woman is reported to have 'died of shock'.

Joe featured 164 times for Liverpool, scoring 74 goals. He was also part of the 1906 league title-winning team. He left Anfield in 1910 after his contract expired and played a season each at Bolton Wanderers and Reading, before hanging up his boots and returning to Liverpool where he lived with his wife Alice and their son, Joseph, at 294 Breck Road. The 1911 Census records his occupation as 'Professional Footballer' – 'Sweet Shop,' suggesting that while he was still registered as a player with the FA, he was now earning a living as a shopkeeper.

However, Joe remained close to Anfield and continued to play various roles at the club and would have been there when David Ashworth arrived. He was eventually appointed as assistant trainer in 1922, a role he retained throughout the title-winning seasons. Joe served the club for 60 years. His various positions included reserve team coach between 1926 and 1928, and manager of the 'A' team in 1931, before he went on to carry out gate and dressing room duties, working in the press box and as a member of the ground staff until 1964.

Billy Connell, Charlie Wilson and Joe Hewitt were therefore pioneering a long tradition of loyalty and devoted service at Anfield, which would be emulated in later years by the likes of Joe Fagan, Ronnie Moran and Bob Paisley. We may never see their likes again.

Two other figures who played significant roles behind the scenes were former player and trainer George Fleming, and groundsman Bert Riley. Both men would be part of the Anfield fabric for decades.

Fleming was born in Bannockburn, Scotland in 1869. Liverpool signed him from Wolverhampton Wanderers in 1901, and he played 83 times for the Reds, scoring six times, and helping to win promotion from the Second Division in 1905.

Fleming made his last appearance on 11 September 1905, having not played enough times to merit a 1905/06 championship medal. After his playing contract ended in 1906, he moved into the backroom staff as a trainer at the age of 37.

Describing Fleming's role at the club, in 1915, former player Alex Raisbeck said, '"Geordie" Fleming is acting in the capacity of trainer. When his playing days were over he had such a regard for Anfield that he could not leave the place. The officials also had a notion of George for he was a good servant to the club from the day he was transferred from the Wolves.

'George looks after the young players at Anfield and they could not have a more efficient master. "Geordie" has forgotten more about football than most players will ever learn. He was a good half in his day and I cannot understand why he was never chosen to represent the country of his birth. He was certainly worth a trial in a representative game.'

Tragically, Fleming became ill in 1922 and was unable to attend a celebration dinner in honour of Liverpool's title win of the same year. He died on 12 August 1922 at his home in Elsie Road, Anfield.

Bert Riley was born on 28 March 1877, in the West Derby area of the city, to parents John and Esther. The family lived in Back Lane. On 30 December 1900 Bert married Mary Constantine at All Saints Church in Stoneycroft, Liverpool. The couple occupied two different terraced houses in nearby Bonsall Road. The cramped addresses occupied by the family were numbers 21 and 37, and both were a stone's throw from the future home of Bill Shankly.

Bert was employed variously as a market gardener and domestic gardener and would have had to work very hard to support his wife and ten children – five boys and five girls – on a meagre income.

He joined the Reds in 1908 and was the father of Arthur, who looked after the Anfield turf until his retirement in 1982. The Riley family had such a strong connection to the club that Bert's mother Mary and sister Hilda both worked at the stadium, preparing refreshments for boardroom guests.

Arthur, speaking on the day of his retirement in 1977, told the *Liverpool Echo* that his father would frequently enlist the whole family in groundwork at Anfield back in the 1920s:

'There were ten of us, five boys, five girls. A fortnight before the start of the season, my father used to take us all to Anfield, give us each a scrubbing brush and we would scrub down every seat in the two stands. It took us a week.'

Prior to joining Liverpool, Bert had previously worked with Percy Young in West Derby. Young was head groundsman at Wembley for over 30 years. According to Arthur:

'My father refused to retire when he was 65. He stayed at Anfield until he was 75, and for his last few years there, he literally ran the place. He died when he was 78.

'In those days, the ground staff did everything as well as care for the pitch. We were responsible for the general ground maintenance and my dad used to work in the office, paying out wages, selling tickets, the lot. He knew every inch of the place, every nail, every nut and bolt.'

In a glowing tribute to Bert, written on 29 December 1934, the *Liverpool Echo* said:

'He is a fixture at the ground because anything to be done is done without fuss or palaver; Bert can be depended upon. Riley was really built in with the bricks at Anfield; he followed a wizened old gentleman 30 years ago, when old Tom Watson and director John James Ramsay used to sit in the wooden hut which stood at the top end of what is now a running track.

'Bert is an expert groundsman; he has studied the weed question, and his experience of years before, when he was connected with a nursery, has helped him in later days. Liverpool's turf is excellent year by year, and the constant attention of the Rileys is the cause of this very important feature.

'Bert Riley not only brings his own resources to the club's help; he has a family of ten, all strong and good-looking people too, and they "live on the ground" working to one end – the service of the Liverpool club. Bert, the father, is a T.T. [teetotal] and non-smoker, a great billiard player, and a cricket fanatic. "The best ever," said one of the officials when we talked of Bert Riley.'

So, blessed with an extremely talented and loyal backroom team, David Ashworth prepared for his first game in charge of Liverpool, a goalless draw with Everton at Goodison Park. Despite going down to ten men in the 78th minute thanks to an injury to Harry Chambers, Ashworth's charges held on for a point. The *Liverpool Daily Post and Mercury* match report suggested an instant improvement under the stewardship of Ashworth and noteworthy performances from Bromilow and Lacey:

'Liverpool were a well-balanced side, and their display was a great improvement upon any of their previous games.

'The defence was rarely in difficulties and Longworth was vigorous and confident. Of the half-backs, no one did better than Bromilow. Pearson and Lewis did not blend well, Lacey and Sheldon being easily the better wing.

'The Everton defence was not really so certain as the Liverpool rear division, and the half-backs were often overwhelmed by the swift movements of the Liverpool forwards.

'The Everton attack had very little sting in it. Kirsopp was a poor leader, Jones and Chedgzoy were badly paired, and Clennell and Harrison were easily subdued.'

This reference to Ashworth's teams being well-balanced was not new, and it would become a hallmark of his Liverpool side in the years to come. After facing the prospect of a potential relegation struggle based on their early season form, the Reds had stabilised and would push on in the second half of the season, managing a fourth-place finish in 1920. The Anfield board could only have been thrilled with their chosen appointment, which was now looking an inspired one. They would now set about reshaping the squad.

The club had added Harold Wadsworth and Jock McNab before the arrival of Ashworth, and in April 1920 they would bring in Peter McKinney from Consett Celtic. However, the 23-year-old would only manage three appearances before leaving the club for New York Giants in 1923. Of equal importance to the Anfield grandees was trimming the squad and moving on players whose best days were behind them.

Between August 1919 and April 1920, no fewer than seven players left the club: Tom Bennett, Arthur Metcalf, Bob McDougall, Fred Pagnam, Sam Speakman, Harry Lowe and Ken Campbell. In moving these men on, Liverpool were able to raise more than £3,250 in transfer fees.

Prior to the 1920/21 season, several players were called upon to take part in a gruelling FA tour of South Africa aimed at promoting the game there. Joining the England squad were veteran Ephraim Longworth and John Bamber. In all they featured in 14 games between 7 May and 9 August 1920. As arduous as that may sound, it was a reduction on the 23 games played by an England select team that toured South Africa in 1910.

This would have been a huge honour for the men, as evidenced by the size of the crowds who turned out to wave the players off at Southampton, as they boarded a ship called *The Union* for the trip to Cape Town. They were also present at a banquet provided by the FA at the Holborn Restaurant in London on the eve of the trip.

However, much like today, the exertions involved in playing for England would take their toll on both players, with newspaper reports suggesting that their form suffered during the early stages of the domestic season. Nevertheless, this was Bamber's best campaign for the Reds in terms of appearances and he would notch up 33 starts in all competitions. Meanwhile, Longworth would post his lowest appearance tally since the 1910/11 season.

The tour was led by two FA Council grandees, J. Lewis (Lancashire) and W.H. Bellamy (Lincolnshire), and the team trainer was a J. Whitley of Chelsea. Though South Africa would later become a fertile ground for Liverpool's scouts, in 1920 the country's football had some way to go in terms of development. The England XI would predictably sweep all before them, winning all 14 games, scoring 63 goals, and conceding just ten.

The stars of the tour were undoubtedly Joe Smith, captain of Bolton Wanderers, who bagged 24 goals, and Stan Fazackerley of Sheffield United, who scored 17 times. Smith was a prolific striker in English football, managing 357 goals between 1908 and 1931, 254 of them for Wanderers. He would also enjoy a successful career in management, spending 23 years in the hotseat at Blackpool. Joe led the club out of the Second Division in 1937 and won their first FA Cup in 1953.

Fazackerley had been an FA Cup winner with Sheffield Wednesday in 1915 and shortly after the tour of South Africa in 1920 he would join Everton. Stan spent two seasons at Goodison, making 51 appearances and scoring 21 times.

The tour would mean that Ashworth and his backroom staff would have to prepare for the 1920/21 season without two of the club's senior players. The pair would return with less than three weeks to go before the opening fixture against Manchester City on 28 August and would no doubt have been exhausted after such a long trip, packed with adventure.

In truth, Ashworth would have little to do with training. Those duties would have been the province of Connell, Wilson and Hewitt. The players would be put through their paces on the Anfield turf, and training would consist of running, sprinting, skipping and handstands, as well as strengthening with weights and ball work.

The manager's job appears to have been focused on recruitment, tactics and formation, with team selection still a committee decision with the board picking the players for each game. This meant the role of coach, trainer and team captain were hugely significant.

The role of the captain during the game was far more important in the 1920s than it is today. In the modern game the man wearing the armband is expected to 'lead by example' and be something of a cheerleader. In the days of Ephraim Longworth, the 'skipper' made tactical decisions and was effectively the manager on the pitch. This would prove to be an essential aspect of the role, particularly as there were frequently occasions when men such as Ashworth, and Watson in earlier years, would not even be present during matches.

In one of his many newspaper columns, Longworth would even argue that the captain should have the right to send off one of his players, should he be deemed to not be pulling his weight. Longworth's views on the game, expressed in print and given a platform in several outlets including the *Liverpool Echo*, were voluminous, and the weight given to his opinions on all aspects of the game is in itself evidence of the importance of the role of captain, although it is doubtful that all of his opinions found favour in the Anfield boardroom.

In 1919, as part of a series entitled 'Longworth's Special Article', the defender would advocate that club directors should have to undergo tests to establish their knowledge of the game, suggesting he didn't always agree with their team selections. His views on this matter seemed to find favour in the sports pages of many newspapers, though the influence of directors in on-field affairs would continue long after Ephraim hung up his boots. At Anfield, it was arguably the arrival of Bill Shankly in 1959 that finally put paid to the practice of teams being picked by the board.

The sport played by Ashworth's Liverpool was a complex affair, as evidenced by the 1919 Referee's Chart, a 76-page booklet which detailed the extensive rules of the game. None appear more complicated than the offside rules, although regulations surrounding throw-ins ran a close second. In relation to offside the FA code stipulated that a player was offside if they were standing ahead of a player taking a throw-in. In open play, they were considered offside if there were fewer than three opponents between them and the opposition goal when possession of the ball was won. This was reduced to two players in 1925.

Longworth was long an advocate of 'defending with your head', by which he meant that defenders should have a good knowledge of the offside rule, and he understood that teams who failed to adapt to changes often suffered. In 1919 he had come out strongly in defence of Newcastle United defender Bill McCracken's tactics of catching strikers offside, which many felt were against the spirit of the game, or 'sharp practice'.

Ephraim did, however, accept that too much 'offside defending' was ruinous to the run of play, suggesting that the tactic should be reserved only for 'desperate situations'. In an amusing turn of phrase, he would liken it to chocolate, which he said was 'nice, but chocolate at every meal would be ruinous for everyone', and to drive home his point he exhorted his readers with this brilliant line: 'For evidence of this just look at those who work in sweetshops.'

Longworth's solution was leave it to the referee to decide whether a defender was using the tactic too often, and if so, he should find the player guilty of 'ungentlemanly conduct'. However, he did acknowledge that referees had enough on their plate interpreting the game's already complex set of rules and regulations. Not surprisingly, Ephraim's views on the offside rule did not always find favour with readers.

His suggestion that an 'offside line' be drawn across the pitch at 25 yards from goal met with fierce criticism, and prompted one reader of the *Liverpool Echo,* John Lewis, to write a lengthy rebuttal, exclaiming:

'Nay, nay Ephraim. I am surprised you would urge that forwards should ever be allowed to go and stand in such a position. Try to remember your own play on the field.'

This was a reference to Longworth's tendency to press opponents in their own half, win the ball and dribble towards goal, something he would not have been able to do with the imposition of an offside line. In 1921, Ephraim advocated for players to wear numbers on the back of their shirts, his principal motive being to allow supporters a greater appreciation of who had the ball, and thereby improve their enjoyment of the game.

There had already been examples of this happening in Australia, Europe, the United States and in some amateur matches in England prior to 1921, but this did not become a feature of the Football League until 1928. In English football the players' team numbers would be printed in the match programme, but with nothing on the shirt, it would often be difficult for supporters to identify who was who, as evidenced by a letter to the *Liverpool Echo* on 10 November 1921:

'For a sensible suggestion I have seen none to best Longworth's in any paper, for a long time, and I hope that his suggestion will be seen and noted by the FA officials and given thought to, and I hope carried out. We pay to see, let us see in the greatest of comfort and know which player is which.'

Longworth had a great deal of respect for supporters who attended games regularly at Anfield and Goodison. Many players of this era felt that sportsmanship was a virtue that they expected of each other, and they also expected it from spectators. Many commented in newspaper articles or in interviews with reporters on the quality and behaviour of support at grounds around the country. Ephraim was no exception, claiming in one column:

'Crowds like footballers are funny things. If you are a home side and you are going strong, whose [sic] like you. And if you're going badly, whose [sic] worse than you! It is the way of the world, and football is not alone in this respect.'

Supporters of modern football would indeed recognise and identify with these comments. However, while many of us simply shrug and roll our eyes skyward, for players like Longworth this represented something of a blight on the game. Thus, his praise for supporters on Merseyside was as fulsome as it was sincere. He once wrote:

'Few, if any [...] could match the city of Liverpool for sporting recognition. They are keenly partisan and like a home victory, but are not afraid to pull their hands out when the opponents give something worthy of a clap.'

Liverpool Football Club, therefore, had not only survived the horrors and privations of war, but in 1919 was emerging once more as a powerhouse of the game. With a tightly knit, experienced and knowledgeable cabal of trainers, a manager with a track record of success, competence in the boardroom and powerful characters like Longworth, McKinlay, Bamber and Lacey on the pitch, the club had now assembled the necessary ingredients to mount a serious challenge for the summit of English football.

However, it was the emergence of the likes of Elisha Scott, Walter Wadsworth, Tom Bromilow, Jock McNab, Harry Chambers and Dick Forshaw that provided the fuel for their ascendency. Anfield was now blessed with a perfect blend of experience and wisdom, mixed with youthful exuberance, cockiness and flair.

In 1921, the likes of Fred Hopkin, who signed from Manchester United, would join the group and dazzle on the wing as a beacon of consistency. And to a lesser extent, local lad and war veteran Danny Shone, who made the step up from Grayson's of Garston in the same year, would also play his part in the club's success. Yet a key ingredient remained elusive, one that has featured in every successful Liverpool team before and since. They now boasted a powerful collection of talented players, but they were not yet a collective.

After stabilising the club during the 1919/20 season, Ashworth and his charges would seek greater consistency during 1920/21 and with that came a chance to forge themselves into a fierce band of brothers. And, it would be that sense of unity, common purpose and comradeship, of which the likes of Wadsworth, Bromilow and Scott spoke often, that would propel the 'Untouchables' into the history books.

10

The Gentlemen of the Board

IN 1920 Liverpool Football Club was 28 years old. Since its formation in 1892, the club had amassed two First Division championships and three Second Division titles. They had also been beaten finalists in the 1914 FA Cup and according to a matchday programme printed in 1937, had laid claim to the 1906 Charity Shield. However, with only two major competitions to compete for, extra significance was attached to regional competitions, and the club would also celebrate success in the Lancashire Cup and the Liverpool Senior Cup.

The Reds had won the Lancashire Cup in 1919, retaining it in 1920 (shared with Manchester United) along with the Liverpool Senior Cup, which they had now won 12 times. Therefore, Liverpool's supporters had tasted success in the years since the club's creation. However, their local rivals Everton remained undisputed top dogs on Merseyside. In 1920 the Blues could boast about their two First Division titles, but their victory in the FA Cup Final in 1906 would have been a huge source of pride and eclipsed anything the red half of the city had achieved. They had also won the Lancashire Cup three times and the Liverpool Senior Cup 20 times (including 1910 and 1912, when they shared the cup with Liverpool). Therefore, the Merseyside 'bragging rights' clearly resided across Stanley Park and at Goodison.

However, off the field, Anfield was a watchword for financial prudence. The club had spent wisely throughout its formative years and in 1918/19 it recorded net profits of £1,666 16s. d. That rose to a huge

£11,945 in 1919/20 and broke all records in 1920/21, when the board reported that the club was in the black to the tune of £12,490 0s. 8d.

During the 1920s, the ground saw several improvements and additions. A report in the *Liverpool Echo* during August 1921 referred to the exceptional quality of the playing surface, the addition of police boxes along the perimeter of the pitch, and improvements to the chairs in the directors' box, which the paper claimed now resembled armchairs and were more in keeping with the club's status. There was also a new bandstand installed next to the players' entrance, which remained there for decades and was even present during the Bill Shankly era.

These improvements continued throughout the decade, and in 1928 the covering of the Kop was finally complete. Windows were added to the rear of the giant terrace to compensate for the reduction in natural light. This now meant that up to 40,000 people at Anfield could be shielded from the rain, and with the entry fee just a shilling, the club was seen to be looking after supporters with more modest incomes. The new Kop, which was now the largest in the country, held 30,000 spectators, all standing. It would be ceremoniously opened by former chairman John McKenna in his role as president of the Football League, and to mark the occasion a huge flag was unfurled over the stand.

Meanwhile, additional refreshment rooms were added around the stadium, and Billy Connell was said to be delighted by the addition of two new training pitches to the rear of the Kemlyn Road Stand, presumably on land that is now the car park. Around the same time a 'Boys' Pen', holding some 4,500 'members of the rising generation', was built in the Paddock area of the same stand.

Behind the scenes, however, the rumblings of boardroom strife could once more be felt, although this time they did not derail progress being made at Anfield. McKenna, a founding father of the club and now a stalwart of the Football League, found himself at odds with the board. At a meeting of the shareholders in 1921, McKenna had lobbied strongly for former player, Matt McQueen, and a fellow director, John Keating, to be re-elected to the board. However, when the voting was counted, the men had lost their seats.

McKenna immediately resigned in protest, ending his almost 30-year association with Liverpool Football Club. It was a desperately sad ending to a storied career at Anfield, although he remained in his position as Football League president to the time of his death in 1936. He was the last of the original triumvirate that also included Houlding and Barclay still at Anfield. It was indeed the end of an era.

Replacing McKenna as chairman in July 1919 was William Robert Williams. Born in Liverpool on 30 April 1868, Williams was the son of a bookmaker. His father and mother resided at 115 Grafton Street in the Toxteth area of the city. Williams's christening took place at St Matthew's in Toxteth on 30 June.

By 1888, he had met and married Jean Bruce Galbraith at St Michael-in-the-Hamlet, also in Toxteth, and in 1901 the couple were living at 25 Great George Place, near to the site of Liverpool's Anglican Cathedral, with their two daughters Florence Catherine and Jeannie, and sons Thomas Valentine, William John and Stanley Ronald. They were clearly a family of considerable means, as also residing at the property was 14-year-old Christine McKee who was employed as the family's servant.

His family are said to have had connections to St Domingo FC, who later became Everton, and would join the newly formed Liverpool as shareholders, when the club split in 1892. In 1903, Williams was elected to the board of Liverpool as a director. However, his business interests included a directorship of a funeral parlour, and he was also a carriage proprietor. By 1911, the family had grown to include another daughter, Hannah Balmer.

He would remain chairman until his death in 1929, at his home, 1 Menlove Avenue in the prosperous Woolton area of the city. He is buried in St James Cemetery in a family plot that includes his wife, who had died three years earlier in 1926. William had bequeathed the sum of £8,676 7s. 3d. to Stanley and Bruce Williams, both undertakers and presumably his sons, along with his address at Menlove Avenue, and his funeral business, at 106-118 Smithdown Road.

His reign at the helm of the Anfield board can be viewed as one of ruthless efficiency and unerring competence. He oversaw continued financial stability, improvements to the ground itself and the rise of one of the greatest teams in the club's history. Their two league championships were no doubt regarded as a fitting legacy of his stewardship by colleagues, supporters and family members alike.

Perhaps the only incident to risk ruffling his feathers in all his years occurred in 1922 and involved accusations of bribery involving members of the playing squad. In an article featured in the *Western Times*, dated 6 October 1922 and headlined 'A bribe attempt on Liverpool?' the paper details the story:

'Three famous players of the Liverpool Football League Club received anonymous letters offering them bribes of £10 each to let Burnley win the match at Liverpool on 23 September. The game resulted in a win for the home team by three clear goals. The players reported the matter to the club secretary, who gave the letters to his directors, and these gentlemen, after consultation, decided to forward them to the police. The players concerned are Elisha Scott, the goalkeeper; Dick Johnson, the centre-forward; and Walter Wadsworth, the centre-half.

'Football authorities in Liverpool are inclined to think that the affair is in the nature of a hoax. The letters bore the Liverpool postmark, but no address, or anything to give a clue as to the identity of the sender.'

Clearly the proverbial storm in a teacup, the incident speaks to the integrity associated with the club and its players. It explains also why the club and the men who represented it were held in such high regard. The honorific 'Untouchable' was clearly intended as a compliment to the players' prowess on the field, but it could just as easily have referenced the probity that had become a watchword at Anfield since McKenna's chairmanship and was continued under the watchful eye of his successor.

Interestingly, two of Williams's sons would also become members of the Liverpool board, with both men also going on to become chairmen and achieving great success in their roles. Stanley had been a director from 1931 before being elected to the chair in 1947, and overseeing the title win of the same year. He also led the club as it reached the 1950 FA Cup Final, which Liverpool lost to Arsenal.

Thomas Valentine Williams, also known as T.V. Williams, was chairman between 1956 and 1964, overseeing the appointment of Bill Shankly and the club's rise from the Second Division. He left the position after Shankly had clinched the Reds' sixth top-flight league title and became life president until his death in 1976. His passing would mark the end of the Williams dynasty, which had spanned more than eight decades.

Another prominent figure who played a key role on the board at Anfield throughout the 1920s was Thomas Crompton. He joined as a director in 1911, replacing John Fare, who had been at the club for many years, and who had presented medals to the championship teams of 1905 and 1906. Crompton was just 38 years of age. *Athletic News* reported his appointment on 17 July 1911, writing:

'Mr Thomas Crompton has been elected to fill the vacancy created on the board of directors of the Liverpool Football Club caused by the resignation of Mr John Fare.

'Formerly a player for Wavertree, St Helens Recreation and Everton, Mr Crompton gained much experience in actual football, and when with the latter club showed much promise as a forward. An injury sustained on the field, however, ended his career as a player.

'Mr Crompton takes a great interest in local junior football, and is a life member of the Old Xaverians Club, with whom he played in one of their recent continental tours. He will have two years to serve on the board, and his experience should prove of service to the Anfield organisation.

'The Liverpool club are to be congratulated upon this excellent addition to their board of management.'

The *Liverpool Echo* referenced his time at Everton, and how injury had ended his playing career. Clearly a well-known and popular figure in Merseyside football, Crompton had a keen interest in junior football and was also a life member of amateur side Old Xaverians.

Crompton was born in Liverpool in 1874. The 1881 Census records him living at Wavertree Road with his occupation listed as 'Scholar'. He remained in the area at various addresses throughout his life, and was employed in several occupations, including clerk and licensed victualler (a seller of alcohol). Thomas had connections with both of Merseyside's premier clubs. A keen footballer himself, he even played four times for Everton as a centre-forward, in January 1899.

Thomas, a tall figure at six feet in height and described as having a roseate complexion and silver hair, would later become chairman from 1926 to 1932. He died in a nursing home two years after the end of his spell, following a short illness aged just 59. He left behind his widow, Mary, and son Oswald, to whom he bequeathed the sum of £12,286 10s. 8d.

Tragically his wife, who he referred to as 'Mother', was on a trip to Australia at the time of his passing. Crompton was succeeded as chairman at Anfield in 1932 by Walter Henry Cartwright.

Like many of his contemporaries on the Anfield board, Thomas had other business interests outside of football, and was a licensee of the Halfway House Hotel in Wavertree, Liverpool. His funeral was attended by hundreds of mourners, including senior figures from the world of football and rival clubs such as Everton, Tranmere Rovers, Preston North End, Newcastle United and the Irish and Welsh football associations. The entire Liverpool board, squad and ground staff also turned out, while the pallbearers included Liverpool stars Tom Bradshaw, Elisha Scott, Arthur Riley, Gordon Hodgson, Jimmy McDougall and Berry Nieuwenhuys.

An obituary, written later in the *Liverpool Echo*, revealed his many sporting and leisure interests, including bowling, billiards and 'conjuring', and it spoke of the personal qualities that endeared him to so many people. This passage is particularly moving:

'He was a lovable character, unusually disposed when his team lost. I never heard him complain, except he would with Friend Bibby and myself rail at the way Fate dealt him a succession of cards unworthy any call.

'The other side of his character was full of love, charm, personality, and, whether he went scouting or seeing an international match, players and people would say, "Do show us the latest?" He was an expert conjuror, and I shall never forget the opening phrase of his act, "Have you seen this one, boys?"'

These popular and competent men helped to oversee a period of sustained stability at Anfield that no doubt provided the bedrock for the club's successes in the 1920s. It's true of any club that success cannot be guaranteed through fiscal prudence and careful stewardship, but in football as in business, it is rarely achieved without that being in place.

Therefore, we can see that Liverpool's rise to prominence during the early years of the decade cannot be attributed singularly to some managerial genius, stellar players, advanced training methods or a great boardroom, but rather it occurred because of all these elements combining at the same time to create something of a 'tipping point' for the club.

The mantra that states 'this club is bigger and represents more than any individual' has been uttered with monotonous regularity by many of Liverpool's more modern heroes, from Shankly to Klopp. The words ring true today, they will tomorrow and, it seems, they have echoed around the walls of the club for more than a century.

11

Creating the Band of Brothers

SUMMER IS almost over, and as a train carriage rattles along the Overhead Railway – or 'Dockers Umbrella' as the locals call it – and past a soot-stained Royal Liver Building on Liverpool's Strand, an artery that courses alongside the Mersey, the city gets ready to welcome the start of a new football season. Thousands of dock workers drawn from across the world load and unload ships and boats sailing from and to all corners of the globe, and the cacophony of industry is deafening. Meanwhile, barely three miles away, at Anfield, William Connell is putting the players through their paces on training pitches behind the Kemlyn Road Stand.

Across the Irish Sea, tensions that would eventually lead to partition of the country had long since passed simmering point and were now boiling over on to the streets of Belfast. On the mainland, the Communist Party of Great Britain is formed at a congress in London, and the Labour Party threatens a general strike if the UK declares war on Soviet Russia. In the middle of this ferment, Liverpool Football Club was preparing to do battle with Manchester City at Anfield on 28 August 1920.

Football itself was in the midst of a revolution of sorts, and the newly formed 22-team Third Division was also preparing to kick off. Southampton, Crystal Palace, Millwall, Norwich City, Queens Park Rangers and Luton Town had all been elected from the Southern League, and in a year's time a northern section would be created.

The Reds had finished a creditable fourth at the end of the 1919/20 season, with their neighbours across Stanley Park languishing in 16th.

There was much for the Anfield faithful to be optimistic about, despite the somewhat volatile situation politically. In truth, after four years of war, many had become numb to such crises and, unless directly affected by them, would have simply got on with their lives as best they could.

The game got under way at 3.30pm and a crowd of 45,000 packed into Anfield to see it. A new entertainment tax, introduced the year before, meant that the minimum cost of attending the match was one shilling, but this did not lead to a reduction in attendances. On the contrary; the average attendance at Anfield had now risen to 40,000. There were also restrictions on how much players could earn, with a maximum wage of £9 per week, though many would not receive even close to that.

Liverpool lined up with Elisha Scott in goal. The Irishman had made just nine appearances the season before, but he was now clearly David Ashworth's and the board's first-choice keeper. He would make 26 appearances during the 1920/21 season. Teams tended to line up in a 2-3-5 formation throughout the period and Liverpool were no exception.

In the directors' box Ashworth cut a diminutive figure, his demeanour in stark contrast to his predecessors, Tom Watson and George Patterson. While the late Watson was a larger than life and hugely charismatic man who had a huge reputation in the game as a winner, Ashworth measured just over five feet tall, and while he had worked wonders at Oldham, his curriculum vitae did not come close to that of 'Owd Tom'. While Patterson was something of an expert administrator, he is said to have lacked the precision of thought and fastidiousness possessed by Ashworth.

Liverpool's new boss would leave nothing to chance and was clearly a deeply superstitious man. An undated press clipping, clearly written after his Liverpool career, tells the curious story of how, since his days at Oldham, he had taken to carrying three 'lucky mascots' in his pocket everywhere he went. They were a tiny ivory black cat, which was presented to him before his first game as a professional footballer, and two chicken wishbones. The first of these had been given to him before Oldham played their opening game in the First Division, and he obtained the second before Oldham reached the semi-final of the FA Cup after defeating Everton 1-0.

So, as Ashworth looked on, no doubt clutching his lucky charms, the 1920/21 season got under way at Anfield, with Manchester City as the sacrificial lambs.

However, as the first half unfolded the boss might have considered jettisoning his mascots altogether. City raced into a two-goal lead thanks to goals from Tommy Browell and Ernest Goodwin. It was a lead they held until half-time.

Ephraim Longworth was furious, and Elisha Scott was said to be 'spitting feathers' at their defensive lapses. Their conversations in the dressing room at the interval must have peeled the paint from the walls, and within four minutes of the restart, Donald McKinlay had pulled one back. The Kop rose to the occasion and the streets around the ground reverberated to their roar.

Liverpool were now flying at City at every opportunity and the visitors were looking very fragile. A brace for Tom Miller would put Liverpool in front, but it would not prevent him leaving the club in a month's time for Manchester United for a fee of £2,000. However, a one-goal lead is a precarious one and with the crowd urging their heroes to finish the job, up popped 'Waddy' to grab the Reds' fourth. It was his debut goal for the club and meant that he and his team-mates could celebrate a very satisfying start to the season.

Given that City would eventually finish as runners-up, the result was a decent one indeed. Across the league, Aston Villa had trounced Arsenal 5-0, the eventual champions Burnley had suffered an opening-day nightmare at the hands of Bradford City, losing 4-1 at home, and Everton had fought out a 3-3 draw with Bradford Park Avenue.

In the city, the local papers were reporting that the cost of boarding the ferry at Woodside, Birkenhead, had gone up – something that may have concerned Elisha Scott who made the journey regularly from his home across the Mersey – and there was an amusing story about the Anfield groundsman who was struggling to keep his goat under control.

Liverpool suffered just one defeat – a 3-2 reverse to Manchester City on 4 September – in a run of 12 games, which included a 5-2 victory over Ashworth's old side, Oldham, and doubles over Preston North End and Everton. The two games against Preston saw Liverpool score nine goals and concede just two. In the first encounter, Harold Wadsworth scored his first goal for the club.

Such was the appeal of this fixture that the gates to the Kemlyn Road stand were closed 30 minutes before the game. Those lucky enough to see it witnessed a rout with Liverpool scoring six without reply.

Harry Chambers opened the scoring in the eighth minute. After brothers Harold and Walter had got in each other's way after a corner, the ball fell to 'Smiler' Chambers, and he smashed it past George Wilcock. A retrospective piece published some years later in the *Liverpool Echo* suggests that Liverpool also failed to convert a penalty in this game. A reader the paper refers to as an 'An Old Liverpudlian' wrote in to say he recalled Chambers deliberately rolling the spot-kick to Wilcock's hands, as the keeper had been injured in the incident that led to the award.

Sadly, this incident cannot be confirmed by the match reports in the local press, but if it happened it is a pleasing example of good sportsmanship. Though quite what his team-mates, manager and supporters thought of it is anyone's guess. The 'Old Liverpudlian' recalls that, though there were 'plenty of rattles and colours', there was 'not so much singing and obscene chants'.

Dick Johnson bagged a hat-trick and Forshaw and Harold Wadsworth completed the drubbing. Preston centre-back Joe McCall was given a torrid time and had to leave the pitch temporarily after sustaining a cut to his face following a clash with Walter Wadsworth. He probably wished he had read Ephraim Longworth's essay titled 'How to place a team in defence', published in the *Liverpool Echo* days earlier.

A week later, Liverpool travelled to Deepdale to face Preston again, and once again Harold Wadsworth was on the scoresheet. This time he was grabbing the winner in the 70th minute after the Reds had fought back from a two-goal half-time deficit to take the points with a 3-2 scoreline. Liverpool were up to third and, after managing a victory and a draw in consecutive games against Sheffield United, they faced two meetings in succession with neighbours Everton.

Liverpool won the first at Anfield in front of a bumper crowd of 50,000, on 23 October, by a single goal from Dick Forshaw scored in the first half. Both teams had to contend with losing significant players for the game. Elisha Scott and Bill Lacey were both selected to play for

Ireland against England at Sunderland, while the national side included Everton stars Sam Chedgzoy and Dickie Downs.

In place of Scott, a 26-year-old Scottish goalkeeper called Harry McNaughton made his first and only appearance for Liverpool. He could at least satisfy himself that he kept a clean sheet.

If the victory at Anfield could be described as dogged, then what followed seven days later at Goodison was considered 'resplendent' by the gentlemen of the local press, and Liverpool's three goals were 'outstanding'. It seems the atmosphere in the city during the seven days between the two games was at fever pitch, and the *Liverpool Echo* captured the mood in a short article by 'F.E.H.' in which he shared a brief ode to the game:

Derby Day; Derby Day!
Once again the rivals play.
Blue on Red and Red on Blue,
With a useful shot or two.
And a cannon now and then,
Just to waken up the men.
Other sports may make for good,
Stir our spirits and our blood,
But our troubles to forget,
None has ever been fashioned yet,
Since the Flood or since the Fall,
As that with the big leather ball!

It is by no means a classic, but it certainly suggests that the games between Liverpool and Everton were as highly anticipated and fiercely contested in the 1920s as they are today. The mood inside Goodison appears to have been good natured, with journalists commenting on the 'hilarity of the crowd' and only minor incidents or rifts noted.

It was by all accounts a game played at a ferocious pace, watched by a 55,000 crowd (setting a new record at Goodison) and with barely a stoppage to mention, Liverpool and Everton went toe to toe for 90 minutes. The difference, according to the *Liverpool Mercury*, lay in the quality of each side's defence.

Both teams created goalscoring opportunities it seems; Liverpool scored three and had another from Chambers disallowed. Everton also fashioned efforts, but Scott in goal was more than equal to them. The paper explained:

'Curiously enough Scott had as much work to do as Fern, and did it better. Chedgzoy caught one rebound of a kick by McKinlay and slammed in a perfect gem of a shot only to find Scott safe. Brewster too, tested Scott to the full, and Grenyer's late on shot, low and curling was just another occasion for Scott to show the best form he has exhibited this season.'

Walter Wadsworth, Tom Bromilow and Don McKinlay were also doing a fine job of smothering Everton's forwards, and in turn setting up wave after wave of Liverpool attacks. The Reds' forward play was ruthlessly clinical, while Everton's defence simply crumbled. Liverpool's first goal, scored by Dick Johnson, appears to have been something truly incredible. Chasing the ball along the wing, he somehow prevented it from going out for a throw-in then lashed a shot that went straight in. It must surely have been a sight to behold, and the watching press could not believe their eyes, as this line from the *Mercury* suggests:

'The ball was actually on the "outside" line, but not over and Johnson's oblique shot beat Fern, a fact which hardly seemed possible.'

Ephraim Longworth, writing in his regular column, described the strike as, 'Possibly the most remarkable scored in many a day. At the distance at which I was, it did not seem possible for Johnson to score.'

In a hint to the type of mentality being fostered in the dressing room, Longworth concludes:

'We may not have star performers. No one wants to be starring if he can be party to such a wholesome and capable game as that served up by our side. Chambers was standing out on a pedestal and Donald M'Kinlays [sic] kicking at full-back was also so great, it entitled him to the word "star". However, as I say, the team do not care a rap about names such as "star" so long as they can combine to make victory well deserved and one that was without a single dirty piece of football.'

It is easy to imagine those same words being uttered by Jordan Henderson today. Indeed, these values are common to all successful teams. Under Ashworth and his backroom team, Liverpool were being gradually transformed from a group of very talented individuals beset by inconsistency and without a clear purpose, into a determined outfit whose belief in hard work and commitment to collective ideals was drawing admiring glances from observers throughout the game.

By New Year's Day 1921, and after 22 games, Liverpool were one of three teams on 28 points and just five points off top spot. A 2-0 victory over Aston Villa on 1 January saw them go third by virtue of goal average, with Everton just a point behind in seventh place. It was tight in the top half of the table and the Reds were more than holding their own.

The country was experiencing something of a baby boom, with the UK recording the highest-ever number of live births, at 1.1 million. Christmas also saw a spectacular footballing occasion take place on Merseyside, with Dick, Kerr Ladies FC drawing a record crowd for women's football of 53,000 to Goodison Park for a match against St Helens Ladies on Boxing Day.

Attendances at games in Liverpool for this period were remarkable, especially in the context of mass unemployment. The national figure would reach one million people out of work by February 1921, and on Merseyside the rate was higher than the national average. Many did find jobs in the port, while factories like Meccano, which produced the first Hornby toy train in 1920, also provided work for families who despite the ending of wartime rationing early that same year were often living hand to mouth.

In parliament the Government of Ireland Act 1920 had received royal assent, and its passing would lead to the partition of Ireland into north and south regions. Each would now have separate parliaments and a measure of home rule. The move would have been a hugely significant issue to Liverpool's large Irish population, and sporadic sectarian clashes on the streets of the city would continue throughout the decade.

At Anfield, though, all focus was on the return of the FA Cup, and a local battle with Manchester United on 8 January 1921. Lining up for United was Tom Miller, who the Reds had sold a matter of months earlier. And he would almost make Ashworth and the board regret that decision.

Tom had been one of the men implicated in the infamous betting scandal of 1915, when players on both sides rigged the game in United's favour. In all, seven players from both teams received lifetime bans from the FA. In 1919, the sanction was lifted on all but United's Enoch West in recognition of the players' services in the war. Whether the affair played a part in Liverpool's decision to sell Miller is difficult to say, but it's entirely possible. Fellow conspirators Jackie Sheldon, Tom Fairfoul and Bob Pursell all left the club too. Sheldon remained until his contract expired in May 1921 and had played in 72 games over two post-war seasons. Miller featured in 24 during the same period. Meanwhile, Fairfoul left in 1915 and Pursell made his last appearance in December 1919, before leaving in May 1920.

The first round tie got under way at 2.30pm in front of a crowd of 36,000. United's Miller, lining up in blue and white stripes, won the toss and elected to kick towards the Anfield Road end in the first half. Liverpool immediately won the ball back and mounted a series of attacks. After one move, a Harry Chambers shot was pushed wide for a corner.

In a local match report, we see an early reference to Tom Bromilow's prowess at set pieces, something he would be recognised for throughout his career. United were rocking and next Walter Wadsworth headed over another perfectly placed corner from Bromilow. Walter was also a standout performer, with this passage in a *Liverpool Echo* report suggesting a typically all action display, with the player involved at both ends of the pitch: 'Wadsworth was in the thick of the fray and the mud, and he gave [Dick] Johnson a snap chance that might have been a goal.'

Ashworth's men were dominant and creating chance after chance, but they were wasteful, with Chambers, Johnson and Lewis all squandering decent opportunities. As so often happens, they were punished for their profligacy in the 26th minute when former Red Miller scored with only his second attempt.

Liverpool had by now established a reputation for raising their performance levels when behind, and they did not disappoint this time. Just seven minutes later United failed to deal with another Bromilow corner and what followed was a series of shots that ricocheted around the box. Wadsworth fired one in and it was deflected out to Chambers who, according to match reports, 'had never hit a ball so hard'.

Chambers was on fire now and went close to immediately doubling Liverpool's tally. The second half saw end-to-end action with United pressing for a winner and the Reds wasteful in attack. Press reports talk about shots flying wide and crashing off the bar, and of Liverpool's forwards failing to take full advantage of Bromilow's set-piece artistry.

An injury to Johnson meant that Chambers had to move into the middle and take up a centre-forward position to no avail. Liverpool were now effectively down to ten men and United saw an opportunity to capitalise, but Wadsworth was in the way, with the Bootle defender brilliantly dispossessing Ted Partridge when the United forward was through on goal. Then it was the turn of Fred Hopkin – soon to move to Anfield – to tee up Miller, who ballooned his shot over the bar and into the Kop.

The game was a typical cup tie and the crowd, wearing rosettes and swinging rattles in the air, lapped it up. They gasped and then held their heads in hands as once more Chambers 'hit an enormous shot that cracked against the crossbar and rebounded towards the Anfield Road end'. Liverpool kept pressing but could not make the breakthrough and the crowd slowly became frustrated.

Their worst fears were almost realised when, with ten minutes to go, Partridge once more bore down on the goal at the Kop end. Wadsworth blocked his run and threw in a last-ditch tackle, but the striker broke free and looked certain to score, only to be denied by a breathtaking save from Elisha Scott, who looked injured as he got to his feet. There was no breathing space, though, as he was immediately pressed into service, saving brilliantly from Billy Harrison, before another shot from the visitors crashed off the post. The Reds were now hanging on for dear life.

However, mercifully, Liverpool held on for a replay, and the gentlemen of the press agreed that a draw was a fair result. The replay took place four days later at Old Trafford and was played in front of crowd of just over 29,000 people. The low turnout can be explained by the fact that the match kicked off in the afternoon when many supporters may have been working. Nevertheless, United took £2,706 11s. 6d. in gate receipts.

The game was played in a torrential downpour that transformed the Old Trafford turf into a mud bath. Writing in the *Liverpool Echo* the following night, 'Stork' said:

'I have heard talk of the Anfield mud heap, but it certainly could not compare to the ground at Old Trafford yesterday. Waders for each of the participants would, I am sure, have been welcomed.'

Another report described the conditions as 'deplorable' and suggested that 'not only was scientific play impossible, but players were often disgusted at their own futile efforts to dislodge the ball from its surroundings of mud and water'.

The home side started where they had left off at Anfield just days earlier. Partridge made up for his earlier wastefulness and put United in front with just 20 minutes on the clock. The first-half deficit would have been much greater had it not been for the antics and heroics of Elisha Scott.

Scott had done everything in his power to keep Liverpool in the game, and his tactics included jumping up and down and dancing on his goal line as the striker rushed towards his goal. Not everyone was impressed, it seemed, but the post-match report in the *Football Echo* leapt to the keeper's defence:

'Some writers object to Scott's dancing dervish, hen-on-hot bricks tactics when the enemy are approaching, but there are those who see method in his seeming madness, holding that nothing flurries an attack more than a really animated opposition keeper.'

The incident reveals something of Scott's genius in goal. To Elisha, football was a serious business and the job he did was every bit as special as any outfield player. In an article about the role of goalkeeper in *Topical Times*, dated 25 February 1938, he said, 'First forget that schoolboy stuff about "any mug" doing for goal. Forget that old joke about it being cheaper to board up the goal. Forget that old tag about footballers (and fast bowlers) being mad.

'Get it into your head that a goalkeeper is as important, if not more so, than a centre-forward. A centre can make a mess of things and a pal will come to his aid. If a goalie makes a mess of things, he's sunk. A goalkeeper is a footballer.'

Scott elevated the art of goalkeeping at Liverpool. His experiences playing as a forward on that patch of wasteland in Belfast all those years before gave him an understanding of what a striker would do in any number of situations. He would insist on playing up front in practice games to 'get in the mind of the forward'. His philosophy was perhaps summed up best with this advice to aspiring goalkeepers: 'Find out what the centre wants you to do, and then don't do it.'

He wrote extensively about his art, explaining, 'Goalkeeping is about anticipation and a knowledge of angles. There are only so many angles a ball can leave a forward's boot and only so much space he can shoot at. A goalkeeper's job is to give him as few angles as possible to shoot at.'

Elisha was also the master of his domain and thoroughly commanded the box. He refused to allow his own defenders to crowd him in the penalty area, often ordering them out of it with what was euphemistically described as 'industrial language'. Some found it funny, others did not.

One such player was Jimmy Jackson, a left-back who played for the Reds between 1925 and 1933. Dixie Dean once recalled how Jackson had turned to him after the Everton striker had scored the Blues' third goal in the game, and after facing a barrage of abuse from Scott who blamed the defender for the goal he was heard to shout, 'William, I shall never play in front of this man again.'

Jimmy, who was known as 'The Parson', was clearly more suited to a career in the clergy, which he duly took upon leaving football. Despite his fierce temperament and foul language, there was no doubting the fact that Elisha was a master craftsman.

His efforts at Old Trafford in 1921 were an earlier example of that, and would ensure that Liverpool went in at half-time still with a chance of progressing. Liverpool equalised in the 55th minute when Bill Lacey headed home a pinpoint corner from Tom Bromilow. Just eight minutes later Chambers, whose performance had been dogged and tenacious, took his reward when he smashed home the winner. Liverpool were now through to the second round and a titanic clash with Newcastle United at St James' Park, on 29 January 1921.

In one of the most eagerly anticipated games of the season, 61,400 supporters turned out see the north-east side triumph by a single goal from Neil Harris. As early as mid-morning crowds had begun to queue outside the stadium and by lunchtime, 'The assembly had assumed the dimensions of an army of occupation.'

Newspapers reported trainloads of supporters travelling from outlying districts, and a considerable following from Liverpool. The turnout swelled the coffers at St James' Park to the tune of £4,479 0s. 9d.

The players walked out to a brass band and reports suggest something of a carnival atmosphere, though the blowing of trumpets and waving of rattles did not seem to impress journalists.

One reporter wrote, 'The time of waiting had elapsed with the strident singing of choruses and the playing of a brass band. There was the usual number of trumpets and rattles, which turned the air hideous, and some of these enthusiasts had gone so far as to array themselves in fancy dress in the colours of their respective sides.'

The game was an even affair, with both sides going toe to toe, and with reputations put to one side for cup ties Newcastle played with great confidence. The home side had a goal ruled out for offside before eventually grabbing a winner in the 65th minute when Harris got the better of McKinlay and lobbed the ball over Scott's shoulder, with the keeper rooted to the spot.

The roar of the crowd was immense, and though Liverpool strived to get an equaliser, time ran out for Ashworth's men. Their cup adventure was over and they had only the league campaign to focus on.

Liverpool lost just three of their last 15 games and finished in fourth place. Their goal average of 1.8 was the second best in the league, but they had relied heavily on Harry Chambers, who had scored 22 goals in 40 league appearances, and Dick Johnson, who weighed in with 13. If they were to progress in the next season they would need to find more firepower, especially as Johnson would miss the whole of the 1921/22 campaign through injury and Chambers would miss nine games also.

Ashworth and the board responded by bringing in Fred Hopkin from Manchester United for £2,800, Cyril Gilhespy from Sunderland for £250, and couple of war veterans who played together at Grayson's of Garston: Harry Beadles and Danny Shone.

Liverpool would also later elevate Jock McNab, who would benefit from John Bamber's misfortune. When the St Helens-born defender was struck down with appendicitis, the former army sergeant McNab stepped confidently into the breach. Rock solid at the back, he had a reputation for seizing possession in any dust-up, with a shout heavily laden with his thick Scottish brogue, 'Ma ball!'

The Untouchables had assembled. It was now time for them to fulfil their promise.

Part Four

Liverpool FC 1921/22: All Hail the Champions

12

Champions Again, at Last!

IN 1921, Britain was engulfed in conflict with the government declaring a state of emergency after the Miners' Federation of Great Britain took strike action in protest at wage cuts. When the union called upon transport union in the so-called Triple Alliance to join the action, the Emergency Powers Act was enacted. In Ireland, the British army clashed with Irish Republican Army volunteers, and by June the number of people unemployed had reached 2.2 million, with two million workers involved in pay disputes.

The population of Liverpool in 1921 was almost twice what it is today, standing at 803,118. Despite the hardships of the time, demand for football was high with Everton raising the prices of their season tickets, and Liverpool telling supporters to get to the ticket office without delay as supplies of tickets were limited.

The city would once again see protests and clashes with the police in 1921 as the unemployed demanded the right to work. They would face the wrath of the local police, with many beaten severely.

In the nearby seaside resort of Southport, Dick, Kerr Ladies were involved in a match that attracted 9,000 spectators. The FA did not take kindly to women's football, however, and effectively banned it in December 1921 following allegation of financial impropriety.

Liverpool had several women's teams and would organise games in defiance of the ban. In March 1922, a women's 'international' match was held at the Athletic Ground, Fairfield. According to reports, the game had the blessing of the mayor and mayoress of Liverpool, who hosted a lavish dinner and dance for the teams – Dick, Kerr Ladies of England and France's Olympique de Paris – at the Adelphi Hotel.

An *Evening Express* editorial suggested that the game would 'injure the dignity of womanhood' and damage respect for femininity among young boys. Football was still predominantly seen as a male sport and too physically demanding for women, a claim that was self-evidently false given the number of women engaged in playing it.

On 27 August 1921 the new Football League season was getting under way. Liverpool kicked off at Roker Park with an inauspicious 3-0 defeat to Sunderland. Meanwhile, the first games of the inaugural Football League Third Division North took place, one year after the southern section had been formed. Among the new division's members were Tranmere Rovers, Stockport County, Walsall, Rochdale and Chesterfield.

Liverpool supporters would welcome a trio of new players to the fold. The most prominent of the three was Fred Hopkin, but this would also be the year that Danny Shone began his Reds career at Anfield. He would be joined by fellow Grayson's of Garston team-mate Harry Beadles. All three men signed in May 1921. Later, in August, the Reds added Cyril Gilhespy for £250 from Sunderland.

Sadly, Cyril would only feature twice in his first season and would miss out on a championship medal in both of Liverpool's title-winning campaigns. A talented outside-right, Cyril's big problem was Billy Lacey who was an established star for the club, so Gilhespy was limited to just two appearances in 1921/22 and ten in 1922/23. In all, 19 appearances were all he made for the club.

Danny and Harry had been impressing local scouts while playing for Grayson's (also known as 'The Shippers') in their first season after the war, in the West Cheshire League. Though the team had finished fourth, winning just five of their 18 games, drawing five and losing eight, the pair had been the stand-out players.

Welshman Beadles would make his debut against Chelsea at Stamford Bridge on 24 September 1921. The Reds won 1-0 thanks to a 15th-minute strike by Billy Matthews. Also from Wales, Billy made only one appearance for Liverpool that season. The club had decided to trial Beadles in the game due to an injury to Harry Chambers.

Beadles had an impressive display and at one point struck the woodwork with a fierce shot. He followed up his debut with a goal in each of his next three games, and like his friend Danny Shone, he would net six times in the 1921/22 season having made fewer appearances, starting just 11 times. Sadly for Beadles, the form and popularity of Chambers meant he faced an insurmountable obstacle in terms of breaking into the first team.

Both men made relatively small but significant contributions to the season after impressing in amateur football. This match report from the *Liverpool Football Echo* dated 27 May 1918, courtesy of Danny's great nephew John English, is perhaps the earliest known record of a report featuring Shone. It describes a 4-0 home win against Runcorn and a Shone goal:

'Ellis scored for the home team after 15 minutes' play from a corner. Runcorn tried hard to get on level terms and Moore struck the crossbar. Grayson's returned and Martin added the second goal. Moore again experienced hard lines and Shone scored the third goal for Grayson's while just before the interval. Martin scored the fourth.'

Danny played mainly as an inside-left but was comfortable in all forward positions. His build was slight, standing at just 5ft 6.5in and weighing 11st 8lb. A keen sportsman, Danny enjoyed bowls and golf. Newspaper reports would later say that despite his diminutive stature, he possessed a 'lethal stinging shot' in his left foot and was a fine header of the ball, a 'good passer' and a 'clever schemer'.

Liverpool had signed Danny as a junior initially, but with Dick Johnson sustaining an injury that would keep him out for the entirety of the 1921/22 season, he would soon find himself in the first team, making his debut along with Fred Hopkin on 27 August 1921 in that 3-0 defeat away to Sunderland. The *Liverpool Echo* described how the Reds' half-backs wasted no opportunity to give the ball to Shone and referred to him as the 'bright fast-shooting boy from Grayson's of Garston'.

Sadly, despite making an impression in the game it would not prove to be his much-desired breakthrough. The *Derby Daily Telegraph* would later report, on 10 September 1921, that Danny would return to the reserves for a spell:

'Danny Shone, the young Garston lad who led Liverpool's attack in the opening game of the season, is having a course of training in the reserves. This youth will be heard of again someday.'

He would go on to score six times in 15 appearances that season. His first goal came in a 1-1 draw with Everton at Goodison Park on Saturday, 5 November 1921.

A crowd of 52,000 watched as Danny opened the scoring for Liverpool in the 38th minute. Everton had the better of the opening exchanges and even had two goals ruled out, so Danny's effort came somewhat against the run of play. The Reds had managed to gain the upper hand when Everton star Dickie Downs was knocked out trying to head a 'hurtling pass' and was forced to leave the field temporarily.

Lacey and Shone both went close, before Danny had the ball in the net only to see it disallowed in frustrating circumstances as the referee had blown his whistle for a foul on Hopkin, as Shone raced through and put the ball in the net.

However, Liverpool had now built up a head of steam and, with just five minutes to go before the interval, Danny grabbed his first goal to put the Reds in front. His strike had added significance as it was the club's 1,500th goal since its foundation in 1892. This report in the *Liverpool Courier* describes how Liverpool's new forward took advantage of a goalkeeping error:

'The steady pressure told, however, and the Reds scored the only goal of the first half about five minutes before the interval. Bromilow drove a stinging ball goalwards, and Fern failed to gather the greasy leather. Forshaw edged it past the falling custodian, but it was Shone who applied the finishing touch.'

Imagine his delirium as he leapt from the turf, fists punching the air, and hearing the huge roar of the crowd. This would have been a spine-tingling moment for the youngster, and after his desperate struggle for survival in Europe only three years earlier, his sense of elation could hardly have been greater.

Though Forshaw saw another Reds goal ruled out for offside, Everton responded immediately and went up the other end to score a leveller on the hour. Here's how the *Courier* saw the goal: 'Refreshed by the interval, the home 11 again began as though they would sweep all before them, but failed to penetrate the opposing defence, and when the ball was netted it was propelled there by Forshaw, who was palpably offside. However, Everton supporters were saved from looking as blue as their wearers of the home jerseys when Chedgzoy forced a corner off Bromilow, and served it up so accurately that Brewster was able to head the equaliser.'

Two weeks later, on 19 November, Danny would find himself on 'cloud nine' after he had bagged his very first hat-trick for Liverpool in a 4-0 thrashing of Middlesbrough, in front of 35,000 people at Anfield. Again, the *Liverpool Echo* chose to highlight Danny's impact on the game with the delightful headline:

LIVERPOOL GO TO TOP OF FIRST DIVISION SHONE'S WONDERFUL HAT TRICK; LACEY PROVIDER THE SUN DID NOT SHINE AT ANFIELD BUT SHONE!

Liverpool had been without Ephraim Longworth, who was replaced at full-back by Tommy Lucas, and Donald McKinlay captained the side in the next three games. Ephraim regained his place for the game against Aston Villa on 10 December, which Liverpool won 2-0. However, when he was dropped again in January 1922, Longworth resigned as captain despite the objections of the board. McKinlay would be an able replacement, though it would represent the end of an era for Longworth and Liverpool.

The *Derby Daily Telegraph* expressed sympathy with Ephraim, suggesting, 'When a captain is left out of the side more often than he plays what can a man do?'

In truth, Ephraim played 27 games in all competitions during the 1921/22 season, three more than he had in the previous campaign. He was now 33 years of age and the most experienced member of the squad, and it seems being dropped had been too difficult a pill to swallow.

The man who had taken his place in November 1921, Tommy Lucas, signed for Liverpool in 1916. Born in St Helens in 1895, Lucas was in his mid-20s and would make the same number of appearances for the Reds as Longworth that season.

The danger man for Middlesbrough was Andy Wilson, a Scottish forward who had two spells at the north-east club, making a total of

86 appearances and scoring 56 goals. Local supporters were eager to see him in action, as was the party of boys from Wallasey Grammar School who had been given tickets to see the game, in the Anfield press box. Little wonder the *Liverpool Echo* suggested that the Reds' defensive line 'marked him fore and aft'.

Danny had already threatened to score before he grabbed his first of the game, heading a corner expertly saved by Tim Williamson in the Middlesbrough goal, but his breakthrough came in the 11th minute. Here's how the *Echo* saw it:

'Shone was not going to be denied, and after dogged runs by Hopkin and some good dribbling by G. Carr, Lacey and McNab paired off as to the manner born. Thanks to the Middlesbrough defence failing to kick clear, a corner was the outcome, and for once in a way it was converted, Shone nodding the ball out of reach of Williamson.'

Danny was immediately surrounded by his team-mates who shook his hand and patted him on the back, and the cheers of the crowd will have filled his heart to bursting. Liverpool began to sense blood and wave after wave of attacks threatened to flood the visitors' rearguard. Hopkin struck the post and then Forshaw went on a mazy dribbling run worthy of a goal, but the move broke down. The Reds had gone five games without registering more than a single goal, and they may have feared the run would continue, but for the magic of Danny Shone.

The *Echo* continued, 'The second goal arose in a rather uncommon manner. Referee Farrar had been prone to let the linesmen control his game, and now when Lacey was tripped a linesman was seen to insist on a foul, whereas the referee saw play would be better if it proceeded.

'The direct result of this was a goal to Shone, whose work was easy once Hopkin had forced Williamson to the ground, the ball rebounding to the unmarked centre-forward.'

With 30 minutes gone, Shone was now on hat-trick but he would have to wait until the second half to claim it. Spectators had barely cheered the kick-off when Liverpool went 3-0 up. This is how the *Echo* described the momentous occasion for Danny:

'The Middlesbrough defence compounded under heavy pressure, and within five minutes of resumption Liverpool had doubled their score, and in the case of the new goals Lacey was again the instrumentalist.

In the first case he kept the ball in play by a super effort, and his run up gave him the chance to centre to Shone. Thus the Garston boy had scored his first hat-trick in senior football.'

All that remained was for Tommy Lucas to wrap up the game with a goal from the penalty spot just three minutes later, after the visitors' Victor Fox brought down Lacey in the area. The local press waxed lyrical about Danny's performance, best encapsulated by these words:

'If evidence were wanted that Shone is a footballer, it came now, when he side-tapped the ball to Lewis – a master pass, and in a way a masterpiece.'

Despite not being an ever-present in the Liverpool team, Danny was a recognisable and popular player with supporters and the public alike. According to his great nephew, Mike Hunter, on matchdays he would leave his house in Freeman Street with his hat and coat, and his boots slung over his shoulders and make the journey to the nearby bus stop. The journey to Anfield would have taken 15 to 20 minutes.

On one of those days, a driver recognised him and, in an example of the Scouse penchant for irony, looked at Shone and said, 'Goodison Park, then, Danny?'

According to Mike, Danny was also a generous man, and at the height of his earning potential would often keep uncashed paycheques in a drawer at his home and would invite his sisters to help themselves to ten shillings each and spend the money on clothing, such as dresses. Danny had three sisters and ten shillings is about £30 in today's money.

He was also a good cricketer, winning medals as a schoolboy. The family still have one medal that he won for his exploits in cricket and dated 1909. He would have been ten years of age.

Also featuring heavily in that game against Middlesbrough was 'Baby' Fred Hopkin, who Liverpool had added to their ranks for the significant sum of £2,800 in May 1921. The deal was shrouded in controversy, however, with United fined £350 for paying him more than the £9 per week maximum wage, and illegally offering to give him a slice of his transfer fee. He was clearly a talented outside-left for United, as evidenced by their willingness to pay him such a generous wage. However, the Anfield board had clearly made their Old Trafford counterparts an offer they could not refuse.

Fred was born in Dewsbury in West Yorkshire to parents Jane and Joseph on 23 September 1895. The family lived at 83 Lumley Street, Middlesbrough, and Fred's father was a boiler smith. By 1911, they had moved to 1 Springfield Road, Springfield, Darlington.

Census records state that his mother was the head of the household and employed as a shopkeeper. His father was now working at a locomotive works as a boiler riveter. Fred, now 16 years of age, was an apprentice shoemaker. However, his spare time was consumed with sports, including hurdling and football.

He won several competitions in hurdling, and his skill and proficiency in the sport would doubtless have helped him escape many tackles as he charged down the wing. An article dated 1926, in the *Derby Daily Telegraph*, describes Fred's talents on the wing:

'Hopkin has turned out to be one of the best investments Liverpool have ever made. His head is now losing its hair, and he may not be as fast as he was, but he can still pull out a rare turn of speed, while as a dribbler he can be elusive. Clings to the touchline, drops perfect centres, and rarely scores a goal.'

Fred started his career at Darlington and played for the side for seven years between 1912 and 1919, though he also featured for Tottenham Hotspur as a wartime guest. After the war, Hopkin signed for Manchester United before joining David Ashworth's Liverpool. When Liverpool travelled to Middlesbrough's Ayresome Park a week after they had beaten the north-east club 4-0 at Anfield, Fred would feature prominently again. The Reds, playing in their rarely seen alternative away kit due to a clash with Boro's home kit, were therefore sporting red-and-white striped shirts with white shorts and black socks, in the *Evening Gazette* on Saturday, 3 December 1921. The accompanying match report read:

'"Unemployment has told its tale on football attendances on the Tees-side," the report said, "and when the game commenced there were not more than 20,000 spectators present, a much lower figure than would have been the case on such an important fixture in normal times."

'Some amusement was caused prior to the match by the appearance of a black kitten, which frolicked about the net at the east end of the field. Was it a good omen for the 'Borough?'

Given that Boro won 3-1, perhaps it was. Fred was never a prolific scorer for Liverpool but despite that their expenditure on the winger, who provided so many dangerous crosses on which the likes of Harry Chambers would feast, would be more than justified. Fred was an ever-present in his maiden season for Liverpool. His many contributions to the team included pace and creativity.

Liverpool were by now competing at the summit of the table, though their defeat at Ayresome Park robbed them of top spot. They were now a point behind Burnley and level with Sunderland. They had won seven of their 16 games so far, drawing seven and losing just twice.

Liverpool were far from prolific in the goalscoring stakes during the opening games of the 1921/22 season. Their 23 goals scored was eclipsed by every other team in the top eight of the division. However, their defence, the best in the league, had been rock solid with the Middlesbrough win being Elisha Scott's fifth clean sheet. They had conceded just 13 goals.

Elisha missed only three games in 1921/22. He was as reliable as any goalkeeper in the league and gave his defenders a tremendous amount of confidence, as illustrated by the words of Tom Bromilow, who described Scott as being as 'safe as the bank of England'.

Writing in *Topical Times* on 27 August 1938, Bromilow sheds light on a player who, while not exactly looking the part, was every inch a master of his trade and utterly obsessed with it. Tom discusses how Scott would arrive at the ground two hours before a game and would be ready for action by the time the rest of the team arrived in the dressing room.

He would compensate for his small frame by wearing three pairs of socks and three sweaters for the game. Elisha would also insist on bouncing the ball on the dressing room floor, handling it intently to get a good feel for it.

These insights suggest that he was one of many in that Liverpool team who thought seriously about the game and how it was played. In many ways, Scott and his team-mates represented the aristocracy of British footballers during this period. That for many, made Scott the King.

On 30 September 1931, the *Daily Mail* suggested that Elisha had given up some of the trickery he had employed earlier in order to put off forwards who were bearing down on him. This passage also referred to his attention to detail and knowledge of his art:

'Scott never exhibits tricks in goal. He catches balls that others would fist; he puts the ball over the bar for a corner when others would be spectacular in clearing. Scott never takes a chance, and if you study those goalkeepers who have gained fame you will find that it was because of this trait. It would be easy to say Scott has anticipation, but telling why he has this gift is much more difficult. Personally, I think it is because he never takes his eye off the ball.

'I do not mean when it is likely to come to him: all goalkeepers must do that. But Scott, if you watch him when there is little chance of him having to save, is moving about in goal in accordance with the position of the ball. He knows that a freak shot will change an angle, so before the ball comes he is protecting the goal from that angle. You never catch him unready.

'Perhaps the greatest test of a goalkeeper is his judgment in running out of goal. If Scott goes he gets the ball. You never see him losing a race and finding the ball going into an untenanted goal. You never see him prancing about the penalty spot when a corner kick has been taken.

'He leaves the backs to do their job and never interferes – but let an opponent get clean through and then see Scott come out. He then comes quickly, and the forward has to be quick or the opening at which to shoot will be very narrow.

'But one could go right through a goalkeeper's task, discuss it in detail, and have to admit with each detail, that that is the way Scott does his job.'

Elisha had forged a great friendship with Walter Wadsworth and Jock McNab. Wadsworth's son, Bill, suggests that it was his father's memories of his team-mates and the bonds between them that he treasured most in later life:

'Dad didn't talk much about the football or winning, it was the players he remembered, especially Jock McNab, Elisha – who could be as brusque as he was – and Tom Bromilow, whom he remembered with a lot of affection. They were all great friends.

'Walter and Elisha were very good buddies, having both signed for the club as young men in 1912. They had fun together and in many ways, they were cut from the same mould: neither suffered fools gladly and they shared a sense of humour.

'On the field Walter and Elisha would always look out for each other, providing cover when necessary. They were similar players in that neither gave any quarter, nor did they expect favours. I was amused to read that after Walter left Liverpool, a defender named Jimmy James wasn't quite as at ease with Elisha as Walter had been. Apparently, he couldn't stand the foul language Scott used, not only to the opposition but also towards his own players!

'Back then, the players didn't earn much so there were no distractions, no celebrity. First and foremost, they were a team and they wanted to win for their club. It's as simple as that.'

Walter's granddaughter, Jacqueline, also shed light on her grandfather's relationship with McNab. Reflecting on an incident later in their Liverpool careers, she said:

'I always think the bond between the two is nicely illustrated in the unfortunate sending-off incident vs Newcastle in 1925, when both found themselves in the dressing room before the match had ended.

'McNab had been sent off for a bad-tempered foul on Newcastle's Urwin. Walter then made a comment on the foul to Urwin, who threw mud at him. Walter replied by punching Urwin. Both were sent off.

'A newspaper writer wrote, "McNab, having arrived in the dressing room sat down and prepared to change into more comfortable clothes when there was a knock on the door. 'Who's there?' demanded Jock in that Scottish brogue so hard for Englishmen to understand. 'It's me – Waddy – I've been sent off too,' came the reply. The pair were commiserating with each other when, a few minutes later, another knock was heard. Again McNab demanded, 'Who is it?' A director who had come down from the stands answered this time, whereupon McNab forgot his troubles and put some humour into the situation. 'Blimey,' he said, 'the bloody referee's sending directors off now!'" I can imagine Walter and Jock as two brothers in arms down in that changing room.'

Walter and Jock were part of a ruthlessly efficient defensive unit, which included Tom Bromilow. Tom, who had made 28 appearances in his debut season, would feature in all but five matches of the following three campaigns, including the two championships. Deployed more often as a left-half, he had quickly developed a reputation as a cultured defender, good on the ball and with excellent distribution.

Outside of football, Tom had many interests. He was a keen cricketer and enjoyed crown green bowling, which he often played with Walter and Jock. However, football had always been his great passion, and that great love for the game would one day lead him into management.

During 1921/22 Bromilow made 44 appearances in league and cup, scoring twice. His first goal came as Liverpool sat fourth in the table, in a 1-0 win over Sheffield United at Bramall Lane, on 10 September 1921. The second was part of a 5-1 blitz of Cardiff City at Anfield, with the Reds well on course for their third league title, on 15 April 1922.

The game at Bramall Lane saw Jack Bamber, who was ill in hospital with appendicitis, replaced by Francis Checkland for his debut. Bamber was clearly a popular player, and the news of his absence disappointed supporters and local reporters alike, with one match report expressing relief that Bamber was making a good recovery.

It was a tense affair with Liverpool seemingly labouring to break down the home side in the first half, but their hopes were lifted after the break when the home side's Harry Johnson was forced to leave the field with an injury early on. They continued to be profligate in front of goal with chances spurned by Lacey and Chambers, before Bromilow finally broke the deadlock in the 75th minute to give Liverpool the points.

Bromilow's second goal of the season came in a flurry of fixtures that saw Liverpool face off against Cardiff just 24 hours after earning a valuable point away to title rivals Burnley, a game in which Bromilow had missed a penalty. That result had left Liverpool five points clear of Tottenham Hotspur with four games to go and Burnley in third, six points behind the Reds.

The championship was so close now that Liverpool supporters could almost smell it. Had Tom scored his spot kick, they may well have started celebrating.

The following day, Cardiff arrived at Anfield and a crowd of well in excess of the reported 50,000 crammed into Anfield to watch Bromilow lead a rout of the Welsh side.

Amid a growing sense of optimism among the home crowd, the opening goal – scored by a former Everton player, Joe Clennell – may have punctured the Reds' bubble and silenced the mighty roar of Anfield. However, thanks to Tom Bromilow, it did not.

With Wadsworth spraying passes around the pitch and Jock McNab holding off Cardiff attacks for fun, Chambers went close to a leveller before Bromilow equalised in the 34th minute. This is how the *Liverpool Echo* reported the goal:

'Up in the left-hand corner in the shade of the Kop, Page and Hopkins had a duel and Page was pitched towards the cement railings. From the throw-in Bromilow made a strong shot that was apparently caught in the variable wind.

'At any rate, Davies appeared to misjudge the flight of the ball, which entered the net after touching the goalkeeper.'

Bromilow had been playing like a man possessed and looked desperate to score to make up for his miss from the penalty spot just 24 hours earlier. His joy would surely have been unbridled as would that of the supporters in the stands.

The goal seemingly lit the fuse and Liverpool exploded into action in the second half. A brace for Chambers in the 46th and 60th minutes put the Reds 3-1 up, and to the delight of the crowd McNab grabbed his first for the club with a 'rasping shot' on the half-volley just 13 minutes later.

The game was won, but Chambers was not interested in that. 'Smiler' was desperate for a hat-trick and with just four minutes to go he got his wish. The final score was 5-1 and, in some quarters, the league title was already Liverpool's.

The local press were now confidently declaring that Ashworth's men were champions, despite it being mathematically possible for both Spurs and Burnley to catch them. The Reds had stuttered on their run-in, losing three and drawing one of their previous ten games, and the hubris on display from local journalists might have seemed misplaced to some. Nevertheless, in a show of brazen triumphalism after the game, the *Liverpool Echo* ran with the headline 'Hail to the Champions, Liverpool'.

It seemed that their supreme confidence was matched by the board of directors at Anfield, who had become so convinced the league championship would soon be arriving that, according to 'Bee', they were already planning a 'social do' to which they would invite as many former players as possible.

There was much talk of omens, and reporters pointed out that when Liverpool last won the league in 1906 they had rounded of the season against West Bromwich Albion, who would be their opponents again at the conclusion of the 1921/22 campaign. It must have felt to everyone connected with the club that success was written in the stars.

Things could have been very different for the Reds had they not found such an able replacement for Dick Johnson, whose 13 goals the previous year had helped Liverpool to a creditable fourth. After news of Johnson's injury broke, the club turned to Dick Forshaw who they had signed in 1919. He would repay them in spades.

Forshaw's 17 league goals made a major contribution to Liverpool's eventual championship triumph. He also managed three in the club's brief foray in the FA Cup. His goal in the first round against Sunderland at Roker Park, on Saturday, 7 January 1922, looked to have booked Liverpool a place in the second round but Paul Stannard levelled in the 70th minute.

As Liverpool did battle in the north-east, the Anglo-Irish Treaty, which ended the war of independence and led to the establishment of an Irish free state in the south, was being ratified. Later that month, a flu epidemic would take the lives of over 800 people.

Football continued regardless and the replay with Sunderland took place four days later at a packed and blustery Anfield. Official records suggest there were 46,000 in attendance to see Liverpool thrash Sunderland 5-0. The influenza epidemic had hit the north-east hard, severely depleting the visitors' ranks, and Sunderland were missing key players.

This and the fact that the Reds played with the swirling wind at their backs in both halves gave the home side a significant advantage. However, once more they would prove wasteful in the opening half.

In truth they could have been two or three up before Forshaw eventually netted on the half-hour. Liverpool and their supporters knew only too well that a single goal wasn't going to be good enough, and with the wind amazingly changing direction in the second period, the Reds' attackers went to town on their beleaguered opponents.

Chambers grabbed two in the 56th and 70th minutes and sandwiched in between was Forshaw's second on the hour. With the seconds ticking down and the huge crowd purring, Walter Wadsworth added Liverpool's fifth with virtually the last kick. The *Liverpool Echo* had the following to say:

'Bromilow was peerless; Wadsworth tackled remorselessly and McNab, after a shaky start, gathered confidence and some sense of touch with his wing adversaries. In the forward line every man worked well with the others ... Forshaw was best because of his deadliness and his willingness to shoot when the chance arrived.'

Frustratingly, though, Forshaw and Liverpool's heroics were to no avail as on 28 January they crashed out of the cup to West Brom. A single goal by Stan Davies, scored in the seventh minute as around 50,000 looked on, did the damage.

From that moment, David Ashworth and his players had only the league title in mind.

The Reds then went on a run of five games unbeaten, including back-to-back victories over Birmingham and a 4-0 home mauling of Arsenal. They then drew 0-0 with Blackburn Rovers at Ewood Park before beating their northern rivals 2-0 a week later at Anfield. The Reds had scored seven without reply during this sequence and Forshaw had bagged five of them.

It was now March, and Liverpool were five points clear at the summit of the First Division. They had won 17 of their 31 games, drawing 12 and losing just two. At Anfield they had been invincible. Though they were not the league's top scorers – six of the teams below them had scored more than Liverpool's 45 goals up to that point – they boasted the tightest defence in the country, conceding just 20 goals. This was the secret of their 'Untouchable' status.

However, with the finishing line almost in sight, there was time for one more stumble on the road to glory. Up next was a home fixture against fifth-placed Bolton Wanderers on 18 March, followed by a trip to Highbury four days later to face bottom side Arsenal.

Both games should have been routine fodder for a Liverpool team reaching peak form. However, they proved tricky and in particular their defeat at Bolton owed much to the scheduling of an international match between the English and Scottish leagues, which took place on the same day in Glasgow.

The Anfielders would be without three key players for the clash: Tom Lucas, Tom Bromilow and Harry Chambers. Two goals from Chambers, who the Reds could certainly have done with at Anfield, helped England to a 3-0 win over the Scots. Meanwhile, Liverpool's reorganised rearguard – thanks to the absent Bromilow and Lucas – struggled to deal with Bolton's attackers.

The newspapers were unsympathetic. 'It could not be argued, however, that the loss of three key players was the main cause of the Reds' first home defeat of the season,' declared the *Echo*, citing the fact that Longworth's return to the side in place of Lucas had actually strengthened their defence. Perhaps, but the disruption to the team could not have helped.

Liverpool had been a machine at Anfield all season, and it seems hard to agree with reporters' claims that the loss of such pivotal performers wasn't the most significant reason for the lapse. Replacing Bromilow was Bill Cunningham, who Liverpool had signed from Blyth Spartans for £50. This was his third and final appearance for the Reds and he had not played since the end of the 1919/20 season. In attack, Harry Beadles was given a run out in place of Chambers.

The game was a bad-tempered affair, and Bolton took the lead through David Jack with a close-range shot in the 15th minute. It was a blow, especially as Beadles had just seen a tremendous effort saved by Bolton goalkeeper Dick Pym. From that moment things got steadily worse and when Jock McNab handled the ball in the penalty area, Liverpool already looked beaten before Joe Smith converted the resultant penalty.

Tempers soon flared and at one point the referee, Mr A.F. Kirby from Preston, had to call all the players together and give them a stern talking to. The Reds could not recover in the second half and crashed to a 2-0 defeat. They may have felt that the visit to relegation-haunted Arsenal would be the perfect way to bounce back, but sadly they would be mistaken.

Perhaps for the first time that season, an element of doubt had crept into the side. In some respects, the slender 1-0 defeat to the Gunners flattered Liverpool. In truth, the home side had peppered the Reds' goal and probably should have won by a far more comfortable margin, but for the heroics of Elisha Scott.

He could do nothing to stop the winning goal, which was scored by Alf Baker in the 30th minute. It was a thunderbolt, blasted in from fully 30 yards, and the striker had fooled both Scott and Longworth by gesturing as if to suggest he would pass the ball before unleashing a shot that sailed past Scott's outstretched arm.

Newspaper articles began to muse on whether Liverpool had what it takes to win the championship, with one reporter writing:

'Liverpool's form of late has given some cause for concern and the manner, if not the margin, of this defeat did not augur well for their chances of winning the league championship.'

Liverpool were under huge pressure after back-to-back defeats and now they faced a trip to Burnden Park on 25 March for a clash with Bolton, who had beaten them at Anfield just seven days earlier. Wanderers were eight points behind Liverpool, in fifth place, with nine games to go. They had everything to play for.

Perhaps angered by their own form, and the criticism they had received in the press, Liverpool put in a performance that was full of grit, fight and determination. In a sign of their wounded pride, McNab would take matters too far, 'incapacitating' Bolton's Ted Vizard in the first half and then being sent off in the second for 'retaliation'. The Bolton crowd did not take kindly to Jock's aggressive style and proceeded to heckle him throughout the game, a factor reporters thought contributed to the red mist that saw him given his marching orders in the 76th minute.

By that point the Reds were 2-0 up thanks to a brace from Dick Forshaw. However, Bolton, emboldened by their numerical advantage, pulled one back within minutes of McNab's dismissal. With seven minutes remaining this was no time for faint hearts and not only did Liverpool hold firm, but in the 89th minute Chambers sealed the points with a fine strike. The game finished 3-1 and Liverpool had righted the ship, for now.

They now faced two matches in the space of a week against Oldham Athletic, who Ashworth knew well. They won the first 2-0, at Anfield on 1 April, thanks to the prolific Chambers and a rare Cyril Gilhespy strike. However, Liverpool would slip once more when they travelled to Boundary Park the following Saturday.

Oldham were fourth from bottom in 19th place. They desperately needed a win, but they could not have hoped for a more comprehensive victory than the one they secured against the league leaders that day. Liverpool had once more had to make do without a player who had been called up to play for England in a 1-0 defeat to Scotland at Villa Park. However, this time, it was difficult to argue they were anything but outplayed, outfought and outclassed.

Liverpool were 2-0 down thanks to a brace from Jimmy Marshall, whose pace had terrorised the defence all game. Then the Reds received another blow with the loss of their captain, Donald McKinlay, through a muscle injury. Now down to ten men and chasing the game, their chances looked slim. To add insult to injury, a spectator in the crowd blew a whistle during an Oldham attack, causing Liverpool's defence to stop, believing that play had been stopped for an offside, and allowing Marshall to run through and score his third unchallenged.

Reports suggest he may well have been offside, but Liverpool's protestations were in vain. The rout was complete with an 88th-minute strike from Athletic's Reuben Butler. The Reds remained top, and with six games to go with a lead over Spurs of six points, the title was still theirs to lose.

For Athletic, the result undoubtedly helped keep them in the division. They would finish the season in 19th place on 37 points, one point above Everton who were 20th and who also escaped relegation that year. However, their result at home to second-placed Spurs nine days later would prove hugely significant in the title race.

As Liverpool entered the last four games of the campaign, they would be presented with a potential championship decider on Monday, 17 April 1922, with the visit of third-placed Burnley. Liverpool began the game on 53 points with Tottenham on 48 and Burnley on 47. If Ashworth's men could secure victory at Anfield and Spurs lost, then the title would return to Liverpool for the first time in 16 years.

The sense of anticipation around the city was palpable and, with 50,000 crammed into the stadium for a late-afternoon kick-off, and many more outside, Liverpool would prove irresistible. Only a stellar performance from Burnley goalkeeper Jerry Dawson and an injury to Harry Lewis which forced him to leave the field saved the visitors from a hammering.

Liverpool took the lead through Chambers in the 22nd minute, and as the ball rippled the net the ground was rocking, with the sound of rattles filling the air. There would be no radios on the Kop and no mobile phones to update supporters on events at Oldham, where Tottenham were also desperately trying to keep their title hopes alive. Instead, just as a banner implores us to do today, Kopites just had to support and believe.

Liverpool took their 1-0 advantage into half-time, but all the talk in the dressing room would have focused not only on the need to continue to defend resolutely as they had for much of the season, but also on the need for a more ruthless edge in attack.

Those on the terraces would have known that Liverpool still had games to spare. Nevertheless, after 16 years of waiting, for many the tension would have been unbearable. The chance to clinch the championship that night, and in an instant see the anxiety evaporate only to be replaced by sheer unadulterated joy, must have been intoxicating.

But in the 62nd minute Burnley looked to have wrecked the party when George Richardson levelled for the visitors. It was a goal of pure impudence and skill. This is how the *Liverpool Echo* captured it:

'The equaliser was a tribute to individual flair. Weaver raced for a ball that he could not centre. He was content to keep it in play and then back-heeled it to Richardson, who also performed a back-heel to level the scores.'

The reporter's words to the modern ear seem almost perfunctory but are entirely in keeping with the matter-of-fact style of the period. Emotion rarely creeps into match reports during this era, though it is often in the subtext or between the lines.

When we consider the quality of the pitch, the weight of the ball and the heaviness of the boots, such artistry of play is hard to fathom, and worthy of so much more than the description above. The subject of pitch quality features in one of Ephraim Longworth's regular newspaper columns at the end of the 1921/22 season. In a wide-ranging discussion about footballers' wage deductions, the weather – which Ephraim felt had been kind to Liverpool – he talked of the 'hard pitches' and the perils of the 'bumping ball' which he claims caused players to lose their temper and pained their feet. That such skill was on view, despite these conditions, is remarkable.

In the modern era, there have been goals scored at Anfield by opposition teams that were so good even the home supporters clapped. We can imagine, despite the stakes being so high, that this may have been one such strike, and in our minds we can almost see the nods of appreciation and hear the faint applause on the Kop.

Amid the grudging respect, however, there will have been mutterings and curses. Men will have chugged on their cigarettes and perhaps chewed their nails as the seconds ticked down. Had their chance gone begging? Or were some simply nonchalant, assured that the vital points would come against Cardiff or in the two remaining encounters with West Brom.

It was said of Liverpool that season that they often played to the needs of the situation. When they were winning, they would ease off. If the opposition got on top and things took a turn for the worse, they could lift their game in an instant, going up a gear and relentlessly harrying and pressuring their foe until they succumbed. The same was true of the supporters, who would often respond to a setback by raising the volume in the stadium.

Liverpool were indeed up against it. Realising his team were down to ten men after the departure of Lewis, Ephraim Longworth took the decision to move further up the field, allowing him to win possession closer to the opposition and set up attacks with greater efficiency. It would prove to be a masterstroke.

With the game heading towards the last ten minutes, one such pass from Longworth found Dick Forshaw who raced towards the goal. As the crowd held its breath, he let loose a shot that flew past Dawson. The net bulged and Anfield had rarely sounded louder.

The resultant cacophony could be heard in the streets surrounding the stadium and beyond. Anfield's glee at Forshaw's winner would soon turn to elation as supporters later discovered that Tottenham had been beaten 1-0 by David Ashworth's former club, Oldham Athletic. The Reds were champions again, at long last.

Now Liverpool had their eyes set on achieving a league record, but they would need a perfect finish to achieve it. It is doubtful anyone around Anfield on Monday, 17 April 1922, cared too much about that though.

13

Celebrations and Speeches

IT IS midway through April 1922, and the English football season is nearing its conclusion. Liverpool are once again champions and the city is gripped with excitement. The title win, with the Anfield club securing 55 points with three games remaining, means that they have an opportunity to surpass West Bromwich Albion's 60-point tally, achieved at the conclusion of the 1919/20 season. To do that, though, Ashworth's men would need to win their remaining three games.

There was also the prospect of a Charity Shield encounter with the winners of the FA Cup Final, which would be contested by Huddersfield Town and Preston North End. The game would be played at London's Stamford Bridge. Across the capital, at Wembley, a new national stadium was being built, and the final of the FA Cup would be played there from the 1922/23 season.

For Liverpool's players, management and board members, though, the focus appears to have been on properly celebrating their historic championship. Whether this had an impact on preparation and performances in the remaining three games is difficult to say with certainty, but it seems likely.

With the title won, and the city of Liverpool basking in the glory, the Reds managed just one more victory, finishing on 57 points. They would record the lowest goals conceded tally in the league, letting in just 36 goals in a 42-game season, with Elisha Scott keeping 17 clean sheets. At the other end they had scored 63 times, not the most prolific record but backed up with a cast-iron defence it had proved more than enough.

The press described them as consistent, if not brilliant. Many pointed to their stinginess in defence and remarked on their 13 draws – ten of which had finished 1-1 and the other three goalless. This was by no means a flamboyant Liverpool team.

Instead they were a machine built from eight internationals and associated spare parts, and assembled with one purpose, to win the Football League. And they had been ruthlessly efficient in achieving their aims. To emphasise this point, another article in *Athletic News*, dated 22 April 1922 and emphasising Liverpool's remarkable consistency, states:

'It is doubtful if they have ever had such an evenly balanced and consistent set of players as at present.'

This is surely a remarkable tribute to the work undertaken by David Ashworth and his backroom staff since his appointment in 1919. Success in sport is rarely the result of individual brilliance alone, and in the case of this Liverpool team it is doubtlessly the case that the whole was greater than the sum of its parts. However, Ashworth's impact is undeniable, particularly in terms of marshalling all of the club's resources towards one common aim.

Following their title-winning heroics at Anfield against Burnley, the Reds travelled to Ninian Park to play Cardiff City. No doubt nursing a few sore heads, they would go down 2-0 thanks to goals in the first five minutes. The game was played in a fierce wind, but the Welsh fans handed the reigning champions a rousing reception, as evidenced by this extract from a clipping, dated 22 April 1922:

'This was one of the fastest and best games seen at Ninian Park this season and the Welsh fans proved themselves thorough sportsmen by the way in which they greeted the league champions.'

If the outfield players were having an understandable off day, their goalkeeper apparently was not. Elisha Scott is said to have had a wonderful game, with reports commenting that only his brilliance prevented Cardiff from winning by an even greater margin.

Such analysis is common when reporting on defeats suffered by Liverpool during the Scott era. There is rarely a focus on the goals he conceded or the mistakes he made – of which there must have been at least a few – instead, match reports often reflect that the score could have been much worse had it not been for Elisha. This was most likely true in a great number of cases, but such reporting says more about the affection and respect that those in the game had for him.

Another example of this was Liverpool's defeat to Manchester City, in the final of the Lancashire Senior Cup, played at Bolton on 12 May 1923, after they had won the second of their back-to-back titles. City scored the winner and took the trophy with a goal four minutes from the end of the game, yet many headlines fixated on the fine performance of Scott. One such headline declares:

'Manchester City Conquer the League Champions' while another, above a report that suggests again that were it not for Scott then Liverpool would have conceded far more, states:

'Scott's Great Display for League Leaders'.

The defeat to Cardiff meant that the Reds had to win the final two games to stand any chance of setting a new benchmark in the history of the Football League. Next up was the visit of West Brom to Anfield for the first of two encounters that would round off the season.

The visitors, undoubtedly aware that Liverpool could still eclipse their points record of just two years ago by winning both games, would no doubt have had extra motivation going into the match at Anfield, and that may well have proved decisive.

Liverpool, playing in front of a crowd of 45,000, flew out of the blocks early. Their frontline featured Harry Beadles, who had also played against Cardiff. It proved to be an inspired selection as the Welshman opened the scoring in the seventh minute. His powerful shot from distance caught the goalkeeper by surprise and he fumbled on the line, allowing it to creep in.

Liverpool had all the play in the first half, seemingly employing a policy of shoot on sight, but could not add to their tally. West Brom's Sammy Richardson sustained a cut to his eye after a clash with Forshaw just before the break, giving the Reds a numerical advantage going into the second half, but they could not make it pay.

The visitors pounced just three minutes into the second half to level the scores. Howard Gregory hit a thunderbolt which cannoned off Tommy Lucas and flew past Elisha Scott and into the net. Then with just three minutes to go and the Reds hanging on for the point, West Brom's Charlie Lewis crossed the ball and Gregory grabbed his second to win the game.

Kopites no doubt left the ground a little deflated, despite the match being a dead rubber. Nevertheless, Liverpool were champions of England and nobody could take that away from them.

The players, however, would have to wait until after the final game of the season to receive their trophy and medals. The presentation would be made by none other than John McKenna, Liverpool's former chairman and founding father, at the Charity Shield match against FA Cup winners Huddersfield Town at Old Trafford. Modern-day supporters will no doubt be delighted to read that Liverpool were handed their third league championship trophy at the home of what is now one of their bitterest enemies.

Before that, though, there was the small matter of the final game of the season, and a trip to the Midlands to once again battle with West Brom. With the league won, and the opportunity of a points record gone, there was only pride at stake. However, that seemed more than enough of a motivator, propelling Liverpool to a 4-1 victory at The Hawthorns.

All five goals were plundered in the first half, with Liverpool racing into a 3-0 lead with just 23 minutes on the clock. The first came in the seventh minute with a flowing move involving the whole forward line resulting in a fine finish by Forshaw. Then it was the turn of Harry Beadles who struck with a 'splendid shot' in the 14th minute, before adding his second and Liverpool's third nine minutes later. Newspapers blame the wind for Liverpool not adding to their tally, and it may have provided the assist for West Brom's only goal of the game.

In the 39th minute, the home team won a free kick just outside the Liverpool area. Stan Davies blasted it through the Reds' defence and, with wind behind it, the ball sailed straight into the Liverpool net. Not to be outdone, just two minutes later, Jock McNab found himself in an advanced position and, spotting the goalkeeper off his line, attempted a somewhat speculative lob, which went in despite Hubert Pearson's best efforts to claw it away.

Liverpool saw out the second half with relative ease and won the game 4-1. One reporter observed, 'After the break, the Throstles did much better against the wind but they were opposed by a resolute defence – the best in the First Division – and Liverpool ran out worthy victors.' Next stop Old Trafford, and the Charity Shield on 10 May.

This would be the last time this game was played at the end of the season in which the league and FA Cup had been won. However, this was the first time that both competing teams had represented the north of England, and thus the venue was moved out of London. Liverpool would lose 1-0, but the only thing anyone connected with the club cared about that day was getting their hands on the league trophy.

They would do so before kick-off, with McKenna, in his capacity as chairman of the Football League, handing the trophy to club captain Donald McKinlay. There was something deeply circular to the presentation, precisely because McKenna was one of the men who built, grew and led the club to its first two league titles. Though he left in somewhat acrimonious circumstances, he will have surely felt a sense of pride in seeing Liverpool's continued success.

Indeed, despite the manner of his departure, McKenna remained a hugely popular figure in the Merseyside game and his contribution to both Liverpool and Everton as well as the Football League meant that when he passed away in 1936, the world of football came out to pay its respects.

His coffin was carried through the streets of the city by three players from Liverpool and three from Everton. Paying tribute to the man he come to know as a friend, Everton's chairman, William Charles Cuff, had this to say:

'He will live long in the memory of all who had anything to do with the governing of football. Fearless, outspoken, and absolutely honest, he was well-named "Honest John". The football world in general is under a very deep sorrow.'

Despite missing out on the Charity Shield thanks to a 75th-minute Tommy Wilson goal, Liverpool would be treated to a hero's welcome on their return to Central Station. In scenes reminiscent of their 1901 and 1906 homecomings, Donald McKinlay would be 'picked up and carried in triumph out of the station'.

Today, supporters of Liverpool create their own banners in honour of the Reds' greatest achievements and most heroic players. Indeed, the idea of displaying anything produced by the club would be frowned on by Kopites in the 21st century. However, in 1922, Liverpool's board of directors commissioned a 'flag' – we would call it a banner – to commemorate their historic championship. And it has a real homemade look to it.

On a presumably red sheet, a white Liver bird stands proudly centre stage, either side of it are the words 'FIRST DIVISION', above its head 'LFC' and beneath its feet 'LEAGUE CHAMPIONS', and below that the club proudly reveals that they have won the title three times, with the seasons '1900-1 1905-6 1921-22'.

The *Liverpool Echo* carried a picture of the banner, surrounded by the club's directors, staff and players, including both Wadsworth brothers and Danny Shone. It would not be out of place surfing the crowd on the old Kop. Perhaps one of the many banner artists could recreate to commemorate the centenary.

The newspapers and football journals were full of praise for the newly crowned champions. *Athletic News*, on 24 April, published several columns and photographs of the teams, all devoted to analysing their qualities. In appraising the forward line, the paper suggested that a tactical decision by the Liverpool board, relating to Harry Chambers's position, had proven crucial, if not pivotal:

'Four men have been seen at centre-forward and three at inside-left. Not until early in January was it determined to retain Harry Chambers at centre-forward and keep Harry Lewis at inside-left. That the directors decided wisely is patent, as Chambers scored his 19th goal on Easter Monday; whereas George Harold Beadles, Billy Matthews (now at Bristol City), and Danny Shone had between them only then accounted for 13 goals.'

While it is true that Chambers could wreak the greatest havoc in a central position, it was important not to overlook the impact of Forshaw in terms of replacing the goals lost due the injury to Johnson. Nor should the contributions of new boy Hopkin and veteran Lacey, in providing the goalscorers with such an abundant supply line. *Athletic News* makes the following observations:

'Dick Forshaw has developed his scoring capacity, and he shot his 16th goal on Monday. Thus Chambers and Forshaw have accounted for 35 out of the 58 goals, leaving 23 among the rest of the team. Now

Fred Hopkin, the outside-left, has never scored, and William Lacey, the outside-right, only once. They have, however, been fertile providers, and if only that industrious forager and untiring initiator, Harry Lewis, had been a marksman, there would have been no criticism to level at the scoring capacity of the champions.'

Nevertheless, this Liverpool team did not possess the most lethal strike force in the division, as the newspaper pointed out: 'Even goals have relative value.' The key to Liverpool's success was clearly the brilliance of their rearguard, and the newspaper continued:

'The defensive division of Liverpool – Elisha Scott, Thomas Lucas, Donald McKinlay, Ephraim Longworth and Edward Parry is wholly international in rank. The brilliance of Scott and his mates has only been equalled by their consistency.'

The reference to Edward (Ted) Parry is an interesting one. Parry, a Welsh international who was capped five times for his country, only featured in 13 games for the Reds. Seven of those appearances over a four-year period, between 1921 and 1925, came in the 1921/22 season. Prior to joining the Reds, he had been an amateur for Colwyn Bay in Wales, before turning professional at the age of 29.

A decent enough full-back, Parry struggled to break into the team thanks in large part to the form of Tommy Lucas, Donald McKinlay and Ephraim Longworth. Ted would have to content himself with the captaincy of the Liverpool reserve team before moving to Third Division Walsall at the age of 33. He later returned to Colwyn Bay.

Athletic News goes on to claim, 'Elisha Scott is unquestionably the world's greatest goalkeeper, and no club has two pairs of backs as reliable and polished as Liverpool. They are not impetuous, lunging, heavy charging players but calculated, surefooted in kicking and just sufficiently forceful in tackling.'

The men in question were of course, Tom Bromilow, Walter Wadsworth, John Bamber and Jock McNab. Contradicting reports written contemporaneously, which refused to attribute the loss of Lucas and Bromilow to international duty as the cause for their only home league defeat, the paper suggests otherwise:

'The one league match lost at Anfield was the penalty of success. On 18 March, Bolton Wanderers mastered the champions by 2-0, but

Lucas, Bromilow, and Chambers were helping the league to smite the Scottish league, and McKinlay was injured near the interval. Liverpool were entitled to sympathy, and they proved that the form was false when they visited Bolton a week later.'

Though clearly written with the benefit of hindsight, this reveals a recognition of the importance of these players to Liverpool's title challenge. However, time and again, reviews of this team highlight the way in which the manager had been successful in blending the various talents of the collective. Take this extract for example:

'No team ever embodied all the talents and all the virtues, in spite of ear-haunting phrases of the past. The success of Liverpool is primarily due to the way the men have blended, have combined to help each other, and have been a happy family.

'It is the old, old story of the bundle of twigs. Their strength has been unity. Eleven of the men who have co-operated have shared in the honours which national associations and the league can bestow, and seven of them in international matches this season.

'The team manager, David Ashworth, has every reason to be proud of the 22 men who have worn the club's red jersey. He has helped them with the fruits of his experience, and they have responded to his advice. Mr Ashworth has followed up his good work as a referee with much success in club life.'

In considering how Liverpool had been converted from an at best average team beset with inconsistency to title winners in a few short years, it is worth reading the words of Tom Bromilow. Writing in the *Fife Free Press and Kirkcaldy Guardian* on Saturday, 2 September 1922, Bromilow muses on Liverpool's defensive performances during the 1922/23 season, and suggests that attack may not always be the best form of defence, and that teamwork and collective effort were the secret behind Liverpool's rise.

'Ever since I have had anything to do with football, it has been continually demonstrated to me that attack is the best defence,' writes Tom. 'That doctrine may, I suppose, be conducted under the heading of trainers, nor, on the face of it, does there seem to be any real reason for quarrelling with the dictum, after all, it is pretty obvious, isn't it?

'On the football field, so long as your side is attacking, then clearly your own goal is not in much danger of failing, for if you can keep your opponents busy defending their goal, then they will have precious little time in which to develop goalscoring schemes of their own. But while, in my opinion, it must always remain true that in a general sense attack is the best defence, it seems to me that there are certain qualifications which should be put down for future reference.

'Before proceeding to point these qualifications, let me first of all explain briefly how it comes about that I am asked to tackle the question of whether attack is really the best defence. As my readers know well enough, the club for which I happen to play managed to win the championship of the First Division of the Football League last season. In doing this, we had a goal record which was, I suppose, a little unusual. However, at the end of the season there were several clubs in the league which had scored more goals than stood to the credit of the Liverpool team, though, on the other hand, there was no club which had so few goals scored against their side. This combination of circumstances led people to ask whether, after all, it was better to concentrate on defence rather than on attack if success was to be attained.'

Liverpool had marched to the title, despite their forwards being outscored by their counterparts in rival teams, and on many occasions they had battled to victory by no more than a single goal. And Bromilow felt that Liverpool's success was owed not to simply possessing a great attack or a solid defence, but in all parts of the team working in harmony.

'The secret to success in any football team is the team spirit,' argued Tom, 'and by that I mean that every man in the 11 should perform the duties of his position to the best of his ability, and a bit more than that – should be perfectly willing to lend a helping hand to a colleague who is in need of assistance. It may be said of this or that football team that there are weak spots in the side, but so long as every man does his level best, with all working harmoniously with one another, then these weak spots do not reveal themselves very easily; an 11 with only moderate individual ability may be a formidable team as a collective force. 'Tis not in a football team to command success, but every individual can do his best to deserve it by trying all the time.'

This is the essence of what many modern supporters recognise as the 'Liverpool way'. It is interesting to note that long before the days of Billy Shankly and Bob Paisley, this collective mentality was evident at Anfield. Indeed, no team can succeed without it. In advocating such an approach, the likes of Shankly and even Jürgen Klopp are standing on the shoulders of giants.

On Thursday, 29 June, at the Adelphi Hotel in Liverpool, a grand celebration banquet was held for the players, in which the club chairman W.R. Williams gave a speech in honour of the team. As he concluded his remarks, the men who had won the league were called to the front, individually, to receive a specially engraved gold watch and congratulations on behalf of the board.

The packed ballroom included the entire 1905/06 championship-winning team and the chairman and secretary of Everton. *Athletic News*, on 3 July 1922, reported the proceedings in detail:

'There was a handsome gathering of shareholders. Mr W.R. Williams presided. A great honour was paid to the team of 1921/22. The players with the unavoidable exception of Scott sat at the centre table and each was presented with a gold watch.

'Equally interesting was the gathering of the league championship team of 1905/06, all of whom were present looking very well. They were Sam Hardy, Alf West, Billy Dunlop, Tom Chorlton, Maurice Parry, Alex Raisbeck, James Bradley, Arthur Goddard, Robert Robinson, Joe Hewitt, Sam Raybould, John Cox, Jack Parkinson, and John Carlin.'

Members of the 1921/22 squad were present, except for Elisha Scott who appears to have had transport problems. Joining them were Ashworth, Billy Connell and George Patterson.

After proposing a toast to the champions old and new, and wishing Everton a good season for the coming campaign, Williams would recall how difficult winning the league had been 16 years earlier, remembering how the celebrations had taken place at the less salubrious Carlton Rooms and how shareholders had been given a ticket for three drinks at the bar. The club, he said, had barely £20,000 in the bank back then.

The newspaper report continued, 'In making the presentation of watches Mr Williams named each individually and made a happy tribute to all. Elisha Scott, he said, was absent through travelling difficulties.

McNab was named as Bob Ferguson's protégé, Bromilow he styled as successor to Makepeace – a happy local coupling that was appreciated by all present.'

Bob Ferguson, like Jock McNab, was a native of Cleland, who had played for the Reds for three years between 1912 and 1915. He was known for his great strength and sound judgement, and this was no doubt a great compliment to Jock. In paying tribute to Tom Bromilow, Williams was drawing a comparison with Harry Makepeace, a former Everton stalwart and England international. Harry was as proficient at cricket as he was at football and played four Test matches for the England cricket team. Tom was also known to be a fine cricketer as well as being capped for his country in football. The report continued:

'He spoke feelingly of the captain, Donald Mackinay [sic], and Ephraim Longworth and William Lacey, and expressed the hope that Lacey would be with them until they won the cup. Tribute was also paid to the newly married forwards, Dick Forshaw and Fred Hopkin, and in the case of Harry Chambers, Mr Williams said he was the last player signed on by Tom Watson before his death in May 1915.'

It was then the turn of Donald McKinlay to speak. As Williams took his seat, and the applause faded, the captain of the team rose to his feet to say a few words:

'Well, gentlemen, this is not a game of mine, speechmaking, but I want to say how grateful and appreciative we are of the words and the watches. If you promise us such a good time as tonight when we win the cup we will bring that elusive pimpernel to Liverpool.'

The celebration speeches concluded with further tributes to the backroom staff, including Charlie Wilson, George Fleming and Bert Riley. In referring to William Connell, Williams observed the trainer had 'grown white in the service of the club'. There followed a touching moment, reported in the *Staffordshire Sentinel* on Saturday, 15 July 1922, in which the board of directors voted to award 1906 championship winners Alf West, James Bradley and Sam Raybould £50 each.

The three men had fallen on hard times and were victims of the steep economic downturn during the 1920s. That the board saw fit to help them out financially is noteworthy, and perhaps a sign of how the club in this period looked after its own.

Liverpool FC had truly become a band of brothers, each with their own backstories, some of them deeply traumatic, but they had been forged together and were much stronger for it. That strength would be tested severely as they plotted the defence of their crown the following season. A shock departure and the return of a champion from a bygone era would see them come through challenges that would derail lesser teams and emerge 'untouchable'.

14

Defence of the Crown

IN 1922, Britain's colonial influence stretched to a quarter of the planet with one in four people living under the rule of the British Empire. However, several independence movements were starting to flex their muscles and in February of that year Egypt would be granted partial independence.

Six months later, on 17 August, Dublin Castle would be handed over to members of the Irish Republican Army. The Irish Republic had now been established, with the people of Northern Ireland remaining part of the United Kingdom. Later, in October, Britain would step back from the brink of war with Turkey, causing the collapse of the Liberal/Conservative coalition government.

Amid the growing challenges to the government's foreign policy was an economic crisis which had led to mass unemployment and food poverty. In November, marchers would begin a protest that would see them walk from Glasgow to London.

Despite the harsh economic conditions, the 1920s saw the continued development and expansion of commercial aviation, and 1922 would also see the creation of the Civil Aviation Authority. Not that football clubs would be flying players around the world any time soon. Though there had been attempts at passenger flights as early as 1913, travelling by aircraft was an uncomfortable and dangerous pursuit.

Planes in the 1920s shook loudly during flight and cabins were unpressurised. Indeed, air travel was often slower than train, and it would not be until the end of the decade that this mode of transport really got going.

Meanwhile, as they geared up for the defence of their crown, Liverpool offloaded Billy Matthews in the summer of 1922, selling him to Bristol City for the sum of £750. He had been at the club for just 18 months as a centre-forward and had managed only nine appearances, scoring four goals. However, Liverpool saw the player as a centre-half, something Billy did not agree with. That seems to have sealed his fate.

Arriving at the club were two new faces, Jimmy Walsh from Stockport County and Jack Sambrook from Wolves. David Pratt would arrive from Bradford City in January 1923. None of them would play a significant role as Liverpool fought to retain their title.

The 1922 accounts showed that the club had presented a very healthy balance sheet to their shareholders and auditors, allowing them to spend the princely sum of £12,477, 9s. 3d. on players' wages and bonuses, and a further £350 on players' benefits. Gate receipts of over £45,000 meant they could cover their wage bill easily, though money received from match-going fans was clearly their principal source of income. There is certainly no evidence, in the accounts at least, of any revenue from advertisers or sponsors.

Of interest though is the fact that the club had invested in war bonds during the First World War and had received interest of £77 10s. on those in 1922. Liverpool were clearly on the right path both on and off the field of play.

After losing the final qualifying round for the Lancashire Senior Cup 3-1 to Bolton Wanderers on 3 May, the Reds embarked on a pre-season tour of Italy. Liverpool took a strong squad but left behind Fred Hopkin, who would get married to Annie Gill that same month, and Danny Shone also missed the trip. A report of the club's preparations appeared in the *Burnley News* on 3 May 1922:

'Touring arrangements of both Liverpool and Everton are now completed. The league champions leave Liverpool on 17 May, and London on the following morning, proceeding via Dover, Calais, Paris, Modena, arriving in Milan on the 19th.

'Their first game will be with Burnley on the 21st, and four other games have been arranged on the 26th, 28th, 1 June, and 4 June, at

Turin, Genoa, Bologna, with the final exhibition at Milan. They return 5 June, and put in a day in Paris, leaving for home on the 7th.'

The club had been paid £100 plus expenses to make the trip, while the players were paid the princely sum of ten shillings per day in expenses. Tom Bromilow's column in the *Liverpool Echo* reveals that the team experienced something of culture shock, and struggled to deal with the heat, particularly in the game against Burnley, during which buckets of water had been stationed around the perimeter of the pitch to prevent the players becoming dehydrated.

When the players could no longer run due to heat exhaustion, Tom reports that sections of the crowd began booing them. Tom's comments on the occasion suggest he was far from impressed:

'What an excitable people these Italians are! Whenever a possible chance presented itself and the shooter failed, he was greeted by a combination of howls of derision or disappointment.' According to Bromilow, 'The players took notice.'

Liverpool stayed at Le Grand Hotel in Maggiore, Milan, before playing five games starting with the 1-0 defeat to Burnley at Campo di Viale Lombardia. They then travelled to Modena to face an Emilia Select XI which featured players from Bologna, Modena, Reggiana and Parma. The game, watched by 4,000 people, ended in a rout for Liverpool, who won 6-1 with a hat-trick from Harry Chambers, a brace from Harry Beadles and a rare Cyril Gilhespy strike.

Despite Elisha Scott saving a penalty against Emilia Select, Liverpool would give a start to reserve goalkeeper Frank Mitchell in the following two games. The Scot, born in Elgin in 1890, played just eight senior matches for the Reds, keeping a clean sheet in all of them. He featured in the following two games of the trip, a 2-2 draw with Liguria and Toscana Select in Pisa, and a goalless draw with Pro Vercelli.

The match against Emilia seems to have been a fierce affair, with an Italian player breaking his arm after being barged over. Bromilow would tell readers back home that he had never experienced an opponent so reckless, and described how they hacked, pushed and kicked at the Liverpool players.

During one of the games, most likely at Vercelli, an approach was made to Walter Wadsworth to become the manager of a Turin-based club, possibly Juventus. He was to turn that offer down, but this does suggest that he was well respected in European football.

The final game of the tour, played in front of a crowd of 15,000, saw the return of Elisha Scott in goal against Genoa in the Stadio Marassi for a 4-1 win by the Reds. Chambers weighed in with another hat-trick and Dick Forshaw got the other goal.

Liverpool now faced a trip back home that would take several days. The new season was just over eight weeks away, meaning just time to briefly rest and recuperate, before training got under way again at Anfield under the guidance of David Ashworth's highly skilled backroom team.

There was to be more joy for Forshaw before the new season got under way. He married Florence Robinson at St Mary's Church in Kirkdale, Liverpool, on 10 June. The *Liverpool Echo* reported he had gone on honeymoon with his bride, to 'Welsh Wales'.

The 1922/23 season got under way on 17 August. The streets around Anfield baked in afternoon sunshine as 40,000 people made their way to the season opener against Arsenal. They came on foot and by tram to see the reigning champions, and as they filled the pubs around the ground, the sense of excitement and pride would have been palpable.

Perhaps few of them would have expected another First Division championship, but all would have been confident of seeing entertaining football. Some will have undoubtedly had their eyes on the much-coveted FA Cup. The competition had eluded Liverpool in 1914, and that loss would have been made more painful by the fact that Everton had earlier won it in 1906.

Returning for the Reds against the Gunners was striker Dick Johnson, who had missed the whole of the previous season. This would mean that Harry Beadles, who had featured in the Charity Shield defeat to Huddersfield, would make way. In addition, Tommy Lucas had sustained a minor injury in a practice match, and Ephraim Longworth would step in.

Hanging over a packed Kop was Liverpool's league champions flag. The Reds lined up with their familiar 2-3-5 formation, with Longworth and McKinlay in front of Scott. Ahead of them were McNab, Wadsworth and Bromilow, in attack Ashworth, Lacey and Hopkin on the wings, plus a front three of Johnson, Forshaw and Chambers.

Arsenal, missing two defenders through injury, were ill-equipped to deal with a Liverpool front line that was full of creativity and goals. The Reds won the toss and flew out of the traps early. However, Arsenal quickly countered and forced Scott into two fine saves. The visitors would pay for their wastefulness after just three minutes when the returning Johnson opened the scoring for Liverpool. This is how the *Echo*'s 'Bee' saw the first goal of the new season, a somewhat scrappy affair:

'First of all Lacey tried to make a lobbing sort of centre, and the ball did not travel far enough, together with which Johnson did not seem to have tumbled to the intended pass. Yet with all this, Lacey's half-hearted pass was converted into a goal, thanks to Johnson following up with intensity.

'The backs were surprised, and Williamson [Arsenal's goalkeeper] when charged was at fault, so that when he missed the ball, Johnson was presented with an open goal.'

The Gunners had barely had time to catch their breath when Liverpool and Johnson added a second, and according to the press, the crowd went wild. Again, Lacey was the provider and Liverpool's front line were running the Londoners ragged.

Eventually, however, Arsenal got into gear and began pushing Liverpool back. Arsenal danger man Bert White flashed a shot just wide and then, after a blunder by McNab, produced a 'miracle' one-handed save from Scott that drew as much adulation from the Kop as the two goals had. It was turning into a tremendous game.

Arsenal, however, were profligate, or as 'Bee' would put it 'all construction and no conclusion'. Their frequent attacks were beginning to rattle the Liverpool back line and soon drew an unnecessary foul from Wadsworth for which the player was reprimanded by the referee.

Arsenal kept up the pressure and soon more heroics from Scott was required, with the Irishman pulling off a string of spectacular saves from Reginald Boreham and Andrew Young. The *Echo* felt, 'It was an astonishing piece of goalkeeping, and the crowd went crazy for it.'

Not content with rescuing his team-mates, Elisha rolled the ball to Bromilow who dribbled upfield before moving to the inside-left position and hitting his shot straight past Williams for Liverpool's third goal. It was a great finish, but all the praise went to Elisha Scott who had pulled off two incredible saves before launching the counter-attack. Bill Lacey was seen to express his disbelief at Scott's heroics to the linesman, while McKinlay offered his thanks to the keeper on behalf of the rest of the team.

Liverpool were in the ascendency and with Wadsworth rampaging upfield it seemed only a matter of time before they added to their tally. Somehow, though, Arsenal hung on for half-time.

Within a minute of the restart Liverpool went four goals in front after Chambers hit a swerving shot from distance that flew straight into the goal. Arsenal hit back almost immediately, and in the 50th minute Boreham reduced the deficit after Scott failed to manage a lobbed ball in the box.

The game was pulsating, and when the Reds were denied what looked like a clear penalty their protests were somewhat muted owing to the comprehensive scoreline. Soon the heat was beginning to take its toll with the players labouring in the strong sunshine.

Johnson bagged Liverpool's fifth and effectively ended the game as a meaningful contest, before Young cannoned a shot that went in off the face of Elisha Scott. With the match ending 5-2, Liverpool had got the defence of their title off to a flyer. They were one of eight teams to win on the opening day and sat third in the table behind Oldham Athletic and Preston North End by virtue of their goal average.

This method of separating teams who were level on points was used from 1889 to the 1978/79 season. It was a simple calculation of dividing goals scored by goals conceded to give the average. Though Liverpool had scored five goals, their two conceded meant they had a goal average of 2.5. Meanwhile Oldham and Preston had won 4-1 and 3-1 respectively.

Liverpool slumped to 16th place, however, following two successive 1-0 defeats away to Sunderland and their opening-day visitors, Arsenal. The press had put those losses down to a lack of energy, confidence and passes from centre-back to the forward line. However, on Wednesday, 6 September the Reds were about to put all that right.

A crowd of around 30,000 took advantage of the light nights of summer and turned out for a 6pm kick-off. Fred Hopkin, on the comeback trail from injury, was not fit enough to play. However, instead of opting to play Beadles in his place, Liverpool went with Harold

Wadsworth, and he did not let the side down. Ernest 'Bee' Edwards was full of praise, writing:

'The little fellow showed his customary pluck, improved heading power, and much stern play against a clever half in Parker. Brother Walter saw to it that "The Kid" had some passes, and in every way the home half-back line got their passes up to their forwards in a manner than one wishes to see.'

Sunderland, known as the '£20,000 team', arrived with something of a reputation having assembled an expensive squad. And when Bromilow slipped in the fourth minute, letting in Charlie Buchan to score, an ominous sense of dread may easily have swept over Anfield.

However, Liverpool took just 11 minutes to get back into the game thanks to a trademark swerving shot from Chambers, which was hit so hard it burst the ball, and by half-time the Reds were 3-1 up. With Longworth feeding Lacey and Johnson with his forward bursts, Forshaw and Chambers were able to capitalise with ease.

Johnson was once again catching the eye of reporters with many commenting on his tight control of the ball, and others remarking on his ability to 'carry the ball close to the foot in his solo dribbles'. It was another forward pass from Longworth that set Johnson up for Liverpool's fourth goal, scored eight minutes after the restart.

Johnson dribbled 20 yards with the ball, keeping his cool as the onrushing goalkeeper raced from his line and a Sunderland defender trailed in his wake, unleashing a clinical shot that effectively ended the game as a contest. However, as far as the Anfield crowd were concerned, the best was yet to come.

With five minutes to go, Donald McKinlay picked up the ball on the halfway line and charged towards the Sunderland goal. As he arrived 20 yards out, with the entire Sunderland back line in front of him, he let loose with his right foot. The ball hit the back of the net and sent the crowd wild. Liverpool took the points, and as fans read the papers the next day the club's ninth place in the league table would have looked a lot more respectable. They may have also liked the write-up of McKinlay's wonder goal too.

'Donal' scored a goal!' 'Bee' wrote. 'It was not the first by this forward-full-back. He has scored quite a number in his time by the aid of free kicks, but I doubt he ever scored a goal that aroused so much enthusiasm as last night. It must be nice to hear the roar of 30,000 people.'

The win over Sunderland appeared to have galvanised Liverpool, and by the first week in October they had climbed to the top of the table. A run of three more victories and one defeat meant confidence was riding high as they prepared to face Everton at home in the first of back-to-back derbies.

Their run had ushered in something of a goal rush, with the Reds demolishing Preston North End 3-1 and 5-2, followed by a 3-0 home win over Burnley, before they lost 2-0 in the next game at Burnley. Liverpool's forwards had been in fine form, with Chambers, Forshaw and Johnson all weighing in, while Wadsworth and Bromilow added a goal each during the run.

The Reds were top on goal average, and only two points separated first place from Everton in 12th. Yet as the final whistle sounded at Anfield on Saturday, 7 October the gulf in class was obvious. Liverpool had run out 5-1 winners thanks to a hat-trick from Chambers and one each for Bromilow, who had scored on his birthday, and McNab.

Liverpool's players, driven on by a tempestuous 54,000 Anfield crowd, were said to have got carried away in the game, with all but McKinlay getting forward to attack the Everton goal. During one Everton counter, the Liverpool captain found himself isolated and in something of a panic hit a back-pass that was a little too powerful for his keeper's liking. It had been more of a shot than a pass and produced a fine save from Scott.

When McKinlay simply responded with a nod and a wink at Elisha, the resultant foul-mouthed blast would have peeled the paint off the picket fence that held back the massed throng in the Kop.

However, it is likely that the spat would have been short-lived. This was a tight-knit group of players who looked after each other on and off the pitch. The *Liverpool Echo* paper reports that prior to the match the football authorities had given the go-ahead for four benefit games for Liverpool players, in which collections would be made. Cardiff would visit Anfield on 21 October in aid of Bill Lacey; on Boxing Day it would be the turn of Oldham for the benefit of Elisha Scott; 27 January would see Middlesbrough arrive to help raise money for Donald McKinlay; and the Reds would play Sheffield United on 30 March 1923, in support of Ephraim Longworth.

The article concludes, 'It is worthy of note that all the collections will be pooled by the players. Thus they are untied in football play and in benefit pay.'

This was truly a collective now, and no on-field spat in the heat of battle could change that. The result condemned Everton to 19th place and moved Liverpool a point clear at the top of the table.

A week later the Reds travelled across Stanley Park to face the Blues once more. They would win by a single goal from Dick Johnson, in front of another bumper crowd of 52,000. That meant over 100,000 people had attended those two games in the space of a week.

Johnson's return had spelled bad news for Danny Shone, who after an impressive debut season the year before would have hoped to make the breakthrough as the Reds defended their title. However, it was simply impossible to deny Johnson his starting place on merit. In all Johnson managed 14 goals in 37 league appearances in 1922/23 and poor Danny would feature just once, in the 2-0 defeat to Burnley at Turf Moor.

Following Liverpool's derby double, Ashworth was forced into a change due to an injury to Bill Lacey that would put the forward out for two months. In addition, Harry Chambers would miss the next game against Cardiff due to a call-up to the England squad.

That meant another opportunity for Cyril Gilhespy, who deputised for Lacey, while Harry Beadles was chosen to replace Chambers. The team did not appear to miss a beat and ran out comfortable 3-1 winners. Gilhespy started the scoring, Forshaw added a second in the first half, before Walter Wadsworth grabbed the third in the 80th minute.

Gilhespy would score again, in a 4-2 home victory over Tottenham Hotspur, during a second-half goal blitz that saw six goals plundered in 45 minutes. Chambers and Forshaw were the other scorers.

Liverpool played four games in November, winning three and drawing one – a goalless draw at Spurs. Sandwiched in between these was a testimonial match for Jackie Sheldon against Derby County, with Liverpool fielding a string side that included Danny Shone. Bill Lacey and former Red Arthur Goddard were the linesmen.

Liverpool won 3-1 and the 6,000 crowd would have raised a decent bounty for the player. Sheldon signed for the Reds from Manchester United for £350 on 26 November 1913. He played 147 times for the Reds, scoring 20 times. Sadly he will always be remembered as one of the key figures involved in the infamous betting scandal of 1915, for which he was banned along with three other Liverpool players.

The ban was lifted but his football career was ended by a terrible leg break. The granting of a testimonial by the club seems to suggest that his name had been somewhat rehabilitated at least at Anfield.

November also saw Britain's second radio station, named 2LO, launched at Marconi House UK. This station would later transfer to the newly formed BBC. The 1922 General Election saw Bonar Law, the MP for Bootle, elected as prime minister. This was also the year that Howard Carter opened the tomb of Tutankhamun at the Pyramid of the Pharaoh.

As the football season moved into December, Liverpool sat two points clear at the top of the table. The expensively assembled Sunderland lay in second place. There was still much to do, but Ashworth's Liverpool were well on course for their second league title in consecutive seasons.

Little did anyone connected with Liverpool know, including the Anfield board, that Oldham Athletic, who were now bottom of the First Division, had already made overtures to entice former manager David Ashworth back to Boundary Park.

On 2 December, Liverpool suffered a setback at home to Newcastle United. Some sources suggest that the game was also designated as a benefit match for Bill Lacey, despite the Football League approving the Cardiff fixture for this purpose. As Lacey was injured, he would have been unable to play in either. The collections held at the Newcastle game raised £40.

A crowd of 30,000 attended and watched in shock as Newcastle took the game to the Reds. Liverpool never really got going in the first half and the visitors scored five minutes before the interval, with a goal from Robert McIntosh. The Reds' defence had struggled and a poor back-pass by Wadsworth put Scott in trouble, the keeper failing to prevent a corner. At the other end, Liverpool's raids on the Newcastle rearguard broke down too easily.

Ashworth's men toiled away in the second period but could not find an equaliser and in the 80th minute Newcastle's Neil Harris put the result beyond doubt after he capitalised on a McKinlay slip and rounded Scott to make it 2-0. Liverpool escaped an embarrassing 3-0 defeat when the referee failed to punish Bromilow after he had appeared to push a Newcastle forward in the box.

The result meant that the gap at the top had narrowed. Sunderland, who had beaten Everton 3-1, were now behind Liverpool on goal average only, while Middlesbrough in third were just a point off the top. Newcastle had moved up to fifth, just a point behind Burnley in fourth.

However, the Reds regained their composure and managed a narrow 1-0 victory in the away game at St James' Park the following week. Once again Chambers provided the all-important breakthrough in the 60th minute. Liverpool had pulled a point clear of their nearest challengers Sunderland, who had drawn 1-1 at Goodison.

Liverpool negotiated their next game against newly promoted Nottingham Forest at Anfield with minimal fuss, winning 2-1 with first-half goals from Dick Johnson and Donald McKinlay. Forest pulled one back in the second half but the Reds saw the game out to maintain their one-point advantage at the summit. Sunderland had beaten West Brom 3-2.

However, the coming days would see rumours emerge of a shock exit from Anfield, with claims and counter-claims that the Liverpool manager was about to leave swirling around the pages of the local press. On 19 December the *Liverpool Echo* published two articles on the same page. One was a strenuous denial from Ashworth, and another suggested he had already accepted a job offer from Oldham. Perhaps fittingly, the contradictory reports had sandwiched an article which reported that Arthur Conan Doyle had found proof of the existence of fairies.

The news was eventually confirmed on 22 December, on the eve of Liverpool's visit to the City Ground to face Forest once again. Liverpool would make the trip with a caretaker manager, which may well have been George Patterson with Connell, Wilson and Hewitt looking after tactics and training. It would have been very much a case of 'as you were'.

They would win 3-1 with a goal from Forshaw and a brace from Johnson, and the victory moved Liverpool two points clear at the top of the table as Sunderland had drawn 1-1 with West Brom. However, the Reds were undoubtedly still reeling from the news of their manager's shock departure.

Reports suggest that the news caught everyone by surprise, including the club's board. Quite how long Ashworth had been talking to Oldham is unclear, as the story only started to filter out days before it was confirmed with the man himself issuing a denial as late as 19 December. Perhaps he was in two minds or maybe waiting until contracts were signed.

The following day, the *Liverpool Echo* ran a piece confirming the news and could barely hide its shock. The news appeared under a headline that read:

BIG FOOTBALL SURPRISE

LIVERPOOL CLUB MANAGER TAKES HIS LEAVE

OLDHAM ATHLETIC'S GAIN

It wrote, 'The "Echo" learns today that there was smoke where there was fire. It will be remembered that we stated yesterday that the Liverpool Football Club manager, Mr David Ashworth, denied that he was to be made successor of Charles Roberts, the ex-Manchester United captain who has been acting as manager for Oldham Athletic for two years.

'Today we learn by special wire that Mr Ashworth has signed as manager for Oldham manager, a side he spent many years with, and with which he was connected when they finished second in the Football League in 1915.'

The paper went on to point out that while Liverpool were at the top of their game both financially and on the playing field, Oldham were 'at their depths'. The *Nottingham Journal* made the same observation: 'Liverpool was astonished by the news for Mr Ashworth was with Liverpool during their happiest times. He leaves a club at its zenith for another in financial difficulties.'

Ashworth was one of the most well-known figures in the English game, particularly in the north, and his departure would have undoubtedly shocked the players and supporters also. Liverpool had made a habit of getting the big questions right over many years. They were a beacon of financial stability and had just won the league title, and they had earned their sense of self-confidence. In accepting Ashworth's resignation, the board would look inward for his replacement, turning to an old boy and a former champion.

15

Matt McQueen to the Rescue as Ashworth Departs

LIVERPOOL'S NEXT game would involve a trip to Oldham Athletic to face their former manager on Christmas Day 1922. The Reds were still led by a caretaker and were apparently in no mood to present David Ashworth or his team with any gifts, running out 2-0 winners – and with rivals Sunderland not playing – moving four points clear at the top.

Athletic News, in its Christmas Day edition, devoted a great deal of space to the story that had rocked football, writing:

'Some surprise has been created by the announcement that David Ashworth, the team manager of Liverpool, resigned that post and is about to return to Oldham Athletic. We say return, because when David Ashworth gave over refereeing his first position as a paid official was with Oldham Athletic. He left for Stockport County, and then joined Liverpool.'

The paper suggested that old alliances and his failure to settle in the city of Liverpool may have played a part in his decision, saying, 'But David Ashworth has many friends at Oldham, and he has never become a resident of Liverpool.'

In truth, Ashworth had never settled anywhere and had spent most of his life living in hotels and digs, something he would continue for the rest of his career. *Athletic News* summed up exactly what Anfield had lost in its report:

'As a team-builder and manager he has been successful with all three clubs. It is not an exaggeration to say that he laid the foundation of Oldham Athletic and that the club has never been quite the same since he went away.

'He accomplished a great deal towards lifting the club into the First Division. In 1913 they ran into the semi-final stage of the Association Cup, and in 1914/15 they were within one point of Aston Villa, the champions of the league.

'To restore the Athletic to this rank will be a hard task, but David Ashworth has never been appalled by work, worry, or even a relatively small revenue. He has succeeded without paying £5,000 for a single player.

'He has an eye for raw material, and, in short, knows his work. Oldham Athletic are lucky to secure his co-operation once more.'

Ashworth's task was indeed a huge one. Oldham, in financial trouble and propping up the rest of the division, were in a poor state. And it's for this reason that his decision-making has been shrouded in mystery ever since.

For decades, the long-held belief was Ashworth left for Oldham to be with his wife and ill daughter, while another theory suggests that his wife was disabled. After all, why else would he leave a club with every chance of securing back-to-back championships?

To answer this question it is important to examine the man, his character and personality. We have discovered that Ashworth was not someone with a habit of settling in one place for any length of time, and he never found a permanent residence in Liverpool.

Ashworth's curriculum vitae includes managerial jobs at eight professional clubs, and his tenure at most of them was short. He left Oldham after two years of his second spell, much to the shock and surprise of the football world, to take up a post at Manchester City. He would spend just 16 months there, and as was the case with all his clubs there was never any reason given for his departure.

Now let us examine the most commonly advanced theory for his decision to rejoin Oldham, a club destined for relegation, that he needed to be close to his wife and family. We can find no evidence of this, and his subsequent departure for Manchester City casts doubt on this as a viable explanation. Ashworth does not appear to have lived at his marital home throughout his career and according to the 1939 Census, taken while he was working as a scout for Blackpool, records him as a guest at a Blackpool hotel, while his wife Annie was living some 38 miles away at 8 Spring Gardens, Rawtenstall, along with her sister Hannah Whittaker.

It seems that Ashworth, just as he had been as a child, was accustomed to life on the road, perhaps returning home for a few days a week. This was unusual for the period, and it would be more common for managers and players to live at home, sometimes many miles from their club, often travelling on the day of a match. We know that Ashworth was something of a unique character, some would even say eccentric, and his need to move around sometimes seemingly on a whim is entirely in keeping with this.

There seems little if any evidence to support the theory that he left Liverpool to be near to or look after his disabled wife or family. If indeed his wife was disabled, Ashworth would continue his nomadic career for many years.

Another reason suggested is that he moved for monetary gain. Given Oldham's financial plight, this seems difficult to believe. It is doubtful that many clubs could compete with Liverpool on salary, much less one mired in difficulties as Oldham were. Certainly, there are no reports or columns in newspaper journals that we have found that provide any evidence that Ashworth moved for money.

David would take jobs at clubs such as Caernarvon, Llanelli and Walsall, all of whom would be unable to offer him significant salaries, and he left them all without reason and often with the boards expressing shock and surprise at his decision. When he left Manchester City, the *Portsmouth Evening News*, dated 26 November 1925, wrote:

'Followers of football in general, and in particular the North, will be surprised to learn that Mr David Ashworth, manager to Manchester City, is to leave the club having tendered his resignation.

'Reasons for the step are not divulged, but the wonderment of the City supporters is heightened by the fact that Mr Ashworth was appointed to succeed Mr Ernest Mangnall only so comparatively recently as July 1924.'

A piece in the *Derbyshire Advertiser*, dated 4 December 1925, hints at possible discord between Ashworth and the boards at both Oldham and Manchester City. In the case of City the author suggests that Ashworth had wanted to improve the squad but was unhappy with the money at his disposal. Speculation among City supporters' forums suggests that the board were growing impatient with him, and he may have 'jumped before he was pushed'.

Did Liverpool's financial prudence, and preference for local talent, drive Ashworth out of Anfield? There is certainly no evidence that the club's board of directors was unhappy with their man, or vice versa, but perhaps he felt they did not share his ambition in the transfer market. That is possible, but his decision to move to Oldham who lacked any financial muscle casts considerable doubt on the theory. Likewise, he would leave City to take over at Walsall, by no means a footballing powerhouse at the time.

Ashworth was clearly one of the most respected men in football throughout the 1920s. He was never short of suitors, despite his penchant for being a wanderer, his inability to rescue Oldham, and his failure to repeat his Liverpool success.

Viewed through modern eyes, his decision to leave Liverpool appears to be a terrible gamble that never paid off. However, a look at his broader career, personality and context suggests that with hindsight it was entirely in keeping with who he was: someone who was never able to settle anywhere for too long before that wanderlust took him over and drove him on to pastures new.

Liverpool soldiered on through most of the winter with their caretaker manager, and the team had done considerably well. When they announced the appointment of the 59-year-old former player Matt McQueen on 13 February 1923, the Reds were three points clear of Sunderland at the top of the table having gone on a 12-game unbeaten run, winning nine and drawing three.

Still, the news of McQueen's appointment was greeted with approval by sports writers and supporters. The *Hull Daily Mail*, reporting the announcement on 14 February wrote:

'At a meeting on Tuesday night the directors of the Liverpool Football Club appointed Mr Matt McQueen team's manager in succession to Mr

(L-R) Elisha Scott, Charlie Wilson, E.A. Bainbridge and Ephraim Longworth at Clevelys. Photo courtesy of Liverpool FC. Colourised by ANT-OGRAPHY via Facebook.

The Untouchables pose for a photo on the beach. Photo courtesy of the Bromilow family. Restored and colourised by Anthony Winson.

(L-R) Jock McNab and Elisha Scott at Clevelys, January 1926. Photo courtesy of Liverpool FC. Restored by ANT-OGRAPHY via Facebook.

(L-R) Bill Cockburn, Jock McNab, E.A. Bainbridge, Elisha Scott, two unidentified men, and Dick Forshaw at Cleveleys, January 1926. Photo courtesy of Liverpool FC. Restored and colourised by ANT-OGRAPHY via Facebook.

Out on the town. (L-R) John Bamber, Walter Wadsworth, Tom Bromilow, Jock McNab. Photo courtesy of the Wadsworth family.

Tom Bromilow arrives for his wedding to Mabel 'May' Kelly in Kirkdale, Liverpool, in 1923. Photo courtesy of the Bromilow family. Restored by ANT-OGRAPHY via Facebook.

Crowds line both sides of the road outside the church, hoping to catch a glimpse of superstar, Tom Bromilow, and his bride. Kirkdale, Liverpool, 1923. Photo courtesy of the Bromilow family. Restored by ANT-OGRAPHY via Facebook.

Police struggle to control crowds of well-wishers at May Kelly and Tom Bromilow's wedding. Photo courtesy of the Bromilow family. Restored by ANT-OGRAPHY via Facebook.

The happy couple, May and Tom surrounded by family at their wedding in 1923. Photo courtesy of the Bromilow family. Restored by ANT-OGRAPHY via Facebook.

Danny Shone, pictured wearing his trademark dickey bow tie outside the family home in Freeman Street, Edge Hill, Liverpool, along with family and friends after a family wedding. Photo courtesy of Danny's family, John English, and Douglas Barlow. This heavily damaged and faded photograph was restored by ANT-OGRAPHY via Facebook.

Tom Bromilow (L) and Walter Wadsworth (R) enjoy a spot of bowls. Photo courtesy of the Wadsworth family. Restored and colourised by ANT-OGRAPHY via Facebook.

THE INVINCIBLES (?) OF MERSEYSIDE.

LIVERPOOL'S PRIDE,
and Sheffield United's Cup opponents of next Saturday.
Back row:—Scott, Forshaw, McNabb.
Front row:—Hopkin, McKinlay, Longworth, Lacey, Bromilow, Wadsworth, Johnson and Chambers.

This cartoon of The Untouchables by Bert Warner in 1923 asks the question, are they invincible?

Standing on the dock of the bay. The Untouchables looking very smart on a team away day. Photo courtesy of Liverpool FC. Restored and colourised by ANT-OGRAPHY via Facebook.

Tom Bromilow, the keen cricketer. Photo courtesy of the Bromilow family.

Tom Bromilow's England badges. Courtesy of the Bromilow family.

Tom Bromilow's League Championship medal. Courtesy of Lee Tracy (Bromilow family).

David Ashworth, perhaps Liverpool's most mysterious and mercurial manager. Photo restored and colourised by ANT-OGRAPHY via Facebook.

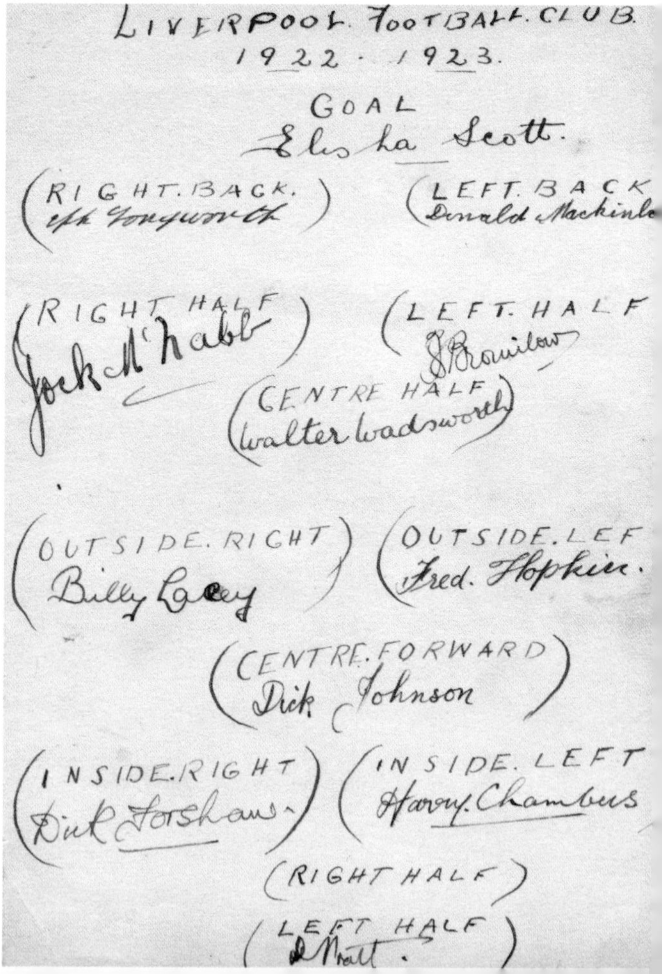

Sheet containing The Untouchables autographs from 1923. Courtesy of Mark Platt.

Merseyside derby at Goodison Park, 4 October 1924. Fans spill from the terrace and line up along the goal line, while Blues player Dougie Livingstone enjoys a joke with one or two lucky supporters. Photo courtesy of the Bromilow family. Restored by ANT-OGRAPHY via Facebook.

Walter Wadsworth is presented with the Division Three Championship in 1927. Photo courtesy of the Wadsworth family.

Liverpool FC in their away kit before a game with West Bromwich Albion around 1925? The team still features, Fred Hopkin, Elisha Scott, Donald McKinlay, and Tom Bromilow. Charlie Wilson can be seen at the back, standing between Gordon Hodgson (L) and Elisha Scott (R). Photo courtesy of Brian Spurgin (Bromilow family)

Liverpool FC 1930/31 team still features Tommy Lucas, Elisha Scott, Tom Bromilow and Fred Hopkin. On the left we can see George Patterson who is once more Secretary/Manager and on the right Ephraim Longworth has now moved into the coaching staff. Photo courtesy of the Bromilow family. Colourised by ANT-OGRAPHY via Facebook.

Left to Right George Patterson, David Ashworth, and Matt McQueen, three men who managed Liverpool FC. Photo courtesy of Kjell Hanssen.

Walter Wadsworth pictured during his time at Flint Town 1928/29. Photo courtesy of the Wadsworth family. Restored and colourised by ANT-OGRAPHY via Facebook.

Walter Wadsworth enjoying training with a skipping rope at New Brighton January 1929. Photo courtesy of the Wadsworth family.

Old pals, Jock and Walter. Picture taken circa 1920, supplied by the Wadsworth family and restored by ANT-OGRAPHY via Facebook.

Willie Steel, Elisha Scott, and James Jackson. Photo courtesy of Liverpool FC. Colourised by ANT-OGRAPHY via Facebook.

Elisha and the Liverpool team of the late 1920s at training near the sea. Photo courtesy of Liverpool FC.

Tom Bromilow in a staged photograph with his tactics board at Leicester. Photo courtesy of the Bromilow family. Restored and colourised by ANT-OGRAPHY via Facebook.

Elisha Scott admires one of Belfast Celtic's many championship trophies. Photo courtesy of Liverpool FC. Colourised by ANT-OGRAPHY via Facebook.

Elisha Scott wearing his Ireland cap at Kelly's Cellars, Belfast. Photo courtesy of Liverpool FC. Colourised by ANT-OGRAPHY via Facebook.

Tom Bromilow with May and Tom's sisters, Annie and Flo, outside the Bromilow family home. Courtesy of the Bromilow family. Restored by ANT-OGRAPHY via Facebook.

Tom Bromilow with son, Terence, born in 1923 and daughter, June Sylvia Vivienne Bromilow born 9 August 1927. June will soon celebrate her 94th birthday. Courtesy of the Bromilow family.

May and Tom Bromilow pictured with May's father, Louis Theo Kelly (who was also father of Everton legend, Theo Kelly) and their daughter, June. Courtesy of the Bromilow family. Restored by ANT-OGRAPHY via Facebook.

Tom Bromilow (R) plays snooker at Burnley with Tommy Lawton. Photo courtesy of the Bromilow family. Restored by ANT-OGRAPHY via Facebook.

Tom Bromilow (R) at the wedding of his daughter, June, to her husband Ralph Ernest Tracy on 14 June 1952. Photo courtesy of the Bromilow family. Restored by ANT-OGRAPHY via Facebook.

Bill Lacey (centre) pictured at Blackmoor School, West Derby, Liverpool, after giving a talk to the children on football in 1968. Photo courtesy of the Lacey family.

Cyril Gilhespy pictured in his garden in 1977 holding a photograph of him and his beloved Liverpool team-mates. Picture courtesy of Rosalind Tatton.

Walter's son Bill Wadsworth shows off a photo of his father in action from 1922 while sharing a joke with children (clockwise from top left) Susan, Jacqueline, David, and Richard, and two of his grandchildren, Tycho and Laya.

John and Matt English, great nephew, and great, great nephew respectively of Danny Shone, who they say will never walk alone.

Bill Sinnott-Lacey (grandson of Bill Lacey) pictured with his wife Jacqueline in front of Bill's Ireland caps.

Harry Chambers' grandson, Dennis Chambers and his wife Karen pictured with Harry's great grandchildren.

Mary Beadles (great, great niece of Harry Beadles) and her friend, Ruth Gray, pictured at a family burial plot, which is Harry's final resting place in Everton cemetery, Liverpool.

David Ashworth, who recently took up a similar position with Oldham Athletic.

'The appointment of Mr McQueen should be a popular one at Anfield, for he has always been in close touch with the Merseyside club. Being a Scotsman, Mr McQueen was one of the first professional players to be signed on by Liverpool, and later he served on the board of directors. In addition, he was for some time a Football League referee, so that his experience in the branches of the sport has been considerable.'

McQueen took over a team that had won 20 of their 28 games, losing five and drawing three. They had an impressive goal average of 2.5 and were virtually unbeatable at Anfield, having lost only once at home. There were just 14 games to go and if he could simply maintain standards, he would deliver the league championship. However, he was inheriting a future rebuilding job, a task that would prove very difficult. The average age of his team was in the late 20s with many players already over 30 years of age.

McQueen's first game in charge was a 3-0 home win over Blackburn Rovers in front of a crowd of just 25,000. Liverpool gave a debut to David Pratt, who they had signed at the end of January. Dick Forshaw put the Rovers to the sword and Ashworth's Oldham held Sunderland to a 1-1 draw. Liverpool's lead was now four points.

Forshaw had scored Liverpool's 1,600th goal in the Football League, and the Reds were now well on course for their second title in successive seasons. McQueen's reign had gotten off to a great start.

Born on 8 May 1863 in Shotts, Lanarkshire, to parents Peter and Margaret, he would later find employment as a coal miner. By 1891 Matt had married Mary, and the couple were living at 5 Gordon Street, Leith, Midlothian, with Matt's brother Hugh. He was employed as a warehouseman, while playing for Leith Athletic.

He signed for Liverpool in October 1892, and the family moved to 6 Elsie Road, Anfield. In Liverpool he would earn a living as an insurance agent as well as playing football for the Reds.

McQueen's younger brother Hugh was also a footballer at Leith, and both men made the journey south to Anfield. The pair had three other brothers and three sisters. McQueen was already a Scottish international, having been capped while playing in Leith, and the brothers would make their debuts in a 9-0 hammering of Newtown in an FA Cup qualifier on 29 October 1892.

McQueen's versatility meant that while he was predominantly a right half-back, he also played in goal for Liverpool on 45 occasions, becoming the only player in history to win medals while playing in both positions. As a player he won the Lancashire League in 1893, and two Second Division championships in 1894 and 1896.

His playing days came to an end in 1899, when he was 36 years of age. Like Ashworth, the man he would later succeed as manager, McQueen became a referee, before joining Liverpool's board of directors on 16 December 1919. He would have certainly seemed like the perfect choice to guide Liverpool through the remainder of the season and beyond.

An ex-player who had also served the club at board level, he knew Anfield inside and out, and would have been respected at all levels. Indeed, according to the *Liverpool Echo*, the man even the players called Matt had beaten off a great deal of competition for the post, including many ex-players. He was, without doubt, the board's choice.

If his first game in the manager's chair had been a roaring success, his next would bring him back down to earth with a bump. Liverpool would welcome Sheffield United in the third round of the FA Cup having dispatched Arsenal 4-1 and beaten Wolves 2-0 to set up the tie.

The game drew a huge crowd of over 51,000 and when Harry Chambers put the Reds 1-0 up on ten minutes, dreams of cup success would have taken flight. However, Billy Gillespie levelled 18 minutes later and Jimmy Waugh won the game for United down at the Anfield Road end in the 74th minute. Liverpool were out of the cup, and Sheffield United would reach the semi-final, before being eliminated by eventual winners Bolton Wanderers, who would be the Reds' next opponents in the league.

The game against Bolton, which took place on 23 March, would be overshadowed to some extent by events off the field. In fact, it was almost abandoned altogether. The headline in the *Liverpool Echo* captured the drama:

SENSATION UPON SENSATION UPON SENSATION

A TERRIBLE COMPLAINT AGAINST 2 CLUBS; ANFIELD ROAD STAND ON FIRE; BRIGADE CALLED TO QUELL FLAMES; SPECTATORS STAMPED FROM BACK OF GOAL

The game got under way on a miserable Saturday afternoon with the rain turning the pitch to mud. A crowd of 25,000 braved the elements and according to reports made the best of it by creating 'a joyful noise' as Liverpool scored two without reply in the first half of the game. In the 22nd minute Forshaw had grabbed his fourth consecutive goal in the league, and Johnson added the second two minutes before half-time, but the real story of the opening exchanges seems to have been the weather, with 'Bee' devoting a few passages to it, like this vivid description of a supporter's encounter with a wayward shot: 'The ball skidded considerably, and outpaced the players, and once, when the ball was put into the spectators, it plumped on to a man's trilby hat and forced the water that had gathered in the ridge up into the air.'

And there was this lovely account of Walter Wadsworth, covered in mud and, apparently, controlling the ball with his behind, much to the amusement of the crowd:

'Wadsworth was a study in black. His face was plastered in mud, and when he jazzed the ball by the use of his rear guard, the crowd was tickled to death.'

Then there was this moment when Harry Chambers had to resort to unorthodox methods to free a trapped ball from the mud and allow the game to continue:

'Chambers was very tactful when he dug the ball out of the turf and lofted it into the air.'

And finally, 'Bee' concluded:

'It was a pity that such a vile day should happen on the very occasion that the grand band of the King's (Liverpool) Regiment had been engaged to play. They have always given the best in music, and therefore their work today was done in difficult circumstances – yet was still of high quality.'

The King's (Liverpool) Regiment were the unit that Tom Bromilow had enlisted and fought with during the First World War. They would have set up in a bandstand that was situated to the right of the players' tunnel entrance and entertained the crowd. This bandstand would remain in place until the 1960s before it was eventually demolished.

The conditions the players endured sound terrible and it is hard to imagine a game like this going ahead today; the risk of injury aside, it would not be considered a great exhibition of the beautiful sport. Nevertheless, to reporters, players and crowds in the 1920s this would have been par for the course, as these matter-of-fact accounts demonstrate.

At half-time the score was 2-0 and as the players trudged off the pitch, soaking wet and caked in mud, it may well have been difficult to tell the teams apart. The supporters gathered on the roofless Spion Kop would have been soaked through with nothing but a trilby hat or a cap to keep their heads dry. However, the weather would soon be the least of their problems.

Liverpool emerged from the tunnel after the interval 'as fresh as paint and clean as lilies'. A quick half-time bath and a change of kit seemed to have revived them, and they were soon back into the action by going 3-0 up within four minutes of the restart thanks to Fred Hopkins's first goal for the club.

'Bee' wrote, 'Hopkins had, as a matter of fact, cut in more cutely than usual, and when he let his left foot go the ball flew into the right hand side of the goal. Thus Hopkin gained his first goal for Liverpool since he joined them two years ago.

'The crowd was only 25,000 strong owing to the weather. However, the crowd to a man raised a joyful noise and for five minutes kept up a roar of applause to celebrate this maiden goal.'

Soon after Hopkins scored, a fire broke out at the rear of the Anfield Road stand, causing thick smoke to waft across the pitch, and supporters were forced by the police to leave the terraced area and into the stand itself. Amazingly, despite the poor visibility, the game continued. Here is what 'Bee made of it in the *Liverpool Echo*, under a dramatic headline:

OUTBREAK OF FIRE
UNCOMMON OCCURRENCE WHERE THE PLAYERS USED TO DRESS

'Just after half-time a fire broke out in the Anfield Road goalstand near the number board. At first it seemed a mere nothing, but later on the smoke threatened to stop the game. The spectators at the bottom end could see little of what was going on, and through my field glasses I could see the police ordering the spectators about and clearing them into the stand.

'There was a general stampede into the stand, and quite an uncommon sight was witnessed of the spectators being more interested in the fire than the game. The Bolton goalkeeper was badly situated as he was in a mass of smoke.

'The fire occurred in the back of the stand, quite near to where the players' dressing room used to be.'

The report continued with descriptions of flashes of action witnessed through a 'smoke screen' that had shrouded the pitch. 'Bee' wrote of Hopkin almost grabbing a second, then through the fog, a 'grand drive by Lacey', a shot by Bolton's John Smith and a brilliant save by Scott, a Bolton player receiving a stern talking-to, and another shot from the visitors sailing over the crossbar at the Kop end. And all of this was witnessed as fragments of play emerging from the thick cloud blanketing the pitch.

Soon fears of the game being abandoned grew before the fire brigade eventually arrived to put out the flames. Seemingly nobody was hurt, and the match was allowed to conclude. 'Bee' thought that Bolton had been so comprehensively beaten that they may have been disappointed the fire didn't stop proceedings:

'The fire brigade from Westminster-road arrived; in fact we could hear them hacking away at the goalstand, so that the fire was now well under control. [Bolton right-half Walter] Rowley was hurt – not for the first time – and Bolton thought it anything but a perfect day, the only bright light being the fire, whose fumes might possibly have abandoned the game.'

A joke among Liverpool fans of the day was that Hopkin was to blame for the fire, and that the shock at his first goal in his 78 games had caused the blaze.

Liverpool's two points for the win proved invaluable as Sunderland had been beaten 3-1 by Sheffield United, so the Reds were in a commanding position at the top of the table with a four-point lead and 12 games to go. They then embarked on something of a mini slump, losing back-to-back games to Blackburn Rovers and Manchester City. While Sunderland failed to capitalise fully, they had reduced the gap by a point and had a game in hand.

The defeat to City took place at Hyde Road on a pitch that was virtually bare of grass. Liverpool lost by a single Horace Barnes goal, but it was the inconsistent application of the rules of the game that vexed Reds veteran Ephraim Longworth. Writing in his regular column, the defender expressed annoyance at how the new throw-in rule was being applied and complained that he had been penalised for placing his foot on the line, while another player had not. He also bemoaned the application of the new offside rule and in particular the impact it had on the workload of the half-back:

'It seems that a team must have a big, hard-working centre-half. That is an assured fact in victory. The poor centre half-back has always had a busy afternoon, but now he finds he has to become a persistent worker fore and aft, and covers more ground than ever before.'

The evolving rules of the game were having an impact on how it was played and as well as defences adapting their tactics to catch forwards offside, so too did wingers, who were now favouring passes played along the ground to the feet of the striker as opposed to high balls whipped into the centre. Here's Longworth on the change in tactics:

'Now it is being borne on me more than ever that wingers are not now sending the ball over to the centre with strength and height. That day seems to have passed. It would seem that a winger's primary duty now is to stand near to the touchline so that he can get the fleeting ball pushed out to him by his comrades. Then he needs to draw the defence and pass inside so that the man who has followed up can take a first-time shot.'

The game was speeding up now, becoming an end-to-end affair, and Longworth was not happy about it. His main concern was that football was becoming too 'tactical' at the expense of skill, and he appealed to the authorities to have a look at the rules. It is not known how supporters felt about this, and we can imagine, using our modern lens, that matches would have become faster, more attractive and exciting because of these rule changes, but we cannot assume that those of the 1920s would have felt the same way.

The Reds then got back into the winning way by beating City 2-0 at Anfield thanks to first-half strikes by Forshaw and Chambers. Kopites travelling home after the match would be cheered by the news that Sunderland had lost to 17th-placed Preston North End. Liverpool were now five points clear at the top of the table with nine games remaining, and even though their rivals had played a game fewer the title was theirs to lose.

Sunderland would prove incapable of capitalising whenever Liverpool dropped points. The Reds won three of their remaining nine games, drawing five and losing one. They would take 11 points from a possible 18 and won the league by six, equalling the record for points won in a single season with 60. Sunderland, meanwhile, lost four of their remaining games, winning five.

The title was won with two games to spare thanks to a 1-1 draw against Huddersfield Town on 21 April. Huddersfield's George Brown put the visitors in front in the 53rd minute but Liverpool were in a determined mood. They had lost just one of their previous seven matches and would not surrender easily. They were four points clear and knew that a win would most likely be enough to clinch the championship.

While it was still mathematically possible for Sunderland to equal Liverpool's points tally, the Reds' superior goal average of 2.31 compared to Sunderland's 1.48 meant that something of a miraculous swing was required for the north-east club to usurp the leaders. McQueen's side would not manage the win but a 73rd-minute leveller from Harry Chambers, which received a 'torrent of applause', would prove enough in the end.

Sunderland had lost 2-0 to Burnley at Turf Moor and the title was Liverpool's again. They had become only the fourth team since the foundation of the Football League to win back-to-back championships, and the first Reds side in the club's history to do so. Since 1900, only The Wednesday (now Sheffield Wednesday) had achieved the feat, and it was little wonder that the prospect of equalling that feat drew a huge crowd.

Official records show that there were 45,000 people in the ground to witness the draw with Huddersfield, though newspaper reports hint that it was most likely much greater than that. McQueen pulled something of a surprise by replacing Johnson with Pratt, and though the latter was a 'willing tryer', in a game where defences were on top, the switch may have worked against Liverpool.

Nevertheless, a point would ultimately prove enough to get the job done. Reports in various newspapers capture the joy bordering on euphoria as the news broke that the title was Liverpool's. The directors' room and players' changing rooms were 'stormed' as supporters and journalists rushed to offer their congratulations and celebrate.

Jubilant Liverpool chairman W.R. Williams, surrounded by well-wishers, the press, players and supporters, told one reporter:

'The team have done wonders. You ask the reason of their success, and I reply that they won because they are a good side, and have proved themselves a good side. It is one of the happiest days of my life.'

There were great cheers, and to roars of laughter, someone at the back of the throng shouted, 'If we win it for a third time does it become our personal property?'

The *Liverpool Echo* reported that captain Donald McKinlay was 'almost too for full words'. Explaining how visiting teams had raised their game against the champions, making it a tough season, he told them:

'It was touch and go now and again and one could see that the boys felt the keenness of the position. We are grateful to all that have helped us to our top position, and we hope that the public realise that we have won again, in spite of being on top early on – a big barrier to success in most cases, as teams came along with the avowed intention of making the league game a cup tie business. However, it is all over now, and I want to thank all the players sincerely for their splendid service in the second championship win in succession.'

Ephraim Longworth wrote about how the team were desperate to get the league sewn up against Huddersfield, and curiously revealed that the players were aware that Sunderland were losing at Burnley:

'I believe there was some broadcasting going on, on Saturday. It appears that someone with a phone to his ear and joy in his eyes was trying to tell Bill Lacey, or anyone else who would listen, that no matter what happened in the game we were playing the championship was ours, because Sunderland had lost at Burnley.'

And echoing his captain's words about the challenges of leading the table for virtually the entire season, Longworth revelled in their ultimate success, saying:

'Naturally the boys are very joyed and bucked about it. It is a natural desire, and though cup honours fleet by us without so much of a glance at us, still we have the consolation of knowing that we have won the biggest and longest test – and that test does not allow mercurial performance to count for everything. It has to be the steady, persistent victorious effort.'

With his closing words, Longworth beautifully and somewhat poetically summed up Liverpool's season. Indeed, both the 1921/22 and 1922/23 campaigns could be described in such terms.

The Reds had won 26 of their 42 games in 1922/23, drawing eight and losing eight to capture their second championship in a row, amassing a record-equalling 60 points. They had plundered 70 goals and conceded just 31, the lowest in the league, thanks to Elisha Scott's 19 clean sheets. At home they were imperious, winning 17 out of 21 matches, losing once and drawing the other three.

It had seemed as if nothing could derail this team; not the weather, the quagmire pitches nor the occasion of defeat. Not even the departure of manager David Ashworth could steer them off course. They were, as the press and their many admirers had christened them, Untouchable.

16

Glory and Adulation as Hero Tom Marries His Sweetheart

AFTER THE outpouring of joy following the draw with Huddersfield, Liverpool would wait until after the final game of the season at home to Stoke City to receive their prize. They had drawn with Stoke at the Victoria Ground on 28 April and would relish the opportunity to end on home turf with a victory against the side from the Potteries on 5 May.

Harry Chambers scored the only goal in the 52nd minute, his 22nd in the league of the season and 25th in all competitions. The match, however, was marred by a thigh injury to Elisha Scott, sustained after the Irishman overstretched to save an over-exuberant back-pass from Jock McNab, with the keeper having to be carried off the field on the back of a ground assistant. Bill Lacey would deputise and managed to keep a clean sheet. At full time, amid scenes of jubilation, Liverpool were presented with the league trophy. This is how the *Liverpool Echo* reported the events:

Hail Liverpool! Football Champions.

English League President Presents The Cup To The Strong And Consistent Anfield Side Amid Scenes of Enthusiasm And Congratulation

RINGING DOWN THE CURTAIN ON EXCELLENT SEASON 1922/23

'There was some enthusiastic scenes at Anfield this afternoon, when Liverpool received the English Football League Cup for the second year in succession. Mr John McKenna, the president of the Football League, made the presentation to Mr W.R. Williams, chairman of the Anfield club, and remarked that it was a wonderful performance to win the league two years in succession, as there was an evenness these days that did not show up in the old days. He congratulated players, officials and all concerned for the wonderful feat.

'Mr W.R. Williams, chairman of the Anfield club, received the trophy amid scenes of enthusiasm that prove the popularity of the side. Players and directors received a rallying shout of praise.'

Liverpool had won the league using only 19 players all season, and some felt their 'immunity to accident' had served them well. However, it was their skill, tenacity and unity that had brought them the ultimate prize.

Manager Matt McQueen would slip away from the trophy presentation as he had not felt worthy of the medal. In his book *Red Men*, John Williams describes the scenes as McKenna presented the players with theirs, when Walter Wadsworth was heard to shout cheekily, 'See you again next year, sir.'

Wadsworth would give 'an eloquent little speech, in his best Bootle accent' that few in the crowd would hear, and presented the former and current captains, Longworth and McKinlay, with replica trophies as a token of the players' gratitude to them. The club had been given permission to award the players a bonus of £25 each for their achievements. This amounted to three weeks' wages.

The club did not contest the Charity Shield in 1923, as they had done the previous season. The format of the contest had changed and the game would be moved to October. It would now be contested between a select team of professionals and amateurs and played at Stamford Bridge.

Chambers was the only player from Liverpool selected to feature. The professionals won 2-0 and Chambers got one of the goals in a game that raised £730 for charity. Despite the apparent lack of enthusiasm for the fixture, with only 11,000 fans attending, the authorities persisted with this format for four more years.

The Reds did reach the final of the Lancashire Cup, played at Bolton's Burnden Park, losing 1-0 to Manchester City, before embarking on a trip to Paris. They featured in two games: the first against Circle de Paris-Gallia at Le Stade Buffalo, on 26 May, and then the following day against Levallois in Paris. The Reds won 3-0 and 4-0 respectively.

There would be more joy in the city as Tom Bromilow, who had now become something of a pin-up and superstar, married Lillian Mabel (May) Kelly on 20 June. His marriage certificate reveals that he was living in 352 Longmoor Lane, Fazakerley, at the corner of Higher Lane, in an ordinary suburb of the city, four miles from Anfield and a short stroll from Aintree Racecourse. His marital home is now a shop. His bride had been residing in 43 Westminster Road, Kirkdale.

Athletic News reported the impending nuptials on 18 June, and the ceremony was covered extensively in Liverpool also. This would ensure a bumper turnout of supporters and well-wishers who gathered outside the church to catch a glimpse of the happy couple.

Athletic News wrote, 'Tom Bromilow, the Liverpool and international left half-back, is to be married on Wednesday to Miss Lillian Mabel May, the daughter of L.T. Kelly, of Liverpool. The ceremony is to take place at St. Athanasius Church, Kirkdale.'

Tom's bride-to-be was the eldest daughter of author of the *Liverpool Echo* column 'Stud Marks'. The paper publicised the wedding in advance, with this notice:

'Wednesday is to be a red-letter day at the north-end of the city. Miss May Kelly, eldest daughter of my esteemed friend, Mr Louis Kelly (Mr Stud Marks of the *Football Echo*), is to be married to Mr Tom Bromilow, the Liverpool footballer, at St Athanasius Church, Fountains Road, Kirkdale. Miss May tied at a Welsh Eisteddfod held at Bootle on Friday, for first place – a happy "finale" as Miss.'

Family mementos and photographs of the wedding day provide a sense of how big an occasion this was, and we begin to realise just how big a phenomenon Bromilow was. Scenes akin to those witnessed during the Beatlemania era of the 1960s would greet Tom as he strode through the gates of the church in his top hat and tails.

Hordes of people had turned up outside the church. In bright sunshine, and wearing their best clothes, they can be seen cramming pavements and any vantage point they could find, desperate to catch a glimpse of the bride and groom. The streets leading up to the venue were lined on both sides, as if people were waiting to see a trophy paraded rather than the wedding of a footballer and his bride. In fact, so many people turned out to witness the event that the police struggled to control the throng.

Writing in his sports notes in the *Liverpool Echo* the following day, journalist, Ernest 'Bee' Edwards said, 'It may have been a Prince's wedding at St Athanasius Church yesterday, so enormous was the crowd that gathered.'

Nine days later, Tom would attend another banquet at the Adelphi Hotel, along with his team-mates. Once more the great and the good of Merseyside football were in attendance, including the chairman of Everton. The guests were treated to music from the piano played by George Freeman, Florence Wray singing, a band, and speeches that, from reports, seemed more like stand-up routines.

Once more, chairman W.R. Williams paid a moving tribute this time to club secretary George Patterson, manager Matt McQueen and trainer Bill Connell. There then followed speeches by Donald McKinlay and Walter Wadsworth, and once again players and officials spoke of wanting to add the FA Cup to the list of achievements.

The whole event seems to show the tremendous spirit of unity of purpose, friendship and togetherness associated with Liverpool Football Club during this period. That fact had been discussed many times in the newspapers over the previous two seasons, but one article, written by 'Bee' in the *Liverpool Echo* on 1 May 1923 and titled 'Football Comrades', is particularly revealing.

'Bee' was a legendary football reporter, and by the 1920s his reputation was such that he enjoyed great relationships with players and officials alike. He was the only journalist to have a phone with a direct line to his newspaper in the Anfield press box. In his article, he tells how he had been given the gift of a silver cigarette case by Reds players McKinlay, Scott, Lacey and Longworth. He then goes on to describe a day he spent with the directors and players of the club, which convinced him that he had discovered the secret to Liverpool's success.

'What is the secret of success?' he asks. 'A day spent with the players and directors of the Liverpool Football Club convinces me. It is the unanimity of purpose, confidence in each other, and above all the spirit of bonhomie that permeates the club.'

'Bee' describes how the players had arranged a surprise party for the chairman on his birthday, at the Sandon Hotel, where they had organised games of bowls. At the end of the evening, McKinlay presented Williams with a set of pipes and a pouch of tobacco and his wife with a silver tray. The inscription read:

'Presented to Mr and Mrs W.R. Williams by the players and staff to commemorate the unique success of winning the League Championship in 1921-22 and 1922-23.'

As a gesture it says so much about the spirit and ethos at Anfield, and why even the departure of David Ashworth could not derail the season. The evening, compered by Wadsworth, ended in song, with first the chairman giving a rendition of 'Mountains of Mourne', followed by McNab, McKinlay, Lacey, Pratt, Connell and Bamber, who all sang for the assembled crowd.

The event would conclude with a stirring speech from Williams, clearly deeply touched by the occasion. He rose to his feet as the players took their seats, and closed with these words:

'If there is a better feeling in any other club than the Liverpool club, I do not want to go there.'

In just 21 words, the Liverpool chairman appears to have succinctly encapsulated the recipe for the club's success in the previous two seasons. It was the result of skill, determination and knowledge of the game. Anfield was blessed with players who were master craftsmen, and a supporting cast of trainers, coaches, managers and directors who were all experts in their respective fields. But the secret ingredient, the glue that held it all together, was the deep bond between all who were connected with Liverpool FC.

They had succeeded because they were a 'good side', as their chairman had said in what must rank as a study in understatement. But they had done so twice in successive seasons, and while earning the respect of all in the game, because they were above all, a band of brothers, and one of the greatest in Liverpool Football Club's illustrious history.

Part Five

All Good Things

17

Whatever Happened to the Untouchables?

IT SEEMS hard to understand how a team whose flame had burned so brightly between 1919 and 1923 could fall into mediocrity in the years after that. The Reds would suffer a 12th-placed finish in 1924, and followed that up with fourth in 1925, seventh in 1926 and ninth in 1927. Matt McQueen would resign midway through the 1927/28 season, leaving George Patterson to become the first man to manage Liverpool in two different eras, a feat repeated by Kenny Dalglish in 2011. Patterson would lead the team to 16th place.

David Ashworth, who had left Liverpool midway through the second title-winning season in February 1923, would fail to save Oldham from relegation. He would then depart Boundary Park in 1924 and go on to manage Manchester City (1924/25), Walsall (1926/27), Caernarfon and Llanelli.

The 1939 Census shows that he was living at 242 Central Drive, Blackpool, and employed as clerk and scout in employment of football club. He died on 22 March 1947 at Victoria Hospital, Blackpool. Ashworth was buried in Carleton Cemetery, Blackpool.

His legacy is therefore a complex one. A mercurial and even eccentric character, Ashworth was undoubtedly a well respected and influential man. Known far and wide in football circles, he will be most remembered as the man who helped build the Untouchables, steering them to the first of their two championships and providing the foundations for their second.

His successor Matt McQueen was a legendary player for Liverpool, and although he would shy away from any praise or recognition for the 1923 title, he undoubtedly maintained the team's high standards, seeing them through the remainder of that season after taking over the reigns in 1923.

In the years that followed, his life would be filled with drama and tragedy. On 1 December 1924, while the Reds were playing Sheffield United at Bramall Lane, McQueen had gone to scout a player in a junior match. He was hit by a taxi outside Tankersley Station, sustaining a complicated fracture of his leg. McQueen would undergo surgery twice at Sheffield Royal Hospital. When infection and later septicaemia set in, his leg had to be amputated on 21 February.

We can only imagine the trauma and anguish this caused him. He would have been gravely ill and though he was discharged from hospital on 22 March, he did not resume his duties until July. We must therefore judge his performance as manager in this context.

More heartache followed in 1926 when his wife Mary passed away after a long illness. Her death coincided with the opening day of the 1926/27 season, with Liverpool facing Manchester United at Anfield. The game drew the biggest crowd in the league that day, and the club lowered its flag to half mast as a mark of respect. Mary was later buried at Anfield Cemetery.

McQueen resigned in February 1928 under his doctor's orders. The club would do away with the role of manager, at least for a period, and *Athletic News* on 12 March wrote:

'Following Matt McQueen's resignation as players' manager, the directors dispensed that role, appointing George Patterson as secretary-manager.'

McQueen can be credited with signing one of Liverpool's greatest strikers, South African-born Gordon Hodgson, who would play 358 times for the club and score 241 goals.

McQueen lived out the remainder of his life at 32 Kemlyn Road, Anfield. The site of his home is now covered by the Sir Kenny Dalglish Stand. He died due to myocardial degeneration, effectively heart failure, on 29 September 1944, having been a regular visitor to Anfield throughout the remainder of his life.

He had remarried and left a generous will of £1,043 14s. 3d. to his widow, Florence. His funeral was held at Anfield Crematorium on 10 March 1944.

Succeeding McQueen was George Patterson, the man who had given Tom Bromilow his chance at Anfield and who had previously made way for David Ashworth. Patterson continued as secretary-manager until he resigned in 1936. He would bow out of football altogether in 1938 due to ill health having spent three decades in the service of the club.

The *Sunderland Daily Echo* carried this tribute to his career on 5 October 1938:

'Thirty years an official of one football club! That is the proud record of Mr George Patterson, secretary of Liverpool FC.

'Mr Patterson has served the club in several positions: assistant secretary, then secretary-manager, but latterly, owing to the increasing duties and a rather severe illness he had to give up the managerial duties which were taken over by Mr George Kay, and confine himself to acting as secretary.

'During Mr Patterson's long stay at Anfield, Liverpool have won practically every honour except that of cup winners.

'Many players who by their performances on the football field have become famous owe their position to Mr Patterson, whose foresight and ability to see the potentialities of young players was responsible for their becoming footballers.'

It was often the case that others would reap the benefits of Patterson's signings. Just as Ashworth and his staff would polish the rough diamonds that were Harry Chambers and Tom Bromilow, so too would George Kay benefit from the talents of Jack Balmer, Berry Nieuwenhuys and others. Both managers would build championship-winning teams around Patterson's players.

Throughout his time at the club, and in his retirement years, Patterson lived in the shadow of Anfield. His home was in Skerries Road, just yards from the Kop. He is said to have sat on the low wall outside his house on matchdays, interacting with supporters as they passed by. He was a hugely popular figure and a significant man behind the scenes in the pre-war history of the club.

Following his death in 1955, Patterson was interned close to home at the nearby Anfield Cemetery. His funeral cortége left from 326 Anfield

Road and would have weaved its way slowly past the stadium where he had worked tirelessly for three decades, then past the streets where he had spent most of his life and on to his final resting place.

There he remained, in an unmarked plot for more than 60 years. However, in 2019, members of the Liverpool FC Historical Group collected the funds necessary to have his grave marked with a headstone. It stands to this day, his record of service carved into the black marble.

Despite his obvious knowledge of the game, Patterson was a man of letters. As secretary his duties would include everything from overseeing ground improvements to player recruitment, including scouting missions. As the game grew, so too did the secretarial demands at a professional club.

The once common role of secretary-manager was being phased out as the role of manager evolved to include tactical awareness and player conditioning. One of the greatest innovators of the role of manager was a Yorkshireman by the name of Herbert Chapman. In 1925, following the removal of Leslie Knighton, Chapman took on the role of team manager. Following Liverpool's back-to-back title wins, Chapman's Huddersfield Town achieved the same honour in 1923/24 and 1924/25. Having established himself as a developer of tactics at Huddersfield, he would take this mantle to a new level at Arsenal.

The offside rule was changed in 1925 and several clubs, including Arsenal, dropped the 2-3-5 formation in favour of 3-4-3, more popularly referred to as the W-M formation, to compensate for the evolution in the offside rule. Despite other clubs implementing the idea, it was Chapman who truly defined the formation, being able to tweak it to suit his counter-attacking ideas. At Arsenal, Chapman won two titles and an FA Cup, before his untimely death in 1934.

In contrast to Arsenal, Liverpool found the 1930s something of a struggle with mid-table being the norm, and would finish 18th and 19th in 1934 and 1936 respectively. After that the club decided to split the role into two separate roles once again, with Kay being drafted in as team manager.

The *Liverpool Echo*, on Friday, 7 August 1936, examined the role played by Kay, and suggested he would be involved in developing players. Perhaps the best illustration of the role of Patterson is a 1931 cartoon that featured in the *Liverpool Echo*. Almost three years into his time as secretary-manager, Patterson is depicted as a clerical man, with a pen in his right hand, and a slip of paper marked 'Transfer Fees' in the other. There is no sign of a football, a pair of boots or a team sheet. His strengths lay away from the field of play, playing his own key role at the club for over 30 years.

Working away behind the scenes, away from the limelight, throughout this period were the backroom team of Billy Connell, Charlie Wilson, Joe Hewitt and Bert Riley. In their own way, these men would toil daily in the cause of Liverpool FC.

Connell lived at 27 Clapham Road, Anfield, and was registered as a 'Professional Trainer, Liverpool Football Club Ltd (Retired)' on the 1929 Census. He passed away on 23 January 1940 and is buried at Anfield Cemetery. He bequeathed £892 19s. 11d. to his sons, builder's foreman William Chandley and dispatch clerk Allatt Connell.

Charlie Wilson would replace the retired Connell as trainer in 1928. In 1935, a report in the *Liverpool Echo* described how Wilson implemented new training methods from the FA training school and attended courses with the FA along with Ephraim Longworth.

In 1939, the *Daily Post* revealed that he had been transferred to the ground staff, and the England and Wales Register records him as living at 21 Sandstone Road, Liverpool. He was employed as a 'General Labourer'. Charlie died at his home on 6 June 1947. His funeral was held at St Anne's Church, Stanley Road, and he was buried at West Derby Cemetery. He had served Liverpool as scout, coach, assistant trainer and trainer.

Joe Hewitt passed away at Sefton Grange Nursing Home on 30 November 1971, after a long struggle with bronchial disease. He had been a dedicated servant at Anfield for 60 years in many roles, including player, coach, club steward and press box attendant.

Bert Riley lived at 3 Alroy Road throughout his life, and the 1939 Census records his occupation as 'Football Groundsman'. He died on 2 December 1956 at Newsham General Hospital and was buried at Anfield Cemetery. As well as working on the pitch at Anfield, Bert would pay out wages and was involved in ticket sales. He left the sum of £2,082 8s. 8d. in his will.

And so to the players who brought so much happiness to Liverpool supporters in the 1920s. What would become of them? Their onward journeys are as interesting as their time at Anfield, and some are tinged with sadness.

Elisha Scott, having spent 22 years at Liverpool, would eventually leave in 1934 to join Belfast Celtic as their player-manager. His last game for the Reds was a 2-0 defeat to Chelsea at Stamford Bridge. However, he would not leave Anfield without saying a proper farewell, taking to the microphone in the Main Stand to say his final few words to the crowd.

To the assembled Kop, many of whom were in tears, he addressed them, 'My friends on the Kop. You have inspired me. God bless you.' Elisha had been left in no doubt as to what he meant to the supporters.

Two earlier attempts by the club's directors to sell Scott to Everton fell through. The first collapsed due to an ankle injury the goalkeeper had sustained and the second would be thwarted by a letter-writing campaign conducted by furious Liverpool supporters. In what Liverpool FC museum curator Stephen Done called an early example of fan power, supporters bombarded the *Liverpool Echo* with complaints, and demanded that the club reversed the decision, which they eventually did.

According to a documentary film produced by Mark Platt for LFCTV, supporters were angry that the directors were prepared to sell to Everton in the first instance, but moreover they found it insulting that a man of Scott's magnitude could be bought and sold just like any other player. Some argued that rather than transfer him, the club should erect a statue of Elisha at St George's Hall. Scott was more than a footballer to the people of Liverpool – he was a legend and an icon.

The relationship Scott struck up with the Kop at Anfield could never be broken. It is said that he would engage the crowd in conversation before and after games, and on the Mersey Ferry as he travelled to Anfield. Many thought they were confidants of his.

One story tells of how a supporter climbed out of the stands during a game at Blackburn, in which Scott had pulled off an incredible acrobatic save, and planted a kiss on the keeper's cheeks. Another describes an encounter in which Elisha had been engaged in a lengthy conversation with a supporter who was behaving like they were old mates.

In the end Scott would ask, 'I am sorry, do we know each other?' 'I should think so,' replied the fan. 'We were talking to each other at the game last week.'

The Kop felt such an affinity with their number one that they dedicated one of their earliest chants to him. 'Lisha, Lisha' would be the cry as he went about his business on the green grass of Anfield.

When he departed from Anfield, Scott would still have many years of football left in him. Amazingly, he was even selected to play for his country in 1936 by which time he would have been 43 years old. Former Liverpool captain Donald McKinlay later declared that Elisha was as good as ever, saying:

'Look at Elisha. I saw him play in goal for the Irish league against the English league when he must have been 44. He played a blinder and, when his team won, looked as though he could have jumped over the crossbar.'

He hung up his boots in 1936 and assumed the sole role as Belfast Celtic's manager. Elisha guided the club to 32 trophies during his 15-year reign, including ten Irish titles, six Irish Cups, three City Cups, eight Gold Cups and five County Antrim Shields.

Tragically, sectarian crowd trouble led to Celtic withdrawing from the league in 1949 as the club felt it could no longer guarantee the safety of supporters. The trouble occurred at Windsor Park in a match against Linfield when fighting in the stands spilled on to the pitch and Celtic's centre-forward Jimmy Jones was injured in the melee. It was a terrible personal blow to Elisha, and he was said to have been devastated by it.

Despite moving on to pastures new, Elisha remained hugely popular among Liverpool supporters of successive generations. In 1939 a survey was conducted among Reds to name the greatest player the club had ever had. Scott's popularity was such that he topped the list. In 2006 he would be ranked 39th in a poll carried out by LFCTV entitled '100 Players Who Shook the Kop'.

However, it was not just supporters who admired the man. His legendary friendship with Everton striker Dixie Dean has now passed into folklore, and the Blues icon would have the following to say about his great rival: 'Elisha was the greatest I've ever seen. You can have

[Frank] Swift, [Bert] Trautmann, [Gordon] Banks, [Bob] Wilson. You can have them all. I'll take Elisha Scott.'

Scott enjoyed many rivalries in the game, but perhaps none more so than with Dean, the prolific Goodison forward. The pair were best of friends off the field and the tales of their many encounters – some real, others greatly exaggerated but entertaining and informative, nonetheless – have been passed down through the ages. Interestingly, though, Elisha would describe a different striker as his greatest challenge – Chelsea's Andy Wilson.

Wilson played 238 times for the Londoners, notching 59 goals. But it was against Scott that he seemed to have the most joy. In 1931, Elisha said of the Scottish forward, 'Everywhere I go he follows me. And every time he has his own way.'

Despite his caustic nature, Elisha made many friends in the game, including journalists who had felt his wrath whenever they wrote something he disagreed with. They admired him and respected him, nonetheless. This extract from 'Bee' in the *Liverpool Echo* on 25 August 1945 is a case in point:

'Next in my parade is Elisha Scott, of Belfast. Friend and schoolmaster John Murray had met him, and his first words were, "How's old 'Bee'?" I would remind Elisha that someone said to an elderly man, "You must be 70," and got the reply, "No, I mustn't!" Elisha was the thorniest of fellows. He wore a surplus of three stockings because he did not want the folk at the back of the goal to call him "Skinny".

'He was also the canniest of card players. He would never go solo unless he had ace, king, queen, jack, ten seven times. When he called solo they just packed up without playing the cards.

'He spent four hours travelling to Nottingham with me one day, vowing I had been unfair to him, saying he "got Dixie Dean in a certain way".

'Four hours' harangue in a somewhat foreign tongue! Arrive at Nottingham, he invited me to a cup of tea with him, remarking, "I got Dixie all right, but not the way you said I did."'

In 1949 a report in the *Derby Evening Telegraph* states that Elisha was likely to accept a job at Portadown, but on 3 March 1950 the *Northern Whig* reported:

'Glenavon decided last night to appoint Mr Elisha Scott manager of their club subject to Belfast Celtic releasing him from his contract. The decision was taken after he had been interviewed at a special meeting of the directors.

'It was stated after the meeting that terms had been agreed upon, and all that remained was for Mr Scott to be released by Celtic. It is confidently expected that this will be done, and if so, he will take up duty at Lurgan early next week.'

Scott passed away nine years later, at Belfast City Hospital, leaving behind his widow Alice and their family. He had lived at 304 Donegall Road in Belfast. A report in the *Belfast Telegraph* on 18 May 1959 describes his funeral proceedings:

'Football fans gathered in hundreds today for the funeral of Mr Elisha Scott, the former Irish international goalkeeper.

'Among those who accompanied the funeral from the house 304 Donegall Road – to the City Cemetery were footballers and ex-footballers and former colleagues. Mr Scott, who died on Saturday at the age of 66, was manager of Belfast Celtic.

'Representatives of the Irish Football Association, the Celtic club, Irish league clubs and of the organisations which used Celtic Park for their matches, were present.

'Among the many wreaths were those from the Irish FA, Belfast Celtic, and the Liverpool FC, for which Mr Scott played for 21 years, before returning home to Belfast to manage Celtic.'

While Elisha's reputation and status in the game continued to grow in the years after he left Anfield, others found adjusting to life without football difficult. One man who epitomised this more than most was Dick Forshaw.

Richard 'Dick' Forshaw had four children to his wife, Florence Robinson. The couple would experience great tragedy early in their marriage. They welcomed their first child, Lilian Grace, into the family on 13 August 1922. She lived to be 82 and passed away in 2004. Heartbreakingly, though, their second child, Raymond Richard, would not survive his birth in 1923.

The couple recovered from that and had another son, Arnold Richard, in January 1926. He enjoyed a long career at sea before settling in Oslo, and passed away in 2009. Their fourth child, Raymond Robert, died in 1963 as a result of a road accident.

Forshaw left Liverpool for Everton when his contract expired in 1927 and spent two seasons at Goodison Park, much to the annoyance of many Liverpool supporters, and his wife. He then enjoyed spells at Wolverhampton Wanderers (1929/30), Hednesford Town (1930), Rhyl Athletic (1930), and Waterford (1930/31). However, in 1932, after his playing career was over, Forshaw fell foul of the law and was sentenced at the Liverpool Courts to 12 months' hard labour.

While employed as a fishmonger, he had been found guilty of the 'fraudulent conversion of £100 for the purpose of gambling', and could offer no mitigation in his defence. The recorder, Mr E.G, Hemmerde K.C., would accuse him of 'peculiar meanness'.

Essentially, Forshaw had taken the money from Richard Green and promised to place bets on his behalf on a horse called Grand Salute, which was running at the Royal Hunt race. The horse won, and Mr Green was due winnings of £2,000, but Forshaw had disappeared.

He had fled to London and was arrested at an address in Kilburn. He initially denied all knowledge of the bet and was remanded for seven days with bail set at £20.

After his release, Forshaw eventually settled in Brighton, living at 187 Marine Drive, Saltdean, overlooking the sea. He died in 1963, leaving £8,730 to John Cyril Bosley. He had led something of a chequered life and the 1930s and '40s were a difficult time for him. However, he seems to have recovered and made a successful life for himself on the south coast.

Another hero at Anfield who would also experience hardship at the end of his Liverpool career was Harry Chambers. Referred to as 'Smiler' because of his constant happy disposition, and possibly an ironic reference to his dental issues, he would find himself in something of a personal slump as he edged towards the exit door.

He had been knocked down by a car while riding a bicycle and had tried unsuccessfully to recover damages for the incident in court, claiming that the accident had caused his loss of form and cost him his place in the team. Unfortunately for Harry, a doctor had said there was nothing physically wrong with Chambers and blamed his loss of form on anxiety.

Towards the end of his Liverpool career there were clear signs that he was falling out of love with his surroundings and even possibly disillusioned with football. Harry believed that a player should work hard in training because of his enthusiasm for the job, not because of the rules. He felt what he called 'the modern footballer' was 'too pampered'. He argued that players were looked after too much, and their surroundings were too luxurious. This, he claimed, made for 'soft' players.

Harry was well liked by everyone at the club and had a reputation for always smiling. His laughter was infectious, but after the accident things seemed to change. He would be transferred and was not happy about the manner of his departure. 'Bee' explained why:

'Once they gave Harry "the bird" at Liverpool. He was very sore about it and told me that if it happened again, he would pack up his kit bag and get out.

'I asked Harry why he was leaving, and his reply was, "Sometimes you get fed up. Well, I'm more than fed up. Not with the team, spectators, the boys, or the directors, ye know; but just fed up. I think if I got away I should do better than I am doing. A change is good for anyone when they have got in a rut. I do not imply that I have been playing a blinder or playing badly, but it seems to me that a move at this critical juncture would do me good and bring me back to my best possible form.

'I told the chairman exactly the position at the back of my mind. I think someone has been good enough to suggest that I haven't been pulling my weight. Well, I am pretty heavy, and I claim to have pulled jolly hard in every game I have played for them. That cannot be denied. However, there it is. I am longing for a change of surroundings, and I hope I shall not be long before I move. Mind you, I have no grievance, no complaints, plenty of pals and plenty of football for the future!'

Harry was allowed to leave Liverpool in April 1928. He was 32 years of age and would sign for West Bromwich Albion where he would be converted to a centre-half. Unsurprisingly, he did not register a single goal while at The Hawthorns.

In addition to West Brom, Harry went to Wellington, had two spells at Oakengates Town, and then played for Hereford United. He finished his playing days at Oakengates as player-manager, remaining there until 1948. He also ran the local pub, the Stafford Arms.

Harry also seems to have worked at a factory in Hadley and continued to play football in Shropshire until his death in 1949, aged just 52. He was buried at Wombridge Parish Church near Oakengates. His obituary in one local newspaper simply read:

'Harry Chambers, of happy memory, is dead. This greatest of all Liverpool players passed away at his home, Oakengates, Shropshire, yesterday.'

Another, more detailed tribute in the *Liverpool Echo* on 30 June 1949, gave a more glowing account of his life:

'Present-day youthful football followers know him almost as well as they know Billy Liddell and Jack Balmer, for their parents and grandparents never ceased talking about this wonderful inside forward, who was in his heyday just after the first First World War.

'"Smiler", as he was known to the crowd because there was always a grin on his face, was not only a scorer of goals but made others play, through his astute generalship and amazing football sense.

'Those who had the pleasure of seeing him will never forget him, and goalkeepers who had to face up to his shots did so with fear in their hearts, for Chambers, thanks to his "pigeon toes", could apply swerve to his shots which was most disconcerting. But it was as part and parcel of the team that Harry was known best. He was one of that wonderful trinity – Chambers, Fred Hopkin and Tom Bromilow – which played such a big part in winning Liverpool two championships in succession.

'He was beloved of the Liverpool crowd, and the way he plied "Hoppy" with a pass had to be seen to be believed. With either head or foot he could "find" his partner no matter where he was, and off Hopkin would go to the corner flag to fling over one of those hanging centres which provided Chambers with so many of his goals.

'On a visit to Wolverhampton last season, I ran across Chambers, and he did not look one whit different from when he sported the red jersey. He told me he had just finished playing with the works team, Oakengates FC with whom he operated at centre-half, a position which fitted him superbly. But Harry could have played anywhere, for he was a footballer born to be great.

'Prior to coming to Anfield Chambers had a fine career as a junior, being capped as a schoolboy. He went on to win 11 England caps. He was the last player signed by Tom Watson. That was in 1915. In the May of that year he joined up, but was invalided home from Salonika. He had a long spell in hospital and after his discharge went to Ireland in 1917 to play for Belfast Distillery in one or two games. He moved on to Glentoran, but finally landed back at Anfield.

'By his pass goes another of the old championship side – undoubtedly the best Liverpool ever had. Two of his contemporaries were the late Dick Johnson, centre-forward, and John McNab, the half-back.'

Chambers played 339 times for Liverpool and scored an astonishing 151 goals. He is rightly regarded as one of the greatest players to ever wear the shirt.

Among the ranks of Anfield's supporting cast was Harry Beadles. The war hero turned footballer left Liverpool in 1924, and enjoyed spells at Cardiff City, Sheffield Wednesday, Southport and Dundalk. According to historian Mal Holme, in later life Harry raised a family and was the manager of a large and prestigious public house owned by Bents Brewery in Huyton, Liverpool. It was called the Hillside Hotel.

After retirement, Harry and his wife moved to Mold in North Wales, and in 1958 at the age of 60, he passed away. He was returned to his adopted home of Liverpool, where he was buried at Everton Cemetery.

Another of those 'bit-part players' was Cyril Gilhespy. He married Edna May Baker in Bristol in March 1926 and the pair had two children, William Cyril Bryan and Gordon Keith, born 1926 and 1928, respectively. By 1939, Cyril was working as a mail order stores supervisor and living at 49 Lyne Grove, Huyton, with Roby. He died in 1985, at the age of 87.

Cyril enjoyed a decent football career after leaving Anfield, with spells at Bristol City, Blackburn Rovers, Reading, Mansfield Town and Crewe Alexandra. However, he is best remembered by Liverpool fans as the man who made 19 appearances for the Reds and scored three goals. Though he never managed enough appearances to earn a championship medal, he will forever be associated with the Untouchables.

One man who was an integral part of that double championship-winning team was Donald McKinlay. The Scot, who had joined the Reds in 1910, would remain in Liverpool after his Anfield days ended in 1929. During his final season the club awarded McKinlay his fourth benefit match as a reward for 19 years of service. The opponents were Manchester City and the game earned him £468.

McKinlay later joined Prescot Cables and played for them in non-league football until 1931. An article on Prescot Cables FC website, written by Glyn Williams in 2012, discusses his time at the club, and says:

'After 19 years of faithful service, McKinlay's contract at Liverpool ran out in July 1929. He was quickly snapped up by Cables, playing for them during the 1929/30 and 1930/31 seasons. He featured mostly at left-back and served, I suspect, as an inspirational captain. He held strong views about captaincy, "In my day I had full control on the field and if there was any decision on changing of positions, I took it. … I told my players, 'If I have to say anything to you, [don't] answer me back and don't start sulking."'

McKinlay lived in 98 Dewsbury Road, Liverpool, and managed the Greyhound Hotel on East Prescot Road. He sadly passed away at Broadgreen Hospital, suffering from carcinoma of the bronchus on 16 September 1959 aged 68. His funeral took place at Anfield Crematorium two days later.

Donald was a stalwart of Liverpool Football Club. Standing at 5ft 10in, he was a keen sportsman and according to a joint Everton and Liverpool match programme published on 16 November 1910, in addition to football he enjoyed cricket in the summer. In later life he enjoyed golf, and music and, apparently, he especially enjoyed playing the drums.

In all he played 435 times for Liverpool and scored 35 goals. Capped twice for his country, he was one of the most consistent performers of the period and a key man in the success of the 1920s and consequently he has rightly been inducted into the club's Hall of Fame.

Similarly, Ephraim Longworth's playing career was one of loyalty and consistency. He ended his playing days for Liverpool a year earlier than McKinlay, in 1928. He had spent 18 years at Anfield as a player and had been capped by England five times. Longworth played 370 times for the club, but never managed a goal in an official game, though he did score three in unofficial wartime matches.

He would go on to be a coach at Anfield after his playing days were over and was even still part of the furniture at the club as late as the

1960s. George Scott, a former Liverpool reserve under Bill Shankly, recalls his encounters with Longworth fondly:

'In 1961, when Gordon Wallace and myself were young apprentices at Anfield, we kept seeing this old chap who seemed to come into the club on most days. I asked Albert Shelley who the old guy was, and he told us his name was Ephraim Longworth, and that he used to play for the club many years ago.

'A few days later, Gordon and I introduced ourselves to Ephraim and he joined us for a game of snooker. He asked if we wanted to play for a shilling and we agreed, confident that we were on to a good thing. Ephraim had a severe tremor in his right hand. He then proceeded to clear the table and took our money with a wry smile and a glint in his eye. Astonished, I mentioned how he seemed to have got his tremor under control.

'He replied by saying, "On no, I forget to tell you, it doesn't happen when I grip a snooker cue." Ephraim would have been well into his late 70s by then. It was difficult to stop Shankly talking about him. He would tell us that Ephraim was a living legend of the game.

'Ephraim used to rub it in to us Scottish lads, telling us that he had captained England when they beat the Scots at Hillsborough having come back from 4-2 down to win 5-4. When I said to him that, as a defender, he could not have been happy conceding four goals to Scotland even though they won, his reply was unprintable.' Longworth's two league championship medals and his runners-up medal from the 1914 FA Cup Final more than earned him his place in the Anfield Hall of Fame. However, he was also something of a student of the game, a thinker whose opinions were sought, listened to and debated by those who loved football.

Ephraim lived in Valescourt Road in the West Derby area of the city and was a member of the air raid patrol during the Second World War. He died on 7 January 1968.

Another of the club's long-serving veterans, Bill Lacey, spent 12 years at Liverpool before leaving in 1924 when his contract expired. He then enjoyed a spell at New Brighton, before returning to Ireland to play for Shelbourne and Cork Bohemians.

However, Bill had come to think of Liverpool as home and he would return there to live out the remainder of his life. Bill attended the engagement of Liverpool's 1960s star Chris Lawler, and celebrated the 1965 FA Cup win with the club. His family have shared a letter he received in 1967 from a headmistress at a local school, after Bill had spent time talking to the children about football and coaching them in the game. Typed on Liverpool Education Committee headed paper and dated 22 September 1967, it says:

> Dear Mr Lacey,
> I thought you might like to have this photograph of yourself, taken with the children.
>
> We think it is very good and we hope it will give you some pleasure to have it.
>
> We enjoyed your visit and thank you very much for coming to stimulate the children's interest in football.
>
> We trust you are keeping very well and will continue to remain so.
>
> With best wishes from us all,
> Yours sincerely
> E.G. Bates
> Headmistress

It is touching to know that Bill's love of football and of the city he came to know and love never diminished. He would have been 78 when he visited that school to talk to the children about football. Some of them will be still alive today. We wonder if they knew what a treat it was to meet him. We hope so.

Bill played 260 times for Liverpool, scoring 29 times. However, he was a Merseyside football hero, having also played for Everton. He is also revered in his homeland of Ireland, and outside a house in Enniscorthy that he once lived in, is a blue plaque that reads:

BILL LACEY (1889–1969)
ROSS ROAD ENNISCORTHY
WAS A DUAL INTERNATIONAL FOOTBALLER
WHO BETWEEN 1909–1924 WON 23 CAPS FOR
IFA XI AND BETWEEN 1927–30 WON 3 CAPS

FOR FAI XI ON MAY 11, 1930 AT THE AGE OF 41 HE BECAME THE OLDEST PLAYER EVER TO BE CAPPED BY AN FAI TEAM. HE PLAYED CLUB FOOTBALL FOR SHELBOURNE, EVERTON, LIVERPOOL, AND LINFIELD

It is a fitting tribute to an Irish football legend, and one his family are rightly proud of. Bill ended his days living at the Basil Grange Nursing Home on Queens Drive, Liverpool. He became ill in May 1969 and died of gastric cancer in Broadgreen Hospital on 30 May, aged 79. Bill is buried in Liverpool.

Lacey's team-mate during those championship seasons, Fred Hopkin, remained at Anfield until 1931. Having made 360 appearances and scored 12 goals, he returned to Darlington where he spent one season. He was 36 years of age. Fred made 36 appearances for the Quakers, who played in the Third Division (Northern), before moving into coaching with Redcar Borough. Fred later went into business as a physiotherapist, working in a room at the back of his wife's hairdressers shop, where he is said to have used a special ointment – described as 'thick black smelly oil' – and heat lamps, to treat sporting injuries.

He passed away in 1970 in his native Darlington, at the age of 74. Though he moved home after leaving Liverpool, an obituary in the *Liverpool Echo* talks of how he would always keep an eye on his former team's progress and would watch them play whenever they came to the north-east.

Another Untouchable who would often keep an eye on the Reds, even attending games, was Jock McNab, who received his one and only international cap for Scotland in March 1923, in a match against Wales.

Following the second of Liverpool's championships in 1923, Jock was injured in a road traffic accident on 10 November and was treated at Bootle Hospital after being thrown through the window of his car. Though he would recover, he missed the game against Huddersfield at Anfield on the Saturday.

In 1927, Jock was married to a Miss Littler, and this report in the *Liverpool Echo* dated 15 June 1927 suggests that many turned out to greet the happy couple:

'John McNab, the Liverpool footballer, was married, today, at St. John's Church, Bootle, to Miss Littler. McNab is a famous figure in local football, and has a way with him that has always captivated the Anfield crowd. Miss Littler is a daughter of a former football official in the city. The church was crowded with football and other friends.'

McNab left Liverpool in 1928 to play for Queens Park Rangers, where he spent two seasons. However, he would return to Liverpool after his stint in the capital, and became a pub landlord in Commutation Row before playing as an amateur for brewery team Higson's Athletic. A small paragraph in the *Liverpool Echo* on 20 November 1930 indicates that he featured in a midweek amateur game in which Higson's defeated Liverpool Co-op 2-0.

On 2 October 1935, Jock also featured in a floodlit amateur five-a-side tournament alongside several ex-professionals, including fellow Untouchables Donald McKinlay and Harry Beadles. The *Liverpool Echo* reported that the competition consisted of four 30-minute games on the Friday, in which goals and corners would count, and the final would be on the Saturday. The playing area, the article said, was 80 yards by 50.

Jock also featured in an annual international bowling tournament between England, Scotland, Ireland and Wales. According to local reports, in 1938 the tournament was played at the bowling green at the Windham Hotel, Bootle. Also turning out to play were former Reds captain Alex Raisbeck and George Patterson.

By 1939, Jock was widowed and had become the landlord of the Jawbone, a pub on Litherland Road, Bootle, and with the outbreak of war he would become part of the air raid patrol. He would manage the Jawbone until his death in 1949 and would often go to bat on behalf of his customers.

Magistrates' records indicate that his licence had been held over in 1941 as Jock had been keeping the pub open beyond the 9pm closing time. McNab had argued that as many of his customers were dockers and did not finish work until late, it was unfair to deprive them of a drink. However, he abided by a gentleman's agreement to observe the rules and had his licence restored.

He died on 2 January 1949 and was buried in Bootle, the place he made home. Jock and Walter Wadsworth remained great friends after their days playing for the Reds. McNab left the sum of £5,044 5s. 3d. to his daughters Mary and Joan. He played 222 times for Liverpool, scoring six goals.

Two of Jock's fellow defenders were both St Helens men: John Bamber and Tommy Lucas. Bamber played 79 times for Liverpool, scoring twice. He left for Leicester City in 1924 and returned to Merseyside three years later to play for Tranmere Rovers, before featuring in the amateur leagues with Prescot Cables between 1930 and 1932.

Bamber would play alongside former team-mate Donald McKinlay during his spell with Cables, and even succeed him as captain in the 1931/32 season. John died aged 78 in St Helens in 1973.

Tommy Lucas played 366 times for Liverpool, managing just three goals from his position at full-back. Though an England international, having been capped three times for his country, breaking into that resolute back line at Anfield was a tall order in the 1920s. He did play 27 times in the 1921/22 season and earned a championship medal but would only feature once during the following campaign.

He was small in stature, could play with both feet and had a powerful shot. He was also known to be a fine tackler. He would benefit greatly as Ephraim Longworth's career came to an end and would feature many times for the club between 1924 and 1931.

He left Liverpool in 1933 and went on to play for Clapton Orient until 1935. He died at the age of 58, in 1953.

The man who had disappointingly missed the first of Liverpool's back-to-back league titles, Dick Johnson, would leave Anfield for Stoke City in 1925.

He remained there for four years, scoring 21 goals in 78 games, before departing in 1929. He then enjoyed a similarly successful spell at New Brighton, managing 24 goals in 74 appearances over two years between 1929 and 1931. Johnson would finish his playing career at Connah's Quay in 1933.

In 1932, while at Connah's Quay, Johnson became seriously ill. This report in the *Liverpool Echo* on 14 July 1932 revealed how friends and team-mates rallied to his aid:

'Dick Johnson, the former Liverpool and New Brighton footballer, is seriously ill. Dick was always a very generous and whole-hearted player, and it is, therefore, pleasing to find friends promoting a bowling tournament for his benefit.

'The match, which is between Harry Baines (Stanley Arms) and Reg Lloyd (Farmers' Arms) will take place at the Farmers' Arms Hotel, Clubmoor, next Wednesday at seven o'clock. Forty-one up is the distance, and Mr John Ward is hopeful of getting there to referee. It is an excellent cause, and Johnson has done much to deserve this of his friends.'

Johnson died at the tragically young age of 38 just six months later, on 14 January 1933. In all he played 80 times for Liverpool and scored 30 times. He will forever remain an Untouchable having helped his team capture that second successive league title in 1923.

Birkenhead-born Harry Lewis made 19 appearances in 1921/22, having made his debut for Liverpool on 30 August 1919 after signing from Birkenhead Old Boys. He therefore qualified for a championship medal. However, he would leave the Reds in 1922 and joined Hull City in 1923, where he played for two seasons. Harry was paid £650 in lieu of benefits he would have received the following season, as part of the transfer.

This article in the *Hull Daily Mail* dated 18 October 1923, explains why it was time for Harry to move on:

'Harry Lewis, the Liverpool inside-left, transferred on Wednesday to Hull City, was a regular member of the team which won the league championship the season before last. During last season an illness kept him out of the first team, and so well did Harry Chambers fill the position when the line was re-shuffled, that Lewis did not get his place again when he was restored to health.

'He has been playing a consistent game in the Liverpool reserves, and for some time has been under observation in the interests of Hull City by a keen judge. Moreover, the Tigers' manager Mr McCracken, is able to speak from personal knowledge of the qualities of the newcomer to Anlaby Road. The Irishman's view is that Lewis will fill "a long felt want".

'Lewis is no more than 5ft 6.5in in height and weights 11st 4lb, but what he lacks in stature is more than compensated for by his foot craft. Lewis, who is a native of Birkenhead, will make his debut at Anlaby Road on Saturday against Stoke. It is understood that the figure paid for the transfer of the Liverpool man, who will arrive at Hull to-morrow, is round about £800.'

After leaving Hull in 1925, and a gap of two years, he joined Mold in 1927 for a single season. Harry died on 11 July 1976, aged 79. In all he made 70 appearances for the Reds and scored 12 times.

There are of course others who made up this squad of players, but sadly did not make sufficient appearances to earn them a medal in either of those championship seasons. Harold Wadsworth, Jack Sambrook, Ted Parry and David Pratt would be used sparingly. However, their names are still worthy of mention, as they would have competed against the Untouchables in training and in doing so would have driven them on to ever higher standards.

Harold would feature for Leicester City, Nottingham Forest and Millwall after he left Liverpool. He died on 2 November 1975, at the age of 77. Jack Sambrook only managed two appearances for the Reds before leaving in 1923. He played for several other clubs, including Stockport County, Southport, Willenhall, and C & L Hills. He passed away on 30 December 1973 at the age of 74.

Ted Parry played 13 times for Liverpool before leaving in 1925 and was also capped for Wales against Scotland in 1922. He went on to play for Walsall, Llandudno Town and Colwyn Bay United. Ted died on 18 November 1976 in Colwyn Bay aged 84.

David Pratt played 84 times for Liverpool, scoring once. He made just seven appearances in the 1923 championship-winning side but went on to have a career with Bury, and Yeovil Petters United. David died on 28 July 1967 at the age of 71.

18

Farewell to 'Waddy,' Tom and Danny

WE BEGAN our journey with three young lads from Liverpool: Walter Wadsworth, Tom Bromilow and Danny Shone. We have travelled with them throughout the pages of this book, learning about the factors that shaped their lives, personalities and helped them to become the men they grew up to be. We have discovered what drew them to football and how they became part of Liverpool Football Club's great history.

Their lives were filled with many challenges, adventures, and great joy. Walter would have suffered great stress as a boy, witnessing his mother's illness and subsequent committal to an asylum, and he would have known what it meant to toil and graft. His work on the docks would have been as good an education in life as anything he learned in school. Football, though, would be his escape and Walter would blossom into a great footballer and a man of some repute, respected by supporters and team-mates alike.

Tom's character was tested to the limit on the battlefields of Europe, and the sights he must have seen, the trauma he experienced, will have lived with him his whole life. Though there is little evidence in his writing or from family recollections that he was ever troubled by his experiences in the First World War, it is impossible to conclude that they did not shape his outlook on life and his development as a footballer and a man.

Danny, the youngest of the three, had a seemingly uneventful childhood, before suffering great peril and almost losing his life in

France during the war. It was to Liverpool and football in general's great benefit that he survived to become part of one of the greatest teams in Anfield history. Danny's contribution, though modest in comparison with Walter's and Tom's, was nonetheless an important one.

Now we must turn to what happened to these men, in the years after they became champions and Untouchables. How did their Liverpool careers pan out and what about their onward journeys, in football and in life?

Walter continued to play for the Reds until 1926. He appeared 242 times for Liverpool in a period that spanned 14 years. His tally would have undoubtedly been much higher had it not been for the war.

Always a fiery character on the pitch, his no-nonsense, tough-tackling style belied a player of great intelligence and guile. Much like Jamie Carragher in the 21st century and Tommy Smith in the 1960s and '70s, Walter cultivated a reputation for being something of a hard man, known for his work rate and effectiveness. But like his latter-day successors there was much more to him than that.

Neither Smith nor Carragher were averse to confronting spectators who they felt had stepped out of line, and neither was Walter. He would famously lose his patience with a supporter who had abused him throughout a game in Sheffield in 1923, climbing into the terrace and punching who he thought was the culprit. Unfortunately he had attacked the wrong man. However, his response was not borne out of simple thuggery, but righteous indignation, as his letter to *Topical Times* revealed:

'Let me state here and now that I hit a spectator, I admit it. I think I was justified because a spectator called me something that I will allow no man to call me. It must not be imagined that because a spectator has paid his bob, he can willy-nilly help himself in the epithets department. He has no justification for something worse than swearing at the players. He has not the right to shout vile words at them.

'I hope the action I took will lead to the offenders learning that they can not lean over the railings and offer vile insults at footballers.

'After the match I begged the people of Sheffield to bring the man to the dressing room to see me. No one came I am sorry to say, and I am more than sorry that the man has not gone to court, because then the facts would be published, and it would be seen by all in the game of football how some spectators carry on.'

This articulate and lucid letter reveals a man of principle, not afraid to defend himself when the need arose, characteristics he would have learned at home and at work, during his childhood and later in his youth. His granddaughter Jacqueline feels that he should be remembered not just as a hard man, but for his skill and intelligence, telling us:

'On the field Walter was well known for his "take-no-prisoners" style of play which reflected his motto, "Ball may pass me but man never!" But underlying his crunching tackles was skill that prompted Sunderland and England player Charles Buchan to describe Walter as the most difficult half-back he had faced. He would say of Walter, "You never know what he's going to do next. He's so unorthodox and seems to 'get there' without disclosing his intentions."

'And this sums up the dichotomy in Walter's character. It is easy to caricature him as simply the original hard man from Bootle who wasn't afraid to put the boot in, but there was far more to him than that. Football obviously meant a great deal to him. But it wasn't just the game he loved, it was the life too, and the team spirit.'

Walter left Liverpool for Bristol City in 1926 at the age of 36 and would become the captain of the team. His manager at City was none other than former Reds captain Alex Raisbeck. Walter would be widely credited with the side's promotion to the Second Division in 1927. In profile of Walter, appearing in *Bristol City From War to War: 1915–1946*, written by David Woods, Wadsworth is described as the catalyst for the team's upturn in fortunes. It also reveals something of Walter's private life:

'The catalyst was undoubtedly Walter Wadsworth, the experienced Liverpool centre-half who signed for City despite concerns over his partiality for alcoholic beverages. Installed as skipper he remained his own man and spent more time knocking back his favourite tipple than he did training. He even drank before games, but there was no denying his ability … Apparently, Wadsworth who was surprised by a director as he sat drinking at a bar before the game, admitted that he usually downed ten to 12 bottles as he reached for another Guinness.'

Such stories would no doubt have been commonplace in football during the period. Indeed, the English game's drinking culture was only really served its last orders at the beginning of the 1990s. However, of interest is the description of Walter as 'his own man'. This was a character who was comfortable enough in his own skin to do things his own way, and he seems to have gotten away with it.

After Bristol City won promotion in 1927, newspaper reports provided an account of a speech Walter had given. They painted a picture of Walter as a much-loved character who marched to the beat of his own drum:

'The speech which got the warmest reception was that of Walter Wadsworth, the captain, especially when he said the secret of Bristol City's success had been that everybody, including the directors, manager, trainer, staff, team, groundsman, and even the old horse which was harnessed to the roller all pulled together.'

Describing the club's promotion, the report went on, 'After a moderate start to the season, a winning sequence was struck and then the players and management were caught up on a flood-tide of enthusiasm, engendered to a very great extent by one of the greatest, if unorthodox, football club captains who ever led a team to promotion. Walter Wadsworth, "Waddy", if you like.'

Walter spent two seasons at Bristol before leaving for Flint Town, where he was employed as player-manager for a season. Then came moves to New Brighton (1929/30) and Oswestry Town (1930/31).

Photographs of Walter training vigorously at New Brighton, at the age of 38, suggest that whatever his drinking habits he was still a very fit man. New Brighton had been in desperate need of a centre-back and he would immediately solve their problem. He eventually hung up his boots in 1931 and would have been 40 years of age.

Walter was living at Chapel Hill Road, Wallasey on Merseyside. His occupation was heavy haulage contractor. He would later move to Bristol, where he spent the reminder of his life. On 8 October 1951 the *Liverpool Echo* reported the sad news of his passing:

'I regret to have to announce the death of Walter Wadsworth, one time captain and centre-half back of Liverpool FC. He has been ill for some time and passed away at Bristol at the age of 61.

'Wadsworth was captain of Liverpool's "double" championship side in the early 20s. "Waddy", as he will always be remembered by Liverpool followers, was as tough a man as ever played football. He asked no quarter nor gave any, yet off the field he had a heart of gold.

'He was one of the trio who received his marching orders in that memorable match at Anfield against Newcastle, when he, along with John McNab and Tommy Urwin, was ordered off the field. It was one of Wadsworth's slogans that "ball may pass me but man never".'

'Wadsworth played more than 200 games for Liverpool. He went into the haulage business on his own in the early days of the war, and became a successful businessman. He left Liverpool and took up residence in Bristol, but he will always be looked upon as a "Liverpudlian".

Walter's friend and team-mate Tom Bromilow made his last appearance for the Reds in a 1-0 defeat to Blackburn Rovers at Ewood Park in 1930. He had captained the club in the 1928/29 season, but he was now 36 years of age and that honour had now passed to Tom Morrison.

However, football remained his true love, and after he hung up his boots he would head into management. Not afraid of a challenge, Bromilow journeyed to the Netherlands to learn his trade and perhaps gain new ideas about formations and training methods. He would spend two years as the coach of AFC of Amsterdam, while continuing to play cricket in the summer.

Tom would return home to manage Burnley, where he stayed for three seasons. He put his experiences to good use, transforming Burnley and revolutionising training. He was an avid student of football tactics – though his daughter, June, recalls that he pronounced it 'tattics' – and he drilled his squad regularly, using table-top boards to outline his strategies. When he left for Crystal Palace, in 1935, the *Burnley Express* penned a very complimentary editorial by way of a farewell:

'Mr Bromilow has been associated with the Burnley club for the past three seasons, and during that period he has done much to bring the town's team once more to the forefront in football history. Only last season he had the distinction of seeing the team reach the semi-final of the English cup, to be beaten in Birmingham by the ultimate winner, Sheffield Wednesday, and in his first season here the team went to the sixth round of the competition.

'During his stay he has introduced new training methods and more or less re-modelled the club. Of the players who were on Burnley's books when he first came to Burnley only Cecil Smith remains.

'He secured the Burnley appointment in October 1932, out of 70 applicants, succeeding Mr Albert Pickles, who had resigned. He had been coach to the Amsterdam FC for the season but, as the climatic conditions did not suit himself or his wife, he was anxious to return to England.'

Tom had two spells at Crystal Palace and managed Newport County twice. However, he would experience tremendous sadness at missing out on the Liverpool job in 1936.

There were said to be 51 applicants and Tom was beaten to the post by George Kay, who went on to win the league for the club in 1947. His family say he was bitterly disappointed by that and had dreamed of managing his boyhood team. While Kay was clearly a success, there is a sense of what might have been, if that superstar defender had been given the chance to emulate his playing success in the dugout.

Bromilow would instead manage Leicester City, but left them in 1945 after an apparent disagreement with the board. The *Birmingham Daily Gazette* reported:

'Mr Tom Bromilow, the Liverpool and England half-back and former Burnley and Crystal Palace manager, is terminating his appointment with Leicester City, owing to a disagreement with the directors over the future policy of the club.'

His final job in management came with his return to Newport, where he spent four years before leaving in 1950. Somehow his differences with the Leicester hierarchy must have been healed, though, as he would finish his career as a scout for the club – a job he undertook until his death at the age of 65, in 1959.

Tom had passed away peacefully on a train while on a scouting mission for Leicester. He was doing what he loved and still passionately involved in football. In 2006, Liverpool supporters who took part in a poll, '100 Players Who Shook the Kop', for the club's website, ranked Tom 98th. Tom made 375 appearances for Liverpool, scoring 11 goals, and was capped for his country five times. On the news of Tom's passing, one of the greatest strikers of the era, Tommy Lawton, paid an emotional tribute, telling the *Leicester Evening Mail* how Bromilow had discovered him, nurtured and coached him:

'Tom Bromilow was a wonderful chap. I endorse everything that Matt Gillies said about him being one of the most lovable of men.'

Gillies, a Scottish footballer, was manager at Leicester for 15 years from 1952–1967, and he had the utmost respect for Bromilow. Tom's funeral took place at the Church of the Martyrs, Leicester, and his coffin was carried by six past and present Leicester players: captain John Newman, George Dewis, Derek Hines, Bill Cunningham, John Anderson and Stanley Milburn.

Tom was clearly loved and admired throughout the game of football. It is therefore fitting that he received such a wonderful send-off in the town he had come to call home.

Danny Shone made 15 appearances under Matt McQueen in the 1923/4 season. However he would make a significant breakthrough during the 1924/25 campaign. He would feature in all 46 league and cup games, scoring 15 goals. In January 1925, the *Derby Daily Telegraph* carried a review of his progress and status:

'Danny Shone, who registered two goals for Liverpool last week, is one of the most improved players in the Anfield camp. When he originally joined the club from Garston's he was thought to be a centre-forward, but subsequently he deputised at inside-left for Harry Chambers, and later, when Forshaw went to centre-forward, became an inside-right. This is his best position.'

After struggling to a 12th placed finish in 1924, Liverpool rose to fourth in 1925. However, Danny would go on to make just three appearances in the 1925/26 season. He would then feature as a regular in the reserves before leaving for West Ham in 1928.

Danny's last league goal for Liverpool was scored at Anfield against West Ham on 10 April 1925. Chambers put the Reds up 1-0 at half-time and Danny Shone sealed the 2-0 win just one minute from the final whistle. His last appearance for the first team was at inside-left against Sheffield United on 19 December 1925. Liverpool would lose 3-1 with Forshaw netting their goal.

The Reds had bettered their previous season's finish, rising to fourth place. Huddersfield would be league champions. Liverpool made it to the fourth round of the FA Cup, going out to Southampton by a single goal. Danny Shone had played in all four rounds, scoring three goals.

Danny's relegation to the reserves would have been a bitter blow, coming after such an incredible season in 1924/25. Though it is not clear why, he was out of favour and would have little option but to move on.

Danny impressed for the Hammers in pre-season, and this report published in the *East Ham Mail, East Ham Echo* and *Barking Chronicle* suggests that Danny had really caught the eye:

GETTING READY FOR KICK-OFF

West Ham United's New Players: Six in first trial match

'West Ham United had six of their seven new players in teams which turned out for the first public trial match on the Boleyn ground at Upton Park, on Saturday.

'And one of them who drew attention was D. Shone, who comes from Liverpool and made a very successful debut in the first team at inside-left, as partner to Ruffell. He plays a cool, calculating game, and showed some very neat passing. He scored a couple of good goals.'

And when Danny moved to Coventry, it was with high hopes and great expectations. The Midlands club were struggling and had endured a miserable Christmas run.

Reporter 'Nemo', writing in his column in the *Midland Daily Telegraph*, on Saturday, 5 January 1929, relayed how a former director had written to him in order to congratulate the present administration on the timely acquisition of new strikers from West Ham. The solution to City's problems, he wrote, was the acquisition of Shone and Loughlin:

'I have written so much concerning the prowess of Loughlin (herewith) and Shone during the last few days that very little else remains to be profitably said.

'If their introduction results in once more bringing the City up among the leaders – as I confidently hope it will – the Christmas debacle will be readily forgotten. It might be mentioned that Shone started his career with the Earle club in the South Liverpool Amateur Alliance, and later went to Grayson's, in the West Cheshire League, from whence he was picked up as a junior by Liverpool in 1921.

'He has gone through a First Division campaign without missing a single match, which puts the stamp of real ability upon him. He has proved very effective during his short sojourn at West Ham and was hailed with delight by the "Hammers'" supporters. He was injured recently but is now declared perfectly fit again. Supporters will have had an opportunity this afternoon to judge of the artistry which he undoubtedly possesses.'

Danny would score his one and only goal for Coventry in his debut match against Brighton and Hove Albion at Highfield Road on 5 January 1929. Playing at inside-left, he impressed in front of a crowd of 15,000.

Shone's final first-team appearance for Coventry City was on 9 March away at Newport County in front of a crowd of 7,000. Coventry lost 2-1. He appeared for the reserves towards the end of the season and his final game for them was on Saturday, 4 May against Millwall's second string in the London Combination. He was not offered a further contract with the club and at the age of 30 he retired from league football, though he later joined Rhyl Athletic for the 1929/30 season.

A cartoon, 'Danny Shone of Rhyl' by George Green, appeared in the *Liverpool Echo* on 5 October 1929. It was accompanied by a short paragraph:

'Everyone at Anfield remembers the bonny little forward, Danny Shone, who scored many popular goals for Liverpool. He went to West Ham and became a big favourite with the London crowds, but has now returned to join Rhyl Athletic.'

Shone had married 31-year-old Mary Lindley (nee Crawley), a widow, on 10 January 1928, at Liverpool Register Office. He was 28 years of age. A report in the local press informed readers of the happy occasion:

DANNY MARRIES

'Shone, the Liverpool forward, was married today to a well-known Wallasey lady. Danny-boy has always shone in the popularity stakes, and he has received the congratulations of a multitude of friends. Shone came to Liverpool FC through Garston six years ago. They went to sign [Harry] Beadles and took the stocky little pair of forwards.'

Unfortunately, the marriage proved to be an unhappy union, and the couple would have no children. Danny's great nephew, Doug Barlow, told us that his grandmother and Danny's sister, Nell Barlow, had said that Shone's wife enjoyed the high life, happily helping to spend Danny's money while he was earning good wages.

In October 1930, the *Liverpool Echo* reported that Danny was back in Liverpool 'looking fitter than he has for a long time', and was anxious to get back into the game, ideally with a local club. Sadly, he failed to get any offers, so over the next two years Danny and Mary had two attempts in business, one in Liverpool, and one in Birkenhead. Both failed and when his money ran out, in 1932, they moved in with Mary's mother. However, she would 'suggest' he leave and return home after just one month.

The split was an acrimonious one, and a short time later Mary took Danny to court to claim maintenance from him. Danny's defence was that he had been unable to find work, but the judge considered he was not trying hard enough and ordered him to pay 7s. 6d. per week, the equivalent of around £60 per week now.

He would experience unemployment and great hardship, forcing him to pawn his league championship medal and commemorative gold watch. However, his sister, Nell found the pawn ticket for the watch and got it back. Danny was unaware that she had done this, and sadly the medal was never recovered.

Census records published in 1939 indicate that Danny was now employed as a shipyard labourer. He would later find employment with Napier's, who were making aeroplane engines in Liverpool. Danny was back in the family home at Freeman Street in Liverpool, and living with Nell.

Sadly, he lost his mother just before the end of the Second World War, in 1944. She was 76. Danny then spent time living with his sisters Sarah and later Nell. Though he was living in very different circumstances, Liverpool Football Club had never forgotten Danny.

On 2 August 1947 the *Liverpool Echo* published a message on behalf of Jack Rouse, assistant secretary of the club, seeking to ascertain the address of Harry Lewis and Danny Shone, to invite them to the 1947 championship celebration banquet on Friday, 8 August.

We have not been able to ascertain whether Danny attended, but it is pleasing to know that 25 years later he was still remembered as an important member of the team that brought so much glory to Anfield.

Shone died on Wednesday, 30 January 1974, aged 74, at Willows Continuation Hospital, Ashton, Preston. On his death certificate, his occupation was given as 'General Labourer (retired)'. Danny played 81 times for Liverpool, scoring 26 goals, and was clearly a very popular character at Anfield and on Merseyside.

19

A Legacy Worthy of Kings

AS WE reach the centenary of the first of the Untouchables' two league titles, it seems appropriate to conclude this book with an exploration of their legacy. What do their achievements mean today, and how significant was the role they played in the storied history of Liverpool Football Club?

We have sadly reached the point where those who were lucky enough to see the Untouchables play have now also passed on. We have only the memories they shared and passed on to their children and grandchildren. A small number of pieces of grainy and jerky film footage have been unearthed, opening a window on the period and the football they played. However, there is no sound accompanying these clips, and we are unable to hear their voices or the shouts of the crowd.

They were certainly revered, and we can see by the accounts of supporters who witnessed their brilliance that they were loved. These comments by Arthur Riley, son of Bert Riley, published in the *Liverpool Echo* in 1977, show just how much they were adored: 'I can name them now … Elisha Scott, Donald McKinlay, Ephraim Longworth, Tommy Lucas, Tom Bromilow, Walter Wadsworth, John Bamber, Jack Sheldon, William Lacey and Dick Johnson. Harry Chambers came into the side a bit later.

'The players I like are those who can beat a mean with the ball. In the days between the wars, every team had players who could do that. There are very few around today but that's why I liked Kevin Keegan as much as any player I've seen since the war. He could beat men with the ball.

'The best I ever saw were Hugh Gallacher and Harry Chambers. Gallacher could get the ball with four or five men between him and the goal and beat the lot in a dribble.

'Chambers – they called him "Smiler" – was one of the greatest Liverpool players ever. He could swerve a ball years before continentals ever thought of it. He could do anything with a ball and played a lot for England.

'He was a character, was Smiler. He got into a bit of bad company and would turn up at Anfield at two o'clock a bit the worse for drink. They'd stick him under a cold shower, and he'd go out and play a blinder.

'That team of the early 20s was equalled by the team of the mid-1960s, with Ian St John and Roger Hunt. I liked those two, and Gordon Milne and Willie Stevenson.

'I think Scott was the best keeper I ever saw although Ray Clemence is a great player. But in those days Scott would have to make six saves while Clemence would be making one ... the game was very different. Scott never trained. All he did was use the punchbag in the Anfield gym.

'We've had some great wing-halves at Liverpool – Tom Bromilow, the master of the body swerve.'

Their contribution to Liverpool is huge and an exploration of it and their legacy is long overdue. To help us in this, we have approached some of their descendants, football historians, writers and key figures associated with the club and invited them to share their views. We hope that the players would be proud to know people are still discussing them so many years after their success, and that their families will draw comfort and pride also.

Jacqueline Wadsworth explained what the Untouchables mean to her family now: 'Bill Wadsworth [Walter's son] summed up our family's view like this: "The players were all characters of their time, but their achievements helped to make Liverpool Football Club what it is today, because greatness doesn't appear overnight – it has to be built up over many years."

'The Untouchables will naturally be forgotten as the generations who watched them die out, but Walter, Jock, Tom, Elisha and the rest of them are, in their own way, just as important as the stars of today and true fans will appreciate their stories and achievements being recorded in this book.'

Lee Tracy, the grandson of Tom Bromilow, describes his journey of discovery as he found out about his grandfather's story. He said, 'I had a very late realisation that my grandad was a good footballer, let alone a famous Liverpool and England player and certainly not that he was the first Scouser captain of Liverpool Football Club.

'Sadly, Tom died when I was two and I only have one recollection of seeing him. Waving at the window of the Leicester house which was only relevant to me as the place we had the most amazing Christmases. In 1959 he was still working as a scout for Leicester City Football Club, and I don't remember anything of the massive shock that must have gone through the family when he died suddenly in March of that year.

'The family never really talked of his amazing career in football and my parents and older brother, Paul Tracy, didn't appear to have any significant interest in the game. Nothing seemed to be mentioned, or if it was, I couldn't relate to it, so it didn't register in my memory.

'The first major step forward in my education about Tom occurred when our class at school was asked to do a presentation on a subject of our choice. I was probably about 13 years of age. My mum, June, suggested doing a presentation about her dad and that I should get all the information from her mum, May, as we knew her.

'My gran wrote loads of notes about his career and turned up some memorabilia to go with it. I turned it into a presentation that went down a storm in a football-loving class, and the teacher, Mr Gates, was a massive fan of the game. I got 20 out of 20 for my presentation and nearly got more because I had brought his First Division winners' medal from 1922/23 in along with a couple of England caps.

'Over the years, my family and I did more research and built up more information about his career. With the advent of Facebook, I have discovered so much more about him, and it has been beyond fantastic to find that so many people share a great interest in that period and my grandad. I feel totally privileged to be part of the "family" that adores the history of probably the most exciting club in the world. Thank you, Grandad.'

Likewise, Tom's great nephew Brian Spurgin only discovered his link to Bromilow later in life. Nevertheless, it is a source of great pride to him: 'During my 55-year history of watching my beloved Reds, I've been privileged to have seen us lift 14 First Division/Premier League titles.

'Back-to-back titles winning teams were taken for granted in the 1970s and 1980s. Knowing that this demanding achievement was carried out by an inspirational squad of players from a bygone era fills me with a sense of immense pride. Having a great uncle who was an integral part of the Untouchables team makes it even more special.

'Tom Bromilow was my paternal grandmother's youngest brother and even though I never had the pleasure of meeting either of them, knowing that they are a part of my heritage makes me feel so proud. How many people can say that their blood relative was the first Scouser to captain our great club?

'The young man who hailed from Kirkdale is a true hero of mine. This special group of players should be honoured by the club in some way so future generations can be given the opportunity to pay homage to them. As the 100-year anniversary approaches they thoroughly deserve recognition for their footballing achievements.'

John English, the great nephew of Danny Shone, is pleased that the story of the Untouchables is now being told in detail and feels that now is the right time for them to be properly commemorated. He said, 'To me, my son and my cousins, Danny Shone, our great uncle, is a family legend. As a small boy growing up in the south of England, I began supporting Tottenham Hotspur. It was the days of Jimmy Greaves, Dave Mackay, Alan Mullery and their manager, Bill Nicholson.

'One day my mother suggested her uncle Dan would be very disappointed if I didn't grow up supporting Liverpool. She explained why and suddenly my allegiance changed. I was a convert and supporting Liverpool Football Club became a rite of passage. Greaves and co. were history – my new heroes were Roger Hunt, Ian Callaghan, Ian St John, Peter Thompson, Tommy Lawrence and Bill Shankly.

'My grandfather and his brothers were Liverpool supporters. One of the brothers lived in Clovelly Road, a stone's throw from Anfield, and they all met there before attending the home matches, many of them featuring Danny.

'I was determined to discover more about Danny. I never got to meet him, but my grandmother told me a lot about him. She remembered the headline in the *Echo* after her brother scored a hat-trick at Anfield against Middlesbrough in November 1921. It was "The Sun Did Not Shine at Anfield but Shone!" The chest of drawers in her box room was full of memorabilia from the day. It was like a treasure trove of both football and family history.

'In the 1990s I started researching Danny's career at Liverpool, West Ham and Coventry. In the days before the internet, I travelled out to the British Newspaper Library at Hendon to dig out football reports from vast tomes of the *Liverpool Echo.*

'I discovered a lot about the man, his life and skills. He was a family man and a generous man. He loved sport. He excelled at cricket as a youth. He played golf, and apparently enjoyed gardening.

'As an 18-year-old boy, Danny survived a serious gunshot wound to the abdomen while serving with the Sherwood Foresters towards the end of the First World War. He recovered and it is astonishing that he went on to have an amazing career as a professional footballer.

'It is a pity that the Untouchables never really seemed to enjoy much recognition or adulation for their achievements. This was, arguably, one of the best Liverpool teams of all time.'

Doug Barlow, another of Danny's great nephews, agrees, and sheds some light on his great uncle's character in later life. 'I remember Danny as a rather reclusive man,' Doug said. 'When we visited our grandparents', he would keep out of the way, he normally went to the pub at lunchtime and would just pop his head round the door to say hello, and then go up to have an afternoon nap. Of course, it may have been that, for a man not used to children, five noisy children in the house were a bit daunting. Every year until he died, he received an invitation to an annual Liverpool Football Club ex-players' evening.'

Bill Sinnott-Lacey, the grandson of Bill Lacey would give anything to be able to watch his granddad play football. 'I was ten years old when my grandad died so from a personal perspective, I remember him as a kind and charismatic man,' recalls Bill. 'I would hear snippets about him being a footballer always accompanied by the phrase "the great Billy Lacey".

'As I grew up, I came to learn about his exploits as a player which were almost like a *Roy of the Rovers* story! In fact, with the dawn of the internet I have been able to explore his career and know more about him than even my own dad did.

'He was one of the few players to make the short journey across Stanley Park from Everton to Liverpool. Grandad was always respectful of the Blues, but his passion was Liverpool. How could it not have been, especially as he had been a player in one of its greatest teams?

'As a family the Sinnott-Laceys are all dedicated Reds supporters so we feel privileged and incredibly proud to have such a club great as part of our family history. In an era where a player's every move is captured by innumerable cameras, what I wouldn't give to go back in a time machine to watch how my grandad played and witness his part in one of our greatest triumphs.'

Football historian and author Peter Kenny Jones feels that the passage of time has been hard on the Untouchables' legacy, with their greatest feats fading from memory. 'As the years ebb by,' he commented, 'the list of forgotten men grows only bigger. Tom Wyllie, Matt McQueen, Ephraim Longworth, Elisha Scott, Billy Liddell, and many others are close to having their memories go into extinction, as sadly too many believe the club began in 1959 with Bill Shankly.

'For a Liverpool team to come out of the ruin of the First World War and deliver back-to-back titles is testament to the men assembled by David Ashworth. The feat of retaining a league title is significant in any era and at any level, and much of the success should be attributed to some true Liverpool greats: Harry Chambers, Fred Hopkin, Tommy Lucas, Tommy Bromilow and Jock McNab.

'As far as their legacy goes, keeping the memories of former heroes and their stories is important. Through honouring and learning about the past, the history will remain alive, and all these men can live forever.'

Christopher Wood, a football historian who spent many years writing for a Liverpool FC history site, feels it is a pity that the achievements of the Untouchables have been largely forgotten, saying:

'Winning the league then retaining it might not be an unusual phenomenon since the Premier League replaced the Football League, but it certainly was in the period between the two world wars. Before the Untouchables' era only four clubs had won back-to-back league titles, with The (later Sheffield) Wednesday being the only club to do it previously in the 20th century.

'A lot of Liverpool's seasons between the two wars could be politely described as mediocre. Yet during this period some of its greatest-ever players represented the club (and, in many cases, their countries). During two 42-match seasons a team which usually included the mercurial talents of Longworth, McKinlay, Wadsworth and Bromilow won 48, drew 21 and lost only 15; and that is without considering the incredible Elisha Scott, who only missed three of the 84 league games.

'What this squad did under David Ashworth and former player Matt McQueen would not be repeated by another Liverpool team until more than five more decades had passed. That proves just how hard it was to go on a run like this in the 1920s and keep it going for as long as they did. These men must not be forgotten. They set the standard for Liverpool teams of the future to try to match and better which, wonderfully, some of them did.'

Jonny Stokkeland, Liverpool Football Club's official archivist, reflecting on the club's incredible history, said, 'More than 5,000 first team, reserves and junior players have represented this club. I think that the Untouchables are forgotten heroes after a century. It will be nice to see them brought once more to the fore.'

Stephen Done is the club's museum curator. He feels that there are moments in the history of the Untouchables that symbolise who we are as a club, and which set the tone for generations to come. He told us:

'If you know your history, then you would know where you are coming from and for those who care about the history of Liverpool FC, there is both a lot to know and so much that helps inform us about who we are and what we stand for as one of the greatest football clubs in the world. These back-to-back league title-winning seasons were pivotal in the development of the club, consolidating the impressive, if rollercoaster, wins of 1901 and 1906 during a period when the club was also just as likely to fight relegation or seek promotion to the top league. The timing was perfect, reminding everyone that Liverpool were a serious team who meant business, building on what must have felt like a distant dream of the near-miss of the 1914 FA Cup Final now overlaid by the horrors of the world war.

'Marching confidently out of the Western Front came the like of Tom Bromilow, who was to rapidly establish himself as one of the club's great star players, and thanks to his family we have been able to enjoy wedding photographs that show how this event attracted the sort of crowds we assume to be a contemporary phenomenon of "celebrity culture". Then there was Elisha Scott, perhaps the name most familiar these days (and rightly so) who continued the fine tradition of excellent goalkeepers that so defines our club to this day, and not for nothing is his name carved on the stone seat in "Anfield Forever" outside the ground.

'There are so many other superb players this book thankfully helps you meet and appreciate, but perhaps what resonates most strongly for me is what happened when David Ashworth (arguably our most enigmatic and mercurial manager) decided to walk away from the club to follow his own ultimately unsuccessful dream halfway through what was surely a second title-winning season. A more cataclysmic shock is hard to imagine, and yet, in a manner that just seems to capture so much of the spirit of Liverpool FC, up stepped Matt McQueen. This most extraordinary of men somehow guided a team now reeling from this shock departure and got them over the finish line.

'How many times since has our team made life hard for itself yet somehow found the inner strength to turn things around in a game, never mind also find the strength to deal with far darker and more painful tragedy? This moment feels emblematic and remains inspirational. They may be the history boys, but they all have tales to tell, and they are worth hearing.'

Mark Platt is a producer at LFCTV and the author of several books about the club. Mark feels that recognition of the achievements of the Untouchables is long overdue:

'It may be an often-overused word in modern football terminology but what Liverpool's team of the early 1920s achieved really is the stuff of "legend". To be crowned champions just once is a feat worthy enough to be the subject of a book like this; to win it twice in successive seasons elevates this side to a status that can only be bestowed on a select few.

'For too long it is an achievement that has been overlooked. When delving into the history of Liverpool Football Club, it is a common misconception to not stray beyond the arrival of Bill Shankly. Scratch below the surface of 1959, though, and there is another six decades of illustrious heritage to immerse yourself in, not to mention many more fascinating stories that are just waiting to be told.

'The heroic deed of the Untouchables is certainly one of the most enthralling. Emerging from the horror of the Great War, they captured the hearts of Liverpudlians, brought unprecedented success to Anfield and set the standard for all who followed in their red footsteps. The fact it took Liverpool over half a century until back-to-back league championships were won again should serve as an ample reminder of just how special this side was.

'Their names will forever be etched in Kop folklore but now there will hopefully be a wider appreciation for this unique band of brothers who plied their trade 100 years ago. Such recognition is long overdue and the least they deserve. What these players achieved and their importance in the overall context of Liverpool's history should never be underestimated or forgotten. This club of ours has been blessed with so many legendary figures yet these double title-winners from a bygone era can still, with some justification, proudly stand shoulder to shoulder alongside them all.'

Peter Hooton, lead singer of Liverpool band The Farm and author of *Boot Room Boys*, is a lifelong Reds fan and Shankly devotee. However, he also feels that the Untouchables need greater recognition. Peter told us:

'When people mention the history of Liverpool Football Club, they are invariably referring to the post-war period, especially the Shankly revolution of the 1960s. But little has been written about the Untouchables, when the Reds won their third and fourth titles back to back in the 1921/22 and 1922/23 seasons.

'Many will have heard of legendary goalkeeper, Belfast-born Elisha Scott, but other players like Tom Bromilow from Kirkdale and Bootle-born Walter Wadsworth should be brought to life. Everyone knows how difficult it is to retain the title and it was the same in those days, so it is interesting to know how the Liverpool team of 100 years ago achieved that.'

Joanna Durkan, a writer with independent Liverpool FC website This is Anfield, reflected on how supporters in the modern era fixate on the post-Shankly years and feels this is a great shame. 'When thinking of the history of Liverpool Football Club one's mind swiftly turns to Shankly, Paisley, Fagan and the illustrious era that was the 1960s, '70s and '80s,' Joanna said. 'They helped build the modern foundations of the club, but as for the ones that came before, you feel they aren't as recognised. That should not be the case.

'When I think of the 1920s specifically, my mind conjures up league titles and the names of Elisha Scott, Walter Wadsworth and David Ashworth, but the extent of my knowledge of the era is certainly lacking compared to other parts of our club's past. I wish it were not so, they deserve to be acknowledged.

'They each had their own stories, failures and successes, that made them the players and the team that they were and I'm sure many of us know very little about these trailblazers beyond the surface layer of statistics and honours. Now that I think about it, it does not sit well with me that a whole period has been largely overlooked, but hopefully that can change now.'

Author Karl Coppack of *The Anfield Wrap* told us how he felt modern supporters should recognise the tremendous characters who played for the Untouchables. 'It saddens me that the side of the early 1920s has been forgotten,' said Karl. 'I suppose many people view our modern history from the day Shankly arrived at the ground and I'm as guilty of that as anyone, but it's important to acknowledge their part in the Liverpool saga.

'I'm no expert on those sides but I know that Harry Chambers shone and is rightly mentioned when the thorny issue of "legends" comes up. Sadly, though, Dick Forshaw's name tends to be lost but he too should be up there. Maybe it's because he went to Everton – much to his wife's chagrin!

'Without him we'd be two titles down. My favourite thing about the early 1920s is the fixture list. Each side played each other one after the other. In other words, if we played West Brom at Anfield one weekend, we'd head off to The Hawthorns the following week. I love that. Get them out of the way and leave them to it. That and playing the Charity Shield at the end of the season rather than at the start of the next one. Different times.'

Adrian Killen grew up in the 1950s, in the same area of Liverpool as Tom Bromilow, Kirkdale. He remembers how his grandparents entertained him with tails of the 1920s and 30s.

'My dad watched the 20s team regularly and risked many a policeman's baton across his backside as he crawled between the legs of the crowd at the turnstiles. He idolised them and I could recite their names by rote as a kid. In fact, I knew them better than that of the first teams of the 50s. Tom Bromilow married in the same church as myself and my mother and father.

'I remember tales like when "big Waddy," refused to sign my dad's cigarette card album, flung it on the wet floor and shut the door on him. As a kid, these were mesmeric stories and, I am certain, had a great influence on where I was heading as soon as I was old enough, and that of course was down the road to Anfield.'

Walter's ambivalence to signing autographs is well known, and this story offers a glimpse of that. However, it also illustrates how supporters of that period revered their heroes every bit as much as we do today. Yet, sadly, their feats are no longer part of the consciousness of modern-day Reds.

David Moen, a lifelong fan and blogger from Monaghan – home of founding father John McKenna – agrees. He feels that the name of one man above all the Untouchables still resonates today:

'Almost a century on since Liverpool won their first back-to-back league titles you could ask any red to name Liverpool Football Club's greatest-ever goalkeeper, and Elisha Scott will likely enter the conversation. The Belfast native was the backbone of an all-conquering red machine that was littered with characters and no shortage of bravery.

'Just a few short years from the horrors of the trenches, this red team came together to win back-to-back First Division league titles, a feat the club wouldn't repeat until Bob Paisley's great side of 1976 and 1977. Alongside Scott, goal machine Harry Chambers, Bill Lacey and company, we had local lad Tom Bromilow who served his time in the trenches before coming home to conquer the green fields of England in the name of Liverpool Football Club.

'Some of us are lucky enough to have witnessed some of the feats of great Liverpool teams from the past, the title-winning teams from the eras of Shankly, Paisley, Fagan, Dalglish and Klopp. But the 1922 and 1923 red vintage deserves to be celebrated and honoured as any other championship side the Reds have ever produced.

'To win one title is difficult, but to retain one and to do so under such trying circumstances, like sensationally losing your team manager halfway through the second season, is quite another challenge. I'm certain no club could repeat that feat today.'

Arnie Baldursson, editor of LFChistory.net and co-author of *Liverpool: The Complete Record, The Liverpool Encyclopaedia* and *Mr Liverpool: Ronnie Moran's Official Biography*, told us what an incredible feat the Untouchables achieved:

'Liverpool had never won the First Division two years in a row prior to 1923 and didn't repeat that feat until 54 years later. A unique blend of players created an unprecedented success for the club who was by no means a dominant force in England in the wake of the First World War.

'The team's greatest strength was its defence that reads like a who's who of Liverpool's greatest players. Elisha Scott, in terms of reputation and influence, deserves being considered the club's best-ever goalkeeper, Donald McKinlay has probably never had his equal on the left side of the defence and if you were looking for consistency similar to Phil Neal's, Ephraim Longworth provided that in his fruitful career at right-back.

'The half-back line, in a position that combined a centre-half and a central midfielder, Tom Bromilow was the artist and by his side hard men Jock McNab and Walter Wadsworth who could have made Tommy Smith blush. On this bedrock, the forwards flourished and together they made history. This is their story, and every Liverpool supporter should know it by heart.'

John Pearman, editor of the *Red All Over the Land* fanzine, singled out Elisha Scott as one of the Untouchables he would have loved to see, and told us how he grew up with stories of the great Irishman from his mother:

'When fans turned up to a football match in the first seasons after the end of the First World War, Anfield still did not have a roof on the Kop, and this was definitely the era of the cloth cap and getting games by tram. In the 21st century football stadiums are, at the top level, almost luxurious but back then going to a game meant braving the elements during the harsh winter months, but I bet it felt just the same when you walked along the roads leading to the Kop or Anny [Anfield] Road. It must have been great.

'When Liverpool won the title in 1921/22 it was the club's third title and considering they'd only been in existence for 30 years (including the war years) it was a remarkable achievement. To go on and defend it was another incredible feat.

'Looking back through the club history there are several players who stood out in this era, but there is one I honestly wish I'd seen play, Elisha Scott. My mother talked of Scott with almost as much fondness as when she spoke of Liddell. How good must he have been and what impact must he have had on the club, when you discover that the club's telegram address was Goalkeeper.

'It is hard for us octogenarians to fathom out, so I do not expect the younger fans to know anything about what it must have meant. The players were the heroes of the day, and what they achieved is just as vital to our history as anything achieved by Bill Shankly and Bob Paisley.'

Perhaps it is fitting to end this book with a quote from someone who has led Liverpool Football Club in the modern era. Peter Moore was chief executive at Anfield between 2017 and 2020. During his tenure he worked to ensure that former players were properly honoured for their service and was involved in establishing the Former Players' Association at Anfield. Peter feels that recognising and honouring the achievement of the Untouchables is very important.

'This club reveres those who have come before us, and on whose shoulders we proudly stand today,' said Mr Moore. 'The double championship team of 1921/22 and 1922/23 had to overcome so much adversity in their lives, with so many team members being active combatants in the Great War.

'We worship, and rightly so, the players of the Shankly era and beyond, but it is important to remember those who came so much earlier and gave hope and joy to post-war Liverpool supporters. We rejoice in their memory, and thank them for their sacrifices, both on the battlefield and on the field of play. They shall never walk alone.'

It is our hope that we have brought back a forgotten era for this and future generations to know and to celebrate. When you think of the history of Liverpool Football Club, we hope you'll now include the Untouchables in your thoughts. They were a band of brothers who fought for Liverpool, and they did so with great distinction.

Bibliography

Baldursson, A., Magnusson, G., *Liverpool: The Complete Record* (deCoubertin Books, 2014)

Barry, J.M., *The Great Influenza: The Story of the Deadliest Pandemic in History* (Penguin, 1920)

Beckett, S.W., *The Team from a Town of Chimneys: Chronicle of Oldham Athletic Association Football Club* (Published by S.W. Beckett, 1982)

Best, N., *The Greatest Day in History: How the Great War Really Ended* (Lume Books, 2020)

Captivating History, *The Battle of Verdun: A Captivating Guide to the Longest and Largest Battle of World War I* (Captivating History, 2019)

Clemente, C., *19: The Official History of Our League Champions* (Reach Sport, 2020)

Collins, T., *How Football Began: A Global History of How the World's Football Codes Were Born* (Taylor & Francis Distribution, 2020)

Fielding, R., *Letters from the Somme* (Kindle Publishing, 2016)

Forwood, Sir W.B., *Recollections of a Busy Life: Being the Reminiscences of a Liverpool Merchant 1840–1910* (https://archive.org/details/recollectionsofb00forw, 1910)

Forwood, Sir W.B., *Reminiscences of a Liverpool Shipowner, 1850–1920* (https://archive.org/details/reminiscencesofl00forwuoft, 1920)

France, D., and Prentice, D., *Everton Treasures – The David France Collection* (Trinity Mirror Sport Media, 2007)

Jones, C., *Whistling in the Dark: The Local Press Response in Liverpool to Spanish Flu 1918–1919* (https://www.balh.org.uk/publication-tlh-the-local-historian-volume-48-number-4-october-2018, 2018)

Ham, P., *Passchendaele: Requiem for Doomed Youth* (Bolinda Publishing Pty Ltd, 2016)

Honigsbaum, M., *The Pandemic Century: A History of Contagion – from Spanish Flu to Covid-19* (Penguin Audio, 2020)

Kelly, S.F., *The Anfield Encyclopaedia: An A-Z of Liverpool FC* (Mainstream Publishing; fifth edition, 2001)

Kelly, S.F., *The Kop: Liverpool's 12th Man* (Virgin Books; UK edition, 2008)

Kennedy, D., *The Man Who Created Merseyside Football: John Houlding, Founding Father of Liverpool and Everton* (Rowman Littlefield, 2020)

Lamin, B., *Letters from the Trenches: A Soldier of the Great War* (Michael O'Mara; reprint edition, 2013)

Lees, A., *Liverpool: The Hurricane Port* (Mainstream Publishing, 2011)

MacDonald, L., *Passchendaele: The Story of the Third Battle of Ypres 1917* (Penguin, 2014)

Mann, T., *Memoirs* (Anarcho-communist institute, Massachusetts, 2015)

Muir, R., Young, H.E., *Bygone Liverpool* (https://archive.org/details/bygoneliverpool00muiruoft, 1913)

Overy, R., *The Morbid Age: Britain Between the Wars* (Penguin; reprint edition, 2010)

Platt, M., Hughes, W., *This is Anfield: The Official Illustrated History of Liverpool FC's Legendary Stadium* (Carlton Books, 2015)

Platt, M., *The Red Journey: An Oral History of Liverpool Football Club* (deCoubertin Books 2017)

Pugh, M., *We Danced All Night: Britain Between the Wars* (Vintage, 2009)

Riley, R., Riley, G., *Liverpool Match by Match: Volume Four 1919–1926* (Tony Brown, 2015)

Thomas, T.J., *The Origins and Development of Association Football in the Liverpool District c1879–c1915* (http://clok.uclan.ac.uk/9733/11/ThomasJohnPreston.pdf, 2007)

Wadsworth, J., *Letters from the Trenches: The First World War by Those Who Were There* (Pen and Sword Military; first edition, 2014)

Walker, N., *From Slacky Brow to Hope Street: A Century of Prescot Football* (Knowsley Metropolitan Borough Council, 1990)

Weir, A., *Latchford Albums* (https://www.flickr.com/photos/bob_latchford/albums, 2012)

Williams, J., *Red Men: Liverpool Football Club the Biography* (Mainstream Publishing; first edition, 2010)

Wilson, A., *The Birth of Liverpool Football Club: Team of All the Macs* (Vertical Editions, 2011)

Woods, D., *Bristol City from War to War: 1915–1946* (Desert Island Books, 2001)

Wurtzburg, M.C. Capt., *The History of the 2/6th (Rifle) Battalion "The King's" (Liverpool) Regiment 1914–1919* (Gale & Polden Ltd., 1920)

Also available at all good book stores

9781785315008

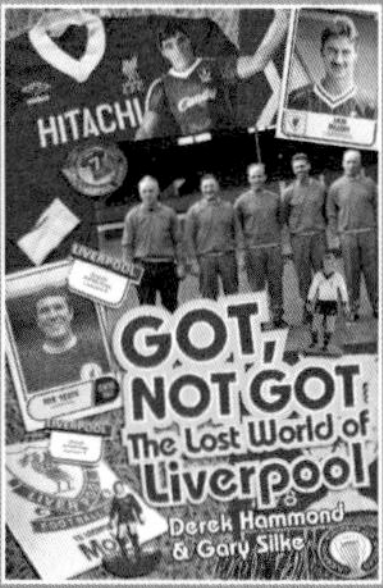

9781909626584

9781785314407

9781785313073

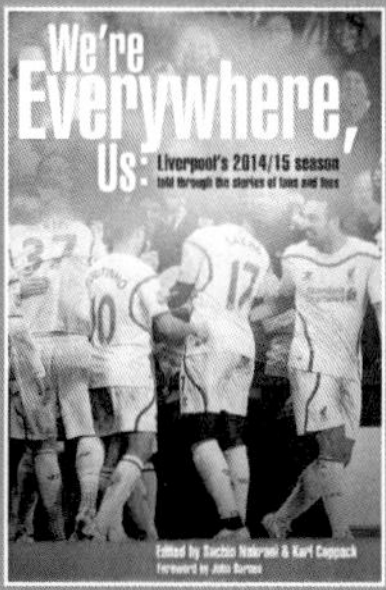

9781785310423

9781908051059

9781908051677

9781905449804

9781785311932